State, Market and Civil Society

State, Market and Civil Society

Issues and Interface

EDITED BY

RAJESH GILL

RAWAT PUBLICATIONS

Jaipur and New Delhi

ISBN 81-7033-890-5

Published by
Prem Rawat for *Rawat Publications*
Satyam Apts., Sector 3, Jawahar Nagar, Jaipur 302 004 (India)
Phone: 0141 265 1748 / 7006 Fax: 0141 265 1748
E-mail: info@rawatbooks.com
Website: www.rawatbooks.com

Delhi Office
4858/24, Ansari Road, Daryaganj, New Delhi 110 002
Phone: 011-23263290

Typeset by Rawat Computers, Jaipur
Printed at Chaman Enterprises, New Delhi

Contents

IV
Corruption: A Challenge to Indian Society

Preface

This volume is an outcome of the national seminar on the theme, *State, Market and Society: Emerging Issues and Interface in India*, organized at the Department of Sociology, Panjab University, Chandigarh in February 2003. The significance of the theme is stands out in the light of tremendous impact of the global market, cultural invasion and information revolution, all over the world, especially in a developing society like India. The ever-extending role of the market, crossing the notions of time and space, entering right into our homes, into our most private lives, 24 hours of the day, has completely overshadowed both the state and society. The failure of a civil society, coming into prominence in countries like India, has further aggravated the problems like the ever-burgeoning gulf between those enjoying the fruits of globalization and others reeling under the painful pangs of hunger, the latter gazing at the state, with wide eyes, full of uncertain future and anxieties.

I am grateful to all the contributors who have been extremely supportive throughout the process of finalizing the manuscript for publication. The volume became possible with the very kind financial help extended by the University Grants Commission under Special Assistance Programme to the Department of Sociology, Panjab University, Chandigarh for conducting the seminar. I also place on record my thanks to Prof. K.N. Pathak, Vice-Chancellor, Panjab University, for being a great help towards the organization of the seminar. My special thanks to Dr. Kiranpreet Kaur, who assisted me with all possible means to accomplish this task.

My thanks are particularly due to Prof. V.S. D'Souza, who wrote such an illuminating article on the theme, touching upon an extremely pertinent theme, i.e., the ethical dimension of the emerging interface between state, market and society. I am also thankful to Prof. T.K. Oommen for contributing a brilliant paper tracing the relationship between state and market on the one hand, and civil society, on the other.

This volume is an outcome of the efforts of my family, my husband and my children, who literally pushed me through towards the completion of the project, relieving me of my mundane activities, and taking these all upon themselves, so selflessly. May God bless all of them!

Rajesh Gill

Contributors

VICTOR S. D'SOUZA is now settled in Bangalore. He retired as Professor, Department of Sociology, Panjab University and authored important books and articles on Social Stratification, Caste, Urban Studies, Family etc.

T.K. OOMMEN, former President, International Sociological Society, retired from Centre for the Study of Social Systems, Jawahar Lal Nehru University, New Delhi. He has made seminal contribution to theorizing in Indian Sociology, Ethnicity and Plural Societies etc.

BIRINDER PAL SINGH is a senior Professor at the Department of Sociology, Punjabi University, Patiala. He has published extensively on the theoretical issues confronting contemporary sociology.

B.S.GHUMAN is a senior Professor at the Department of Public Administration, Panjab University, Chandigarh. His research focus has been mainly upon the contemporary challenges posed by liberalization to the different aspects of Indian society.

S.S. BHATTI belongs to the City Beautiful, Chandigarh and retired as Principal, College of Architecture, Chandigarh. He has made enormous contribution to Art, Literature and Philosophy, particularly by problematizing the issues of development, modernization and technology-induced social change.

ANU CELLY is a senior Lecturer at the Department of English, Panjab University, Chandigarh. The focus of her research has been on gender imaging in popular culture, primarily the electronic media.

SUDIP MINHAS is a senior Lecturer at the Department of English, Panjab University, Chandigarh. She is keenly interested in the feminist theory and its post-modernist nuances.

MADHURIMA is a Reader in Sociology at the Department of Correspondence Studies, Panjab University, Chandigarh. She has an extensive research experience in the field of domestic violence, Indian family and gender issues.

PEEYUSHI DIWAN JAIN is a legal expert, teaching at the Department of Laws, Panjab University, Chandigarh. She specializes in the interface between Indian Constitution and women's issues, particularly in India.

KUMOOL ABBI is a senior Lecturer at the Department of Sociology, Panjab University, Chandigarh. She has to her credit extremely interesting publications on family and gender images in media and its socio-cultural implications.

A.S. GILL is an expert in Management Studies. He specializes in the areas of liberalization and Indian export industry, corruption in Indian industry, etc.

RAJESH GILL is Professor in the Department of Sociology, Panjab University, Chandigarh. She specializes in the areas of urban studies, gender studies, poverty, slums, governance and research methodology.

Introduction

RAJESH GILL

Most of the modern theorizing on state was devoted to demonstrating that its particular form of social organization was indeed the true and permanent expression of the nature of society. But, the fact is that a particular version of the state – the nation-state – sought to create society in its own image. Thus, from a late modern perspective, the state appears as the primary and the social sphere to be controlled by it. Of late, however, the nation-state project has lost momentum and the welfare state has been challenged as a result. The nation-state was never wholly successful in becoming society, unable to completely muffle the clamour of the interest groups. The state, whose legitimacy depended upon the universality of its benefits, is questioned for its legitimacy when the state loses its universalistic appeal and appears to serve sectional interest. The immense control of the state over society was recognized even by Marx and his followers. Gramsci (1957) sought to account for state control over the whole way of life of a nation-state society with the idea of hegemony. Althusser (1971) developed an elaborate structuralist account around repressive and ideological state apparatuses.

With the dissolution of the modern project the nation-state loses control of the forces it previously contained. As a consequence, fragmentation occurred for which various forces were responsible. Of these, the most important is the autonomy of economic relations, namely, market.

The market principle came into direct conflict with a static state since it necessitated the barriers to economic exchange with the outside world, besides expanding the sphere of market relations within the state. Market relations do not respect human boundaries, whether territorial or moral. Markets work on the principle of potential supply and demand from anonymous third parties. Globality becomes an ever-present aspect of human calculations once the limits of action are the globe itself.

Free trade, with the dismantling of state control over activities, reduction of trade barriers, free export and import of capital and foreign exchange, results into a process of denationalization rather than internationalization. The delinkages which globalization induces, force us to restore to concepts, the meanings which modernity concealed. State has a wider meaning when nation-states acknowledge law beyond their frontiers, state identity beyond particular governments, or the binding nature of inter-state activities. State activities are therefore to that extent denationalized, polycentric and to some extent decentred, without central control. The global shift leads thus to a reconceptualization of the state. It disaggregates the linkage of nation and state. In the global age, the state is decentred, crosses nation-state boundaries, penetrates and is realized in the daily activities of ordinary people. In this sense, a world state develops to parallel the growth of world society.

It is significant to note however that unlike modernity, globalization hardly implies a unidirectional process, especially in view of globalization, etc. In the global age nations may become less than, but also more than, nation-states. The rhetoric of 'black nation' or 'Islamic nation' is an assertion of a group identity transcending nation-state boundaries. Nationalism escapes the frame of nation-state structures into a cultural space defined in terms of globality rather than territory. Global communication technology makes it easier both to sustain links at a distance and to sustain and affirm cultural identity within the global cultural space.

What globalization has definitely done is ensuring the supremacy of the market over both state as well as society. Neo-Marxists, e.g., Lukacs and Marcuse, while talking about the autonomy of economic forces over society and individuals, argued that this process results into the establishment of an all-pervading cultural system, which is 'inauthentic' in that it imposes on people ways of living, which are a denial and distortion of genuine human needs. The degrading of the subjective experience of individuals by the alienated culture creates a 'maimed consciousness' of individuals in modern capitalism, and their 'regression' to a child-like state of dependency which destroys their capacity for original thought or actions. What comes out finally is the 'mass culture'. Weber too felt concerned about the tendencies in capitalism to curtail the freedom of individual to make free choices. He argued that modern societies have subordinated themselves to a new and equally powerful set of constraints, the source of which is rationality itself. The more social life is organized according to rational principles, the less the individuals can exercise choice, freedom or spontaneity in their lives.

The overarching role of market and mass culture created by it is further emphasized by Simmel when he brings out the 'tragedy of culture'. All cultural objects, viz., gods, the state, language, the market, money etc., created by humans for their own use, have the capacity to assume an independent existence, to appear objective and immutable, and ultimately to dominate their creators. Since the process of rationalization demands constant innovation and the production of new ideas, the result is a huge and ever-growing 'stock of objectified cultural elements' which comes to seem overwhelming and threatening to individuals. An unprecedented array of cultural products is available in such rich and overburdened cultures yet our contact with most of them is fleeting and superficial. It is not only that the individual cannot make choices, but more important is that these choices are for the most part superficial and restricted. The individual's freedom is largely illusory, an illusion projected and perpetuated through popular culture – leading to something called 'pseudo individualism'. People are shaped to think only as the society allows. This actually turned the spirit of modern capitalism, i.e., rationality into its very opposite, irrationality.

Hence, state, market and society stand today in totally transformed nexus. The relationship is certainly not fixed but most fluid. In this strong interplay between state and market, culture has pushed itself as a strong force, shaping not only the societal options but the state and market options too. The interface between state, market and society needs therefore to be understood in the contemporary context, for which the theories of modern capitalism, positivism, insisting upon rational forces, do not hold much water. The post-modernist discourse on the other hand too suffers from its inability to capture the reality, which is much more than merely decentred, detextualized and absolutely fluid.

It is in this context, therefore, that the present work has been compiled. Various papers in the volume address to the different facets of the interface between state, market and society and the issues emerging out of it. The book has been divided into four sections. Section I focuses upon the conceptual issues concerning state, market and society and has five articles, providing the conceptual framework. Victor S. D'Souza, in his paper on 'State, Market and Society: The Ethical Imperative' shows concern for the failure of the republican constitution of India to transform the society in the form of a civil society. Instead, today, all the democratic institutions stand discredited. D'Souza emphasizes upon the need to de-emotionalize the parochial undemocratic values of our caste-ridden past, and charge the new values of democracy with a new motive force that can impel people to act in a civilized way. The new institutions of state and market are the new forms of agencies which need to be operated by Indian people turned into citizens.

The role of state, civil society and market in the process of development is examined by T.K. Oommen and he looks for a comprehensive consensus as a result of this interface. Beginning with the different approaches to development exhibited by the capitalist democracies on the one hand, and the socialist economies on the other, Oommen traces the evolution of the Third World through the anti-colonial revolution. He argues that all the three politico-economic systems have failed to forge a participatory process of governance, thus falling short of the objective of a civil society. Based upon a very systematic analysis, Oommen concludes that the role of these three pillars of society needs to be examined afresh in the light of contemporary scenario, where state's role in planned development has become nebulous while the private sector is showing apathy towards the developmental agenda.

Birinder Pal Singh discusses the interface between state, market and society in terms of the complete overpowering of state and society by market, through a vulgar exhibition of wealth and affluence all over the globe, pushing the moralistic role of the society to the background. The agenda for national and societal development that used to come from the state (polity) is now set by the market, which has emerged all strong.

B.S. Ghuman analyzes the social implications of privatization in the Indian context. Acknowledging the methodological handicaps in systematically studying the impact of privatization on society, Ghuman makes an interesting attempt in his paper to identify the social issues of privatization by combining empirical evidence from other countries. He argues that while privatization in the earlier phases resulted in rapid economic gains for the nations, its long-term effects are proving to be disastrous, especially for the less fortunate and deprived sections within societies. The interface between business and social worlds is portrayed by Rajesh Gill in her paper. She demonstrates how the increased commercialization in modern times has brought the two worlds closer, with the lines dividing the two getting blurred.

Section II deals with the rural-urban interface in the context of state, market and society. S.S. Bhatti, a renowned architect by training and philosopher by temperament, examines the contemporary Indian society, reeling under the serious threats of political corruption, commodification of culture and increasing impoverishment of the masses, especially in the rural India. Bhatti introduces a number of terms in his essay in order to bring home the irrelevance of idealized notions such as 'welfare state', 'materialism' etc. The rural-urban interface in contemporary Indian society is further analyzed by Rajesh Gill in her paper on "Rural-Urban Interface in Market, Culture and Society: The Case of an Urbanizing Village." Gill, on the basis of an ethnographic account of an urbanizing village near a large city, narrates how the city brings to its periphery not only market and commercialization, but an erosion of social fabric, which gave a distinctive character to the rural life.

Emerging gender issues in the wake of contemporary state and market are discussed in Section III. Anu Celly, an expert on English literature, portrays how in the name of liberalization, the flood gates of mindless consumerism have unleashed anew, the instincts of avarice and materialism to inveigle us into living beyond our means, lending to all our moves and deeds, the ethics of profitable transaction as the ultimate objective. Celly argues that cinematic images, which conceptualize women as an archetype or an artefact, need to be decoded rather than to be lapped up, with a level of 'consciousness-raising'. What is required, according to her, is a redefinition of our responses to the most potent and wide reaching impact of the media-generated sub-text that has increasingly become an apparatus for hegemonic interventions on the nature of identity and agency.

Sudip Minhas, again an English literature expert, in her very interesting paper, 'Mandir and Mandira', questions the persistent discourse on womanhood and femininity, portrayed through the marketing of cricket by glamorizing and vulgarizing the body of a woman. Of course, the woman is herself a willing actor in this context, yet, how she is being easily abused in the process of commercialization and advertising, needs to be seriously taken up as an issue.

Another very pertinent gender issue is taken up for a socio-economic analysis by Madhurima and Piyushi in their paper on rape. They insist upon the need to take the problem of increasing incidence of rape not merely as legal, but also a social and attitudinal, which needs a treatment at the level of change of mindsets. They recommend that rectification of the patriarchal social vision to the problem would go a long way in psychological rehabilitation of the victim as also in exposing the perpetrators before law and society.

The experiences of Indian women in local governance after the implementation of 73rd and 74th Constitutional Amendment Acts are highlighted by Rajesh Gill in her paper. Having entered the arena of political power and decision-making, it is not an easy task for the women at the grassroots level to break the patriarchal structures both in the rural and urban settings, and exercise the empowered status achieved by them. Gill unravels many problems these elected women representatives face, while discharging their duties and sharing a common platform with men, for whom the situation is quite uncomfortable.

How market, commercialization and societal hypocrisy have digressed the very pertinent issue of gender justice in a forward state of Punjab is brought out by Rajesh Gill. She argues that in a blind feminist search for gender empowerment, the woman in Punjab stands today commodified, demystified and disempowered, under the immensely heavy weight of the newly found masculinity, so akin to the traditional discourse. Media has turned the image of woman into an accessory, a shadow, having a meaning only in the presence of a man.

Kumool Abbi, in her paper 'State, Market and Gender in India', discusses how the women stand marginalized in the changed market system, particularly agriculture. Drawing heavily from a large number of empirical studies, she brings out the mechanisms through which it has become all the more difficult for women to sustain their families and employment within the altered market equations.

Rajesh Gill, in her paper, examines the changing spaces within and outside the family as a result of electronic media. She argues that television is working as an isolating force, especially in upper class families, locating individuals in their private spaces, away from other members within the family as well as outside. It has altered the intra-familial spaces right from the husband-wife duo to the relationships between parents-children and the siblings themselves.

The last section takes up the most important challenge Indian polity and society confront today, i.e., corruption. A. S. Gill, in his interesting analysis, shows how corruption in Indian bureaucracy has served the needs of the market players – exporters in this case. Unfortunately, however, it has only tarnished the image of Indian industry in the global market, calling for immediate and serious treatment of the problem. The paper makes a positive contribution by suggesting practical strategies to eliminate corruption from the Indian polity and society, thus enabling the Indian market to gain greater competence at the global scene.

Rajesh Gill brings out the mechanisms through which corruption, in the Indian context, has been almost legitimized in mundane life, both in the public and private domains. She argues that the idea of good governance cannot be an easy alternative to the present system of governance, soaked with corruption at every level, thus asking for some harsh measures, accompanied by a general awakening. The wielders of power can certainly not be expected to make the system of governance transparent and decentralized, thus putting their established positions to risk.

I

Conceptual Issues

1

State, Market and Society: The Ethical Imperative

VICTOR S. D'SOUZA

The theme of this seminar "State, Market and Society: Emerging Issues and Interface in India" is indeed a complex one, and if we add to it the unavoidable phenomenon of globalization, it will become really perplexing. It is obviously a changing scene and the changes have become more and more out of hand ever since India attained independence from the foreign rule and adopted a radically new form of state. The change was radical in the sense that for the first time in the history of India, sovereign power that always vested in the ruler, passed into the hands of the people, and the state functionaries now became the representatives of people. The common people, who had now become legally free and independent citizens but never had the capacity for democratic decision-making, were saddled with the responsibility of electing capable representatives to govern them. It was a pious hope of the constitution-makers that appropriate political institutions and legislation would bring about the necessary transformation in the citizens' way of thinking and behaving.

The change in the Indian polity is in tune with the global trend of shift in the civilization pattern from an authoritarian to a liberal

---

Valedictory address delivered at the National Seminar on State, Market and Society: Emerging Issues and Interface in India (Panjab University, Department of Sociology, 21-22 February, 2003).

democratic one. It lays down the agenda for changing social relations based on status to ones based on contract; those based on localized trust to one based on universalized trust. In short, it is a change in the very consciousness of the Indian people to inculcate them with the new ideals of freedom, equality and universal brotherhood, to which they were never exposed before in their social, political and economic environment.

The envisioned social, economic and political order may be acceptable to the people. But, the process that has been politically manipulated in bringing about revolutionary changes has thrown up a mess that seems to be detestable. The problems that we have been discussing in this context, therefore, represent the birth pangs of a new social order mismanaged by its midwives.

As sociologists we have a burden of analyzing the nature of the problem and suggesting possible solutions. In doing so, we should first of all recognize the limitations of our analytical methodologies such as functionalism, social action approach and positivism. Any one approach to an analysis of a complex reality such as problems of fundamental societal change that affect both meaning and behaviour of people would not be appropriate because it would only give us a tunnel vision that would befuddle our understanding of a multiplex problem. The problems that we have been dealing with involve, besides changes in culture and society, also radical changes in the consciousness of people. In this context, even for an understanding of the problems involved, we would have to combine insights from different methodological paradigms.

In all traditional societies including ours, consciousness was moulded by religion that has shaped the traditional moral order. I daresay that by and large Indian sociologists' understanding of the role of religion in India is clouded by the views expressed about religion by the renowned classical sociologist, Emile Durkheim. In his classic sociological study on religion, Durkheim (1976), on the one hand, emphasized the role of religion in the moral order and hence in social order, but on the other hand, through his positivist and structural functional approach, divested religion of its spiritual significance. He has, however, rightly emphasized the fact that no social order can be long-lasting unless the norms and rules of society are internalized in individual consciousness. He has also pointed out that such internalization takes place when the members of the society believe that the norms of the society are prescribed by an awe-inspiring external power such as a deity.

But Durkheim, who was a positivist in his approach, has dealt a blow to the belief in the metaphysical concept of the deity itself that had been the lynchpin of the morality of religiously-oriented people everywhere. This he has done by postulating that the external power reckoned as a deity is none other than the society itself projected as an external being. To buttress his arguments he has further put forward the spurious concept of collective consciousness of society distinct from the generally accepted concept of inter-subjectivity.

Apart from diminishing the spiritual significance of religion, Durkheim's view of the moral order, while emphasizing its importance in society, has underplayed the role of the individual in social interaction. Therefore, his path-breaking positivist methodology, so far as sociology is concerned, can analyze only the influence of society upon the individual. We have therefore to realize that it is the methodologies we generally adopt that give us the impression that state, market and society are autonomous. The same impression is given when we adopt the functionalist view whether it is of the consensus or the conflict variety. In other words, any methodological paradigm that is based on social reality as observable facts gives rise to the dilemma of underestimating the role of the individual in social interaction, for the individual is endowed with an inner consciousness that is also crucial in social interaction. But, the inner world of the individual that is the realm of meanings and values is not amenable for observation as social facts.

Yet it is significant that Durkheim recognized the importance of an awe-inspiring object that could induce the individual to internalize the norms and laws of society, so that they are obeyed as the commands of a deity that controls the individual's destiny. Neither law nor norm of the society that goes against the interest of the individual can succeed if it has to rely upon the constant vigilance of the rulers, unless it is rendered intrinsic to the individual. In the absence of the belief in a spiritual power, some of the former totalitarian regimes used to impose upon the common people ersatz or artificial symbols for veneration, such as the embalmed body of Stalin exposed in the famous Lenin Square in Moscow. In the atheist Soviet society, the newly married couples used to visit the Lenin

Square for attesting to their marital vows. However, the perfect law and order noticeable in the streets of Moscow and elsewhere in society was no doubt possible only because of the consciousness on the part of the Soviet citizens that the secret service agency was ever vigilant.

I have made this digression to call attention of sociologists to the role of the individual in the functioning of the state, market and society, which has assumed a special significance after establishment of the republican form of the state. What are implied is a radically new set of social skills and values required on the part of Indian citizens to be able to operate in the radically new set of institutions. The republican state, the modern contractual market and the democratic society require on the part of the citizens a totally new moral order. Whereas the moral order that was intrinsic to most people until then was one based on the caste system sanctified by a dominant religious world view that became repugnant to the new social order.

Integral to any moral order are the evaluative concepts of good and evil, and standards of right and wrong that are confounded with facts, values and beliefs. People sharing a common cultural and moral order also trust one another and form a moral community. If we delve into ancient history, we would discover that in the remote past, inbreeding groups of people occupying a given territory such as tribes, devised their own moral order with their cults of beliefs enshrined in primitive religion.

With the development of economy and division of labour, it became possible for several localized communities to be united into a larger inter-dependent society with a central state authority. In such a multicultural society with fragmented trust confined to tribal communities, unity needed to be accomplished by force that was subsequently legitimized by freezing the different roles and positions of various cultural groups in a hierarchy of social status and a hierarchical moral order. This complex exercise in the Indian context was carried out by the combined efforts of the warrior and the priestly castes. It is such a social and moral order that has been skilfully captured and described by Srinivas in his popular concept of sanskritization, both as a process and as social order (Srinivas, 1996; 1998)

Obviously, the Brahmanic Hindu religion has played the major role in fashioning the moral order of the caste system that ultimately got established throughout the Indian subcontinent as it suited the prevailing political and economic institutions. In this manner, militarism and caste system became the hallmark of Indian civilization. Even the Muslim and British ruling dynasties belonging to religions that renounce caste system compromised their religious values to their political and economic interests. What I am emphasizing is fact that the so-called unity in diversity of the Indian society in the past was economically interdependent and occupying a contiguous territory. Such a unit created a society of people of collective identities in which basic unit in society was caste or tribe, the smallest culturally and spatially identifiable group that was assigned a distinct role and status. Consequently, it was difficult for a person to distinguish between one's individual or core identity and collective identity.

The British rule, however, besides vastly expanding the scope of the interdependency among territories and people, also introduced political, social and economic reforms that infringed upon the caste system but not enough to replace it. What is more significant is the fact that it created a new middle class intellectuals that with their minds stirred by their interaction with two qualitatively distinct cultures: their own and that of rulers. It is this select class of elite who imbibed the freedom-loving values of the culture of their rulers and fought for freedom for themselves from their bondage. Freedom struggle was steered by Mahatma Gandhi, who, by combining the best human values of the West and of India's past, led a non-violent struggle thereby creating a new moral climate in India that laid the foundation for India's freedom as well as the vision of a new social order. Thus, the freedom struggle envisioned the republican polity, contractual market and a civil society capable of democratic decision-making – a totally different social order from what had existed before.

What had existed before was an authoritarian political order in which the political authority flowed form top downwards. The individuals in society had no autonomy for electing their political representatives. As a matter of fact, their consciousness was moulded in such a way that they were not socially equipped to do so. Indian culture and society were intertwined in such a way that in the interaction between individual and society the latter influenced the former. In other words, the political, economic and religious institutions overpowered the individuals. In such an overpowering social structure, the individual identity itself was overpowered by the collective identity of the caste or tribal groups that were hierarchically integrated in the caste structure. Let alone the autonomy for the individual to elect her/his political representative, the individuals in India lacked even the social capacity for making a democratic/contractual choice in the economy or in the polity.

Here it may be useful to call attention to the basic distinction between the genesis of democratic order in India and in England – the country from which India got its inspiration. In England, in particular, and in Europe, in general, the mindset of individual identity and values of freedom, equality and universal brotherhood, which is the bedrock of a democratic society, was already there since the spread of Christianity to the whole European continent. However, its ability to transform the society into one capable of democratic decision-making was inhibited by the authoritarian polity reinforced by the pre-modern economy. It was in the 17th century when radical changes took place in the European economy that the individual could cut loose from the stranglehold of the feudal economic order and clamor for political autonomy. A new form of society called 'civil society' came into existence in which the individual could exercise both economic and political autonomy.

Therefore, in India, the inauguration of the democratic rule is a case of putting the cart before the horse. The leaders of Indian freedom struggle were no ordinary people. They had imbibed the best of both western and Indian traditions and were liberated from the shackles of the prevailing Indian social structure and prejudices of collective identities. As enlightened individuals, they could translate the political and economic institutions of democracy first with a socialist bias of Jawaharlal Nehru and subsequently with the liberal model that is of relatively recent origin. As for the appropriate social transformation of individuals and society, going by their own democratic fervour, they had piously hoped that institutions would change individuals and society. Accordingly, the republican constitution of India mandated the responsibility of transforming the society in the form of a civil society, upon the political process.

Over half a century of functioning of democratic institutions, we see a tremendous amount of change in state, market and society. But, what is of concern is that the change is not in the direction expected in a democratic society but one that is portraying a distortion of the society based on the caste system as well as of the democratic institutions. Today, all the democratic institutions stand discredited. We are all familiar with the tragic consequences resulting in problems noticeable throughout the country. What I would like to do on this occasion afforded to me, is to make a few observations about what needs to be done to stem the rot.

The forms of the state, market and society, envisaged in the Indian Constitution, are the ideal types of social arrangements for the realization of the goals of freedom, equality and universal brotherhood. These goals are translated into human rights and duties that have to be secured through the appropriate institutional frameworks. What the constitution takes care of are the agencies for realizing the goals. But, we should not forget that there are also agents involved in the operation of the agencies, and, in this case, they happen to be the citizens and their representatives. For the operation of these institutions the agents involved should be equipped with practical wisdom, a certain kind of ethical mindset to negotiate the institutions which by themselves are just mechanism that could also be misdirected for unintended purposes. That is what the Indian democratic institutions have turned out today. We have the institutions, but we do not have the appropriate skills to operate them. What we are faced with today is the crisis of moral order.

In the smooth functioning of state, market and society, the appropriate moral order of the individuals involved is a crucial dimension that is taken for granted in a well-established society. When there are long established traditions, it becomes intrinsic to the individual, like one's instincts, but in authoritarian societies the conduct expected of the persons is linked with external or extrinsic symbols so that it is amenable to the supervision of authorities. So also, when religious institutions exercise control over their members, they resort to extrinsic devices. The caste system fashioned by Brahmin Hinduism is an extreme case of an extrinsic moral order. It branded members of different caste groups with different degrees of dignity and codified the conduct appropriate to different castes. In this manner, the individual identity was forged with the collective identity. For obvious reasons, in pre-independent India, Brahmin lawmakers became invaluable advisors to the ruling dynasties of all religious persuasions not excluding the British rulers hailing from a democratic country.

Over the centuries, the extrinsic moral codes of the caste system had become intrinsic to the Indian psyche. It only shows that our cultures have a tendency of perpetuating themselves and so human beings can be imprisoned in cages of their own making. Rene' Dubos, the renowned microbiologist and experimental pathologist who demonstrated the feasibility of obtaining germ-fighting drugs from microbes, has provided us interesting illustrations for the evaluation of human nature. He tells us that there is much in common between the collective life of termites, or shoals of fish, and the type of group behaviour in human population obscurely referred to as mob psychology. In other words, there is also a biological dimension to the collective life of humans. They share with higher animals like apes, the ability to transform life conditions by social evolution, in contrast to the conservatism of social insects.

It is true that humans can learn much more faster and they can also spread their learning among other humans. But, this superior ability however does not make humans qualitatively distinct from higher animals. Human cultures too, like the culture of animals, have a deterministic tendency and that is what is emphasized in sociology, namely, the influence of society upon the individual. This tendency is a part of the instinctive nature of human behaviour.

But, what distinguishes the human beings from all other creatures is their proneness to alter or even abandon certain ways of life thereby make possible or greatly accelerate revolutionary changes. The human individual is unique in the possession of a free will that enables her/him to rise above one's culture and change its course if it is perceived as objectionable (Dubos, 1972). In traditional societies, not many people were able to rise above their cultures. Therefore, we can identify some illustrious exceptions in world history. They include the Vedantic sages of the Ganges Valley who criticized the bizarre cultural practices of their period, and founders of new religions that freed their followers from the bondage of traditional cultures, for example, Buddha, Jesus, Muhammad and Nanak to name a few.

Similarly, under exposure to the cross-cultural setting during the British rule, several leading lights of Indian society such as Swami

Vivekananda, Raja Rammohan Roy, Ishwer Chandra Vidyasagar, Jyotirao Phule, Gandhi and Ambedkar were able to cut loose from their decaying culture and assumed the role of social reformers. Such individuals could be clearly distinguished from the rank and file of the society at large inasmuch as the latter had not the free will to change from their existing condition. Individuality consists in the capacity of looking at oneself as one who is 'becoming' and not merely as 'being'. But, the pre-modern Indian society based on the caste system defined every person as a foreordained 'being' bereft of the opportunity of 'becoming'.

The leaders of the freedom movement defined the future Indians as individuals who would become different from what they had been in the past in the way that the leaders themselves had become by a fundamental change in their consciousness. They visualized a society that was radically different from the one in which they were brought up. There was a fundamental change in the conception of the 'good society' as envisioned in the India's republican constitution that is to be evaluated by the new yardstick of the values of freedom, equality and universal brotherhood. The new ideals are totally in opposition to the values of caste system that was ruling in the consciousness of the Indian people at large. What was required therefore was a new moral order.

The institutions of the republican state and the contractual market system may be in conformity with the kind of good society that is envisaged. But these contrivances can yield the desired results if people operate these institutions with the new values. Where are those values to come from? They have to come from the society and culture they are living in. Are the institutions of the state and of the market economy capable of transforming the society with the new values? As they are functioning today, the so-called democratic institutions have lost their credibility, not because they are defective as mechanisms but because of the ethical inadequacy of the persons operating them as well as the people at large in society whose representative they are. All the more regrettable is fact that the very guarantor of our social security, the judicial system itself is in jeopardy for the same reason. In March 2003, the Maharashtra government was obliged to honour with gallantry award a film actress for testifying in a magistrate's court to her statement made before the police that should have been the duty of any ordinary citizen.[1] The spirit of the freedom fighters has long since evaporated and people are caught up in their old ways.

In times like these it behoves us to look back upon the Indian leaders who were responsible for giving us the new vision to see what moved them to free themselves from the culture of their forebears. It was partly the democratic values of their rulers in their home country but largely a view of Indian history when there was a manifestation of such ideals in India's past. Those ideals were suppressed time and again by the ethos of the caste system that was congenial to the ruling and priestly classes. So much so that the Indian elite during the British rule needed to view the enlightened values of the rejected past through the eyes of the western oriental scholars. Those were the values that were suppressed by the dominant Indian culture that was fashioned in the pattern of the caste system that suited the pre-modern economy land authoritarian political order, as they were perceived as disruptive of the prevailing order.

The ethos of the caste system that was consistent with an authoritarian social order is precisely what is suppressed by the new constitution that has also led to a revamping of the political and economic institutions whose pattern could be easily copied from other functioning democratic countries. But for their operation they also need people with a proper ethical disposition – people who believe in the new ideals of individual freedom, equality land universal brotherhood in the spirit of commitment to their fulfilment. And thereby lies the rub. As this is, in my opinion, the crux of the problem, I should like to crave your indulgence for some more time to enable me to elucidate the problem.

It is true that the new structures of state and market are fraught with forces that bring in their train certain fundamental changes in the traditional social and cultural behaviour. They give rise to spatial and social mobility that topple the moral order of caste system by breaking up the spatial and social arrangements of the joint families and the caste-based hierarchical set-up of the village community. The earlier arrangements were shaped by a belief and emotional attachment to values such as men are superior to women, members of a given caste possess the same degree of dignity and different castes, different degrees, and these characteristics are hereditarily determined and perpetuated.

I have discussed elsewhere in a publication entitled *Indian Family at the Crossroads* (D'Souza, 2001), how such a process works and how, along with the change, it also engenders dialectical contradiction between the old values and the new ones that are needed for the smooth functioning of the family. Such a material change leads to the dialectic of marital adjustment between husband and wife who have now acquired individual identity and economic autonomy but in a milieu of consciousness moulded according to the traditional family values. The traditional superior-subordinate relationship of dualism between husband and wife is now turned into one of duality of equality between the two, requiring a different pattern of marital adjustment. Many of the gender-related problems that are now increasing could be attributed to such a change.

In this context, I would like to call your attention to the fact that human consciousness does not necessarily adapt itself to material changes – a point that Max Weber was trying to address to Karl Marx in his celebrated work entitled *The Protestant Ethic and the Spirit of Capitalism* (Weber, 1976). Material changes are complementary to changes in the consciousness or meaning, but they do not automatically trigger each other. The failure of the totalitarian Marxist and fascist models attest this hypothesis. The democratic models that have succeeded in the West are in societies that had tried to bring alive in their political and economic institutions the Christian ideals of freedom, equality and brotherhood. These democracies too are now threatened by the neglect of the source that motivated them (Fukuyama, 1999). Facts such as these should open our eyes to the necessity of an appropriate moral order for the proper functioning of democracy.

It is therefore significant for us to realize that we have a republican form of state and economy in the absence of a democratic moral order. In this context, it is ominous to ponder that ever since the assassination of Mahatma Gandhi, the most prominent among the freedom fighters who had recognized the urgency for a moral transformation of the society, no consorted efforts have been made to change the consciousness of the Indian masses. Gandhi was an illustrious example of those who recognized the importance of changing the consciousness of Indian people in the formation of a civil society. He realized the importance of transforming the multicultural Indian society into the democratic mode.

The imprint of the caste system in the Indian psyche cannot be wished away, as its memory is bound to persist. What is needed is to de-emotionalize those values and charge the new values of democracy with a new motive force that can impel people to act in a different way. The ethic that is needed for people to function in a democratic society requires a transformation of the conscience of a person equivalent to a conversion experience. It is an ethic that can release people from the bonds and bondage of the collective consciousness of the familism[2] of the joint family and of the clan, caste and caste system as a whole.

Although a discussion on the democratic moral order is central to my discourse, time constraints preclude me from a detailed treatment of this concern, and so we have to be content with a brief idea. The democratic moral order is presaged on three pivotal moral principles: (1) Rationality that is assumed to be universal in human beings and that obliges a person to regard that every person as an end in himself/herself, not a means for arbitrary use by this or that will. A rational person should be able to discern the rightness or wrongness of acts not as determined by their consequences but by their imperatives or rules by which they are guided. This is the principle of moral imperative as defined by Emmanuel Kant. (2) Capacity to extend the empathic expression of sociability or the sentiment of trust, to persons beyond the bounds of one's own cultural group. Sociologists refer to this tendency as spontaneous sociability. (3) The third principle is individual autonomy whereby one feels free to take independent moral decision.

It can be shown that these moral principles are also implied in the major values of freedom, equality and universal brotherhood that are also basic to democracy. But it is important to discern that not all these principles of morality or the values of democratic society are present in every kind of culture and society. Still more important to reckon with the fact that the constituents of neither the moral principles nor the democratic values are consistent among themselves. In the successful democratic societies from which India has copied its democratic institutions, as Max Weber has brought out in some of his studies, these principles and values were finally honed with the teachings of Jesus (Munch, 1994: 180-198).

When the sense of autonomy and freedom emerges from material changes in the economy and political institutions, it mostly results in conflict and hatred that alienates the individual from the group. Such tension calls for a new value complex that can enable the individual to transcend the narrow loyalties of collective identity and to acquire the wider loyalty of the individual identity to the whole society. In the 17th century Europe, when the economy was palpably changing and people in the lower feudal orders acquired autonomy, they already had a value complex of the providential moral order of Christianity. The moral and political philosophers could discern the flaws of the feudal society and provide new designs for the evolving society. I should not like to dwell on the different visions that arose as a result of the different views as regards the genesis of those values, and as to whether the source of those values was metaphysical or material. In England, however, the design of the new political and economic order emerged in conformity with the Christian providential moral order.

The Indian freedom fighters had an ambivalent attitude towards Christianity that was the motive force underlying the democratic values of their rulers. They appreciated their Biblical values but rejected their religious identity that was compromised in the colonial rule. Therefore, Gandhi and several others who had imbibed their democratic values from the West tried to justify them with values of India's past that were rejected because the prevailing economy and polity were not ready for them. As pointed out by A.L. Basham (1981:485), though Gandhi might have been sensitized to his idea of non-violent resistance by the Bible and discourses of Tolstoy, he presented it in the garb of Indian values drawn especially from Jain tradition notwithstanding the fact that he professed the Hindu faith. Interestingly, after his death, oppressed people in Christian countries practise Gandhi's ideas more than his own.

But, the fact remains that there are enough values lying buried in India's history from which one can draw inspiration for sensitizing the Indian masses with the democratic ethic. What then is needed for the resolution of our problem? M. N. Srinivas, who had devoted much of his writing in describing Indian society with its caste ethic, had come to the conclusion that caste system is the structural basis of Hinduism. Therefore, in discussing the changes in the Indian society that are inimical to the caste system, he had raised the question about the future of Hindu religion. Significantly, in what appears to be the last piece of writing of his distinguished academic career that was published in the *Economic and Political Weekly* posthumously after he passed away, is entitled "An Obituary on Caste as a System" (Srinivas, 2003). In this paper, he had come to the conclusion that the essence of the caste system is the *jati*-based division of labour that is being eroded in the new economy beyond repair – a view that I have also tried to test and verify in several of my writings (e.g., D'Souza, 1981). Srinivas has recognized that sanskritization, the Hindu religious strategy of integrating different castes in a unity, is no longer tenable.

However, in being careful to point out that what has demised is the caste as a system, Srinivas is mindful of the separate social existence of castes as cultural groups and hence recognized an alternative strategy for their integration. He has therefore suggested that now is the time to turn back to the various religious movements of the past such as Buddhism and Jainism and the Bhakti cults that were precisely aimed at the abolition of caste distinctions. Such religious reforms were aimed at integrating the morally fragmented caste society of their time. They could not succeed in their time because of the opposition of the economic and political forces. It is now obvious that the values of these religions are congenial to the democratic order. Gandhi and other modern Hindu reformers were trying to transform Hinduism itself to suit the democratic ethos.

To conclude my discourse, in which I have brought together many different ideas each requiring a separate paper, I should like to make a summary statement in a sociological jargon. The new institutions of state and market are new forms of agencies. They have to be operated by Indian people turned into citizens. The Indian people in the past were acting as passive agents, not as citizens, under the control of the old forms of agencies of the authoritarian state and pre-modern market exchange based on status. The term 'citizen' itself implies an active agent in society. The transformation of Indian elite from passive agents reconciled to an authoritarian social order into active agents fighting for freedom took place in a setting of cross-cultural interaction. Those elite freedom fighters introduced the modern forms of state and market apparatus that needs active agents for its operation. The new apparatus has succeeded in breaking down the old agencies, which has shaken the lethargy of the passive agents but has not equipped them with the capacity and skills necessary to handle the apparatus itself. In short, the Indian society is caught up in a crisis of moral order. The modern democratic state and market are still extrinsic to the Indian psyche. For their success they need to be rendered intrinsic to the Indian society.

Notes

1. The film actress Preity Zinta was presented the Red and White Bravery Award by Maharashtra government in March 2003.
2. For an illustrative discussion on the paradox of family values see Fukuyama, 1995. TRUST. London: Hamish Hamilton, pp. 61-127.

References

Basham, A.L. 1981. *The Wonder That was India,* Calcutta, Rupa Paperback.

D'Souza, Victor S. 2001. *Indian Family at the Crossroads*. Surat, Centre for Social Research.

— 1981. *Inequality and Its Perpetuation: A Theory of Social Strafication.* New Delhi, Manohar Publications.

Dubos, Rene'. 1972. *A God Within (a positive philosophy for a complete fulfilment of human potentials),* New York, Charles Scribner's Sons.

Durkheim, Emile. 1976. *Elementary Forms of Religious Life.* Translated by J.W. Swain, London, Allen & Unwin.

Fukuyama, Francis. 1999. *The Great Disruption (Human Nature and Reconstruction of Social Order),* New York, Simon & Shuster.

Munch, Richard. 1994. *Sociological Theory,* Vol. I. Chicago, Nelson-Hall Publishers.

Srinivas M. N. 2003. "An Obituary on Caste as a System". *Economic and Political Weekly*, Vol. 38, No. 5.

— 1998. *The Cohesive Role of Sanskritization and Other Essays,* Delhi, Oxford University Press.

— 1966. *Social Change in Modern India.* Berkeley, California University Press.

Weber, Max. 1976. *The Protestant Ethic and the Spirit of Capitalism.* Translated by Talcott Parsons, New York: Scribner's.

2

State, Civil Society and Market in Development: Towards a Comprehensive Consensus

T.K. OOMMEN

I believe that we can meaningfully discuss the theme of interface between state, market and society as partnership between state, civil society and market in development. Therefore, I am inclined to spell out the reciprocal roles of these three agencies – state, civil society and market – in the context of development I am arguing for a comprehensive consensus.

Although human society has been in existence for three million years, the discourse on development is barely three hundred years old. Initially, development was sought to be achieved through the instrument of industrialization. This in turn meant two things. First, substantial replacement of agriculture by industry and the rural population by urban population. Second, the progressive displacement of animate energy by inanimate energy. The three elements – industrialization, urbanization, technologization – conjointly gave birth to the notion of modernization, irrespective of ideological variations, that is, capitalism and socialism, wherein industrialization was a common refrain.

While both capitalism and socialism invoked industrialization as the primary tool of development, the former combined it with multi-party democracy and the latter with one-party democracy, giving birth to two models of development. The 'natural' modernity of capitalist democracies combined the process of economic growth with equity through welfare states giving birth to the First World. The state played a central role in development in capitalist welfare states but adequate space was conceded to market and civil society. In contrast, the 'enlightened' modernity of socialist states rolled up the state, civil society and market into one entity, firmly positioning the state at the commanding position. However, the socialist states pursued economic development with a firm thrust on distributive justice and equality. The Second World is the product of this process.

If the 'bourgeoisie revolution' produced the First World and the 'socialist revolution' created the Second World, the 'anti-colonial revolution' gave birth to the Third World. Most of the Third World countries opted for one of the two modernities, but India opted for the Third World, combining planned economic development of the Second World and multi-party democracy of the First World.

However, all the three worlds had industrialization as their common aim. In fact, development came to be measured in terms of the level of industrialization. But, the devastation caused by industrialization on environment produced a new trend in development thinking. Development produced a 'risk society' as the whole world is exposed to ecological problem. Globalization of risks through global ecological hazards, export of polluting industries and scrap waste materials, the risks of bio-genetic engineering, etc., are fast spreading. Understandably, sustainable development became the new refrain. It is in this context that development assumes a new meaning and needs to be put on the agenda.

But, which agency should take the responsibility of launching and sustaining development? In the socialist states, the state was the only agency engaged in development. But, in welfare states, voluntary associations, popularly referred to as non-governmental organizations (NGOs), too got involved in the task of development. In concrete terms, this meant introducing a set of income-generating measures for the poor, which it was hoped, would eventually make them economically self-sufficient and even autonomous. The leadership for this was provided either by development bureaucracy of the state and/or by 'altruistic' professionals. But, both groups were drawn from the middle class and they viewed development essentially as a non-political, techno-managerial activity. In this model of development, people's participation had no space; the beneficiaries of development were defined as clients and targets. In fact, development itself was defined as a function of capital and technology, while development goals were recognized in terms of urban middle class aspirations. If the people did not show the expected level of enthusiasm and aspiration about this strategy and goal of development, they were instantly dubbed as conservatives and change-resistors. Understandably, this paradigm of development castrated the people of their participatory potential. However, gradually, a new understanding about development crystallized; it dawned on a few of the experts and bureaucrats as well as the people at large, i.e., to be authentic, development ought to be participatory.

The above realization ushered in a new phase of collective action. Accordingly, for this paradigm of development, the critical inputs are not capital and technology but mobilization and protest. The middle-class experts of the NGOs and the developmental bureaucracy of the state are replaced by a set of militant, ideologically-oriented social activists. The focus was on conscientizing the deprived of their legal and political rights as equal citizens. Development was defined as a human right of the poor and not as charity or as a benefit bestowed on them. It was viewed as political activity.

This understanding of development brought in the much-needed focus on people's participation. But it also suffered from several defects. First, it did not clearly articulate a political theory, leave alone a political strategy, of capturing state power through the electoral process or through revolutionary means. It operated in the extra or non-parliamentary space, demanding effective implementation of the existing laws or at best proposing new legislations in response to the changing situation. Second, notwithstanding the above, since law making and its implementation are a state monopoly, the protagonists of this paradigm invariably took a negative stance towards the state which turned out to be dysfunctional. Dysfunctional because not only will the state not wither away, it cannot be wished away either. Further, the state will attempt to co-opt or repress the activists, if they constitute a nuisance or threat, both of which are detrimental from the perspective of the cause they pursue. If co-optation leads to their ideological castration, repression may result in their physical annihilation. Their success, therefore, would depend on keeping the required amount of pressure on the state by acting as a countervailing power.

Third, protest and the resultant mobilization are not substitutes for capital and technology although both are essential for development. Protest and mobilization are only instruments to moderate the hegemony of capital and to determine the choice of technology. That is, it should be squarely recognized that protest and mobilization are the means for achieving participatory development. What I am suggesting is that to be effective and meaningful collective actors should give adequate weightage not only to democracy but also to development.

A democratic polity, by definition, is one in which the hiatus between the government and the people does not exist. It is a system in which the people also participate with their representatives in the government to create a common future; it is tryst with destiny, to recall the evocative phase invoked by Jawaharlal Nehru. Political institutions, development plans, technology, information and knowledge etc. are inputs and instruments through which the destiny is to be achieved. But, when these institutions, instrumentalities and inputs do not deliver the goods and instead, become agencies of oppression, people's action becomes imperative. This is the context of the contemporary collective action, which is common to the whole world. It is indicative of the failures of the 'liberal expectancy' of the First World, the 'radical expectancy' of the Second World and the 'nationalist expectancy' of the Third World.

The elite of all the three worlds, notwithstanding the variations in their modes of recruitment and social composition, have failed to incorporate the people – the masses – into the participatory process and to create an open, civil society. Instead, the state, the government and even their political parties have become instruments in the hands of the elite to perpetuate themselves in positions of power and acquire privileges and perks. The people have become aware of the abysmal gap between what the system had promised and what it delivered and they are demanding the correction of this aberration.

Admittedly, established institutions have become suspect and even stigmatized. People's actions in contemporary societies are piloted through agencies variously labelled as non-party organizations, voluntary associations, people's committees etc., and all of them want to avoid the 'iron law of oligarchy' which has sapped the vitality of established institutions. This provides the moment for promoting participatory development through the agency of civil society.

It follows from the above that we need to establish the much-needed balance between the logic of development and the demands of democracy. The situation has been complicated by two contrasting tendencies. Development fostered the cult of affluence and the ethic of consumerism leading to the concentration of wealth in a limited number of polities and in the hands of groups and individuals within them. On the other hand, democracy nurtured the notion of decentralization and the process of participation. The assumption on which the liberal democracies of the First World have been built, namely, that political democracy can be sustained without economic equity, is being seriously questioned. The premise of the Second World, namely, that the ideology of distributive justice in the economy and a concentration of authority with the party-state can co-exist, was stripped naked leading to its very collapse. The widespread belief in the Third World that in the name of the abstract notion of 'nation-building' the rising aspirations of the people can be contained and kept at bay indefinitely, has come to grief. Today, people demand that economic content should be provided to political democracy; on the other hand, they insist that food without freedom is not worth consuming! It is against this background that we must situate the near-universal legitimacy obtained by democracy and the dismantling of the Second World leading to the emergence of the Global Age. The new instrument of development is the Structural Adjustment Programme (SAP). Its ideological high point is articulated through the Washington Consensus which maintains that economic growth is best pursued through open trade, export-led growth, de-regulation and more liberalized financial markets. Substantively, this implies the clear differentiation between state, civil society and market.

The principle of progressive autonomization between state, civil society and market is based on three assumptions. First, state is a coercive agent and motivated by authority. Therefore, the process of acquiring and exercising power should be well-defined and regulated through legal mechanism. Second, economic activity is motivated by material incentives and is to be regulated by the market mechanism in terms of free exchange. Third, civil society is the space for free voluntary activity for citizens, the space between market and state, which can moderate the authoritarianism of state and the rapacity of market. While endorsing the relative autonomy of state, market and civil society, I want to emphasize the need for reciprocity between them. And this calls for a comprehensive consensus.

If human welfare is the true measure of development and the purpose of good governance is to create a humane society, we need to clearly articulate the reciprocity between the three pillars of society – state, market and civil society. But, unfortunately, at present, they are drifting apart. The current ethos is one of shrinking state, expanding market and assertive civil society. However, this mood is against the very grain of human society because human beings are three-in-one entities. They are at once citizens, consumers and communitarians.

Citizen is the creature of state; one cannot meaningfully think of entitlements, duties and rights of citizens without reference to a state. Market produces consumers, much of their needs and aspirations are created and sustained by the market. Civil society prompts the emergence of communitarians, ideally the communitarian spirit of interrogation is informed of altruism. If the ongoing process gains momentum, we will enter a world torn asunder between the citizen, consumer and communitarian. And this should be arrested.

The role and responsibility of citizen will reduce with the shrinkage of state, the salience of consumer will increase with expansion of market and the vitality of communitarian will not be very relevant in the changed situation. That is, the hegemony of market will adversely affect not only the citizen and the communitarian but the consumer too. The citizen may opt out and become apathetic and alienated. The communitarian may limit his involvement and participation in society, become a retreatist and a recluse, out of sheer disgust. The consumer may tend to catch up, to cope with the intense global competition becoming an atomized individual indulging in consumerism. This is a dangerous protent.

Why should this scenario emerge? Because of the contradictory expectations we have from each of the three societal pillars. We want that the state should promote and facilitate high quality of life for citizens. The state is expected to be responsible, responsive, transparent and decentering. But, at the same time, it is desired that the state should roll back and shrink. A shrinking agency cannot be responsible and responsive.

On the other hand, the expanding market is not charged with the responsibility of being a promoter or facilitator of high quality of life. Rarely does one hear the need for market institutions to be responsible and responsive. The Berlin-based Transparency International measures corruption of governments. It does not extend this exercise to corporations. Decentralization is a constant refrain put to the state but not to the private sector. The tyranny of Presidents and Prime Ministers fill considerable spaces in our media but the authoritarianism of chief executive officers of corporations rarely come for comment. An expanding agency should not be let off without its share of social responsibilities. If taxes collected by the state from citizens are to be invested for their welfare, the profits made through consumers should also be shared with them. We need to postulate a consumer-friendly market ethic.

Institutions of civil society come for frequent approbation in the media. But, are they free of the malaise which beset institutions of state and market? The fact is civil society like the curate's egg is partly good and partly rotten. Civil society, which produces communitarians who participates in caring and sharing activities, also produces criminals, crooks and communalists. The NGOs and even the media are not always transparent. None is above reproach, beyond blemish. Therefore, we need a consensus, which is comprehensive enough to encapsulate the roles and responsibilities of state, market and civil society. This, I suggest, is the philosophy behind building partnership between state, market and civil society to bring about development.

II

In this context, I think, it is important to focus on rural development. Mohandas Karamchand Gandhi used to say: "India lives in her villages." Even today, after considerable progress in industrialization, 71 per cent of

India's population are rural according to the 2001 census. Therefore, rural development in India is synonymous with development.

True, M.K. Gandhi advocated a village-based development process. But it has been castigated for several reasons. I shall list just two of these. First, development was, and continues to be, wrongly equated with industrial urbanization. Second, leaders like Pandit Jawaharlal Nehru and Dr. Baba Saheb Ambedkar viewed the Indian village as an intellectually and culturally backward entity, indeed a den of ignorance and illiteracy and a habitat, which perpetuates both physical and mental ill-health.

The paradox is that Gandhiji himself did recognize this. He admitted that "the approach to many villages is not a refreshing experience. Often, one would like to shut one's eyes and stuff one's nose: such is the surrounding dirt and offending smell." However, he refused to accept this state of affairs as a fait accompli, as an irredeemable situation. Gandhiji wanted to change the village radically and held the view that "if the village perishes, India will perish too". And he did not advocate village primitivism. He wrote in 1936 that "there would be no objection to villages using even the most modern machines and tools they can make and can afford to use". Therefore, he only wanted to save rural India being exploited by urban India, the villages "from catching the infection of industrism".

However, Gandhiji insisted that "nothing will be allowed to be produced by cities which can equally well be produced by villages". And, when the villages are developed "... there will be no dearth in them of men with high degree of skill and artistic talent". Therefore, what Gandhiji advocated was the co-existence. He has not even advocated village self-sufficiency. He held the view that "it will be possible to reconstruct our villages so that villages collectively not villages individually, will become self contained".

I have spent a little time to explicate Gandhiji's position because he was/is widely misunderstood and misrepresented even by his outstanding contemporaries like Nehru and Ambedkar. But, there were others who shared his perception. Permit me to cite just one case. William Digby, the British scholar-administrator wrote in 1901, i.e., a century ago: "There are two Indias: the India of the Presidency and the chief provincial cities, of the railway systems, of the hill stations... there are two countries: Anglostan, the land especially ruled by the English, in which English investments have been made and Hindustan, practically all India fifty miles from each side of the railway lines." It will be dishonest to insist that there have been no change in the past one century but it is a truism that the basic wedge between Bharat, that is, rural India and India, that is, urban India, persists obstinately. That is why, we need to make a special effort to bring about development of rural India.

Now, the question arises who should undertake this stupendous task? I have allued to independent India opting for the third way to bring about development. Planned economic development launched through Five-Year Plans in which the state played a crucial role was and continues to be an important instrument in this context. And people's participation was consciously solicited by the state in the formulation and implementation of Five-Year Plans. The *modus operandi* invoked to elicit participation was indeed unique. Usually draft outlines of Five-Year Plans are circulated to ensure the widest possible discussion. The rationale of this procedure was enunciated in the First Plan: "Planning in a democratic state is a social process {in} which, in some part, every citizen should have the opportunity to participate. To set the patterns of future development is a task of such magnitude and significance that it should embody the impact of public opinion and the needs of the community... The draft is intended to be a *document for the widest possible discussion*" (italics added).

The process of planned development through people's participation was intended to bring about distributive justice as is evident from the following statement from the draft outline of the Second Plan: "The benefits of economic development must accrue more to the relatively less privileged classes of the society and there should be progressive reduction of the concentration of incomes, wealth and economic power."

These laudable objectives, notwithstanding and in spite of introducing institutional clusters such as the Community Development Programmes (CDP), Panchayati Raj Institutions (PRIs) and co-operatives, it cannot be said that participation by the weak achieved a high pitch in rural India. The basic reason of non-participation of the poor in the developmental process is the lack of economic content in India's political democracy.

The state in India had recognized the inadequacy of PRIs in promoting participatory development as articulated in the Fifth Plan documents. It notes: "In actual practice.... the resources envisaged have not had adequate impact on the direction or tempo of development." Therefore, the strategy was radically changed when the Seventh Plan was launched in 1985 which recognized the importance of "education in all its aspects, and people's participation in development programmes through their own organizations, holding the key to rapid and sustained social and economic advance". Thus, a major change of tool to elicit people's participation has been recognized. The role of civil society in development came to the accepted by the state and the proliferation of NGOs started. The Seventh Plan (1985-90) document advised NGOs to "...give greater attention to mobilize locally available human and financial resources, identify people in the poorer and vulnerable occupations like farmers, rural artisans, scheduled castes, scheduled tribes, agricultural labourers, girijans, bonded labour, upgrade their skills and give them the tools to make them economically self-sufficient as well as productive."

Thus, the high point of state-civil society partnership was achieved by the Seventh Plan which ended in 1990. It was precisely at this point of time that liberalization of the Indian economy was initiated. The last decade of 20th century (1990-2000) was somewhat ambiguous with regard to the role of the three agencies – state, civil society and market – in the context of development. The state's role in planned development agenda and the civil society largely became an interrogator of the policies of state and market.

Given the above scenario, this is the most opportune time to think about the roles and responsibilities of the three pillars of the evolving society. In this context, the partnership between civil society and private sector (i.e., market) is particularly relevant. The private sector should squarely recognize its new role and responsibility in development, particularly rural development. The expanding private sector needs to nurture a new ethic; a shift from exclusive profit-orientation to sharing the profit with the wretched of the earth. This is the mission of the moment.

3

State, Market and Society: Some Emerging Trends

BIRINDER PAL SINGH

The relationship of state, market and society may be seen in the context of the growing and expanding institution of the market which is both apolitical and amoral. The politics sets goals both for the market and the society. An important function of the state is to implement these plans and projects for the development of society. The society, on the other hand, enforces morality amongst individuals/people for a just social order. In the present times, the growing power of the market, supplemented by the multinational corporations, has become virtually autonomous. It has weakened the political power of the state and broken the moral authority of the society. Both these institutions, viz., state and society, have been relegated to the background. The withdrawal of the state is distinctly visible in the developing societies. In the name of globalization, all forms of alternative politics and society are being crushed. Under these circumstances, to assess what picture is more likely to emerge in the near future in our country and more so in its northwest region, is the desired objective of the present paper.

In earlier societies, the state had appropriated the duty to look after the affairs of society involving the rudimentary stage to meet the basic needs of the people necessary for their survival. Most of the times the market was never a permanent institution there though it was a regular one even if the periodicity of its organization varied from a week to six months or year. Its organization or establishment was often associated with fairs and festivals that attracted a large gathering of people at a single place: security of life and material from external invasions in the first place followed by internal administration pertaining to the maintenance of law and order. In such societies market did not make a dominant institution.

Enter capitalism and we find the emergence of a perennial and a permanent institution of market that has grown with the development and expansion of the capitalist economy. It has now become a place that is no less than a fair. People often go there for recreation and spending leisure. It is an open exhibition displaying consumer goods of all sorts in a manner that would attract the customer passing by the store. Window-shopping forms an integral part of the modern market as actual shopping. Today's window-shoppers are tomorrow's potential buyers. The market has now become the only place in the present-day society to offer the latest commodities to its people. Those who have the potential to pay in terms of a currency, carry goods with them, while others have to content with gazing only. This lack of equal opportunity for all consumers gives rise to social deviance and violence of a sort.[1]

In the contemporary civilized society market has universally acquired prominence over all other institutions. It forms the pulse of each nation-state. The modern economy operates through the market and regulates all social relations including the personal. The market dominates both the state and the society. It extracts maximum benefits from the state in the form of subsidies and sureties etc. and garners profit by producing and retailing the commodities to people at large.

From the times of the foremost economist of the liberal state Adam Smith, the economists have been debating on the relationship between the state and the economy (market) or the effectiveness of the government intervention very passionately. For some, the state must stay away from intervention and let the market forces operate freely on their own for the best economic results. For others, converse is true. According to them, markets need to be regulated and spearheaded by the government not only for the development of a healthy society but also for the robustness of the economy itself. In the words of Amit Bhaduri:

> Since under generalized commodity production of capitalism, every product including labour power becomes a commodity bought and sold in the market, the market is presumed to reflect the economic aspect of the functioning of the capitalist society. From this point of view, analysing the role of the state in relation to the market also implies an analysis of the economic relations between the state and the society.[2]

In the present-day capitalist economy the debate about the relationship between the state and the economy has become more sharp in the wake of economic leaps taken by certain small nation-states, for instance, the Asian Tigers. According to the World Bank, Japan leapt from the thirtieth richest country in per capita income in 1962 to eleventh in 1986; Taiwan from eighty-fifth to thirty-eighth and South Korea from ninety-ninth to forty-fourth. It is expected that by the early 21st century Japan, Taiwan, South Korea and China will probably have as much weight in the world economy as North America or Europe. Taiwan and South Korea will be as rich as Great Britain and Italy.[3]

This probable projection seems to be an issue of concern for the economists, especially in the West. That is why, they have given a number of theories to account for the rise of the Asian Tigers. Besides the two major economic institutions of the world, namely, the World Bank and the International Monetary Fund, numerous other economists like Hugh Patrick, Edward Chen, Milton and Rose Friedman and John Fei are the strong supporters of the Free Market Theory that subscribes to the primary role of private entrepreneurs and least intervention on the part of the government. The Simulated Market Theory subscribed by Fredrick Berger, Jagdish Bhagwati and others hold that more than liberalizing the markets the governments of these countries intervened more positively to offset other distortions caused by certain policies to create conditions "simulating a free market". The third type of theories refer to the governed market put forth by Parvez Hasan, Edward Mason, Henry Rosovsky and Chalmers Johnson etc. They believe that it is the directive role of the state in economic development. The government participates actively in all business decisions.[4]

Three largest nation-states in terms of the demographic statistics and geographical area, namely, India, China and the erstwhile USSR had resisted the blatant dominance of the market in the initial stages of their development but finally succumbed to its pressures as is distinctly visible in one of the major consequences of globalization on them. The demise of the former USSR marks the ascendancy of the world capitalism. India under Nehru opted for the mixed economy – a combination of private and state capitalism – that he thought would usher in new vistas for development and modernization in a hitherto backward country. This approach to economic development was criticized right from the very beginning. The fears of its critics have come true.

The Indian economy was finally liberalized during the late 1980s. It could not withstand pressures – both external and internal. The former in the form of appropriation of the national economy by the multinational corporations, directly or indirectly in the name of globalization and the later in the form of misappropriation of political office by its incumbents for self-aggrandizement. When 40 per cent people of the country are living below the poverty line, the so-called august members of the parliament (MPs) are busy in enhancing their perks and privileges. It is sheerly ludicrous, to quote an example, that they had obtained for themselves 25,000 units of power, 2,000 kls of water and one lakh telephone calls free in a single year. Dipankar Gupta has calculated that it "would mean roughly 275 calls a day. Assuming a twelve-hour waking cycle for MPs, that would mean about twenty-three calls an hour. If each call lasts for about three minutes, their diurnal clock has already run out of sand. This is literally an embarrassment of riches."[5]

Such a lavish lifestyle and display of power of money and political authority has become increasingly vulgar over the years. Recently, a party leader championing the cause of the poor and the downtrodden has allegedly spent Rs.10 crore on her birthday celebrations. The extent of public money involved in scams unearthed over the last decade is earth shaking. For the political elite, amassing private property is the only objective. Both the nation and its people have been left to themselves. The most prosperous states in the country are finding it difficult to pay the salaries of its employees. How would "development of the people and for the people" take place under such circumstances?

The external pressure comes from the world economy. Lenin had remarked that when a small peasant in a remote corner of the world brings his produce to the market, he immediately gets linked to the international market. In the modern society no one indulging in organized production can afford to stay away from the market. Hence, in the era of globalization, once the borders of a nation-state become vulnerable to the external markets, there is no option left for the developing country but to liberalize its economy. It means more access to multinational corporations which have tremendous capacity, both economic and political, to out-manoeuvre any company, howsoever strong that may be, in its own right. The protagonists of free economy uphold the logic of the market that corrects all errors creeping into it. For these economists a market is a perfect institution based on reason and rationality. Such people undermine the role of politics. But Joseph Stiglitz argues that markets are afflicted with imperfections due to asymmetries of information. Thus, the only way to overcome such imperfections is through good politics. Hence, he recommends "good economics with good politics".[6] Do we have a blend of good politics with good economics, both within the nation-state and without?

My fear is that we have none. Neither internally the politicians are committed to good politics nor the external institutions like the World Bank (WB) and the International Monetary Fund (IMF) are interested in good economics for people's development. To expect the external forces to do good economics is demanding too much from them since they are there to garner profit. The only hope lies with the former that is missing in most of the developing countries. Keynes had expected the World Bank to do good economics alone. But it is far from that in practice. Stiglitz writes:

> I had always been interested in economic development and what I saw radically changed my views of both globalization and development. I have written this book because while I was at the World Bank, I saw firsthand the devastating effect that globalization can have on developing countries, and especially the poor within those countries.[7]

The WB and IMF had been pursuing the policy of development which suggests, following Ann Krueger, former chief economist of the World Bank, that the only way for progress is free trade, without any barriers. She saw "government as the problem". But Stiglitz suggests its anti-thesis. He cites instances of small countries like Botswana and Ethiopia besides the Asian Tigers whose political elite effectively intervened in the aid plans from these world bodies and protected the interests of their own countries and their people. He writes about the East Asian countries: "The countries had been successful not only in spite of the fact that they had not followed most of the dictates of the Washington Consensus, but *because* they had not."[8]

These remarks from the former chief economist of the World Bank and a Nobel Laureate need to be taken seriously. His criticism of the processes of globalization, unleashed by these two premier institutions, viz., the WB and the IMF, should be seen as writing on the wall. That, "the IMF itself had become a part of the countries' problem rather than part of the solution". And,

> '...people refer to the economic and social storm that hit their nations simply as "the IMF" – the way one would say "the plague" or "the Great Depression". History is dated "before" and "after" the IMF, just as countries that are devastated by an earthquake or some other natural disaster date events by "before" or "after" the earthquake.[9]

Stiglitz also criticizes the very method of economic development followed by these two world institutions. They constitute their own teams of experts to provide guidelines to the recipient countries without involving the local experts. He writes: "The standard IMF procedure before visiting a client country is to write a draft report first. The visit is only intended to fine-tune the report and its recommendations, and to catch any glaring mistakes."[10] The IMF follows the 'one-size-fits-all' policy of development.[11] Such policies of the harbingers of globalization have pushed country after country into severe economic crises. Such crises could however be avoided if the market and the government of the client country play a complementary role. That is why, Stiglitz suggests active and committed participation of the governments in the developing countries to regulate their markets. Do we have such a responsive government and a political elite committed to the people's development?

Bureaucracy forms the second line of defence in steering the country on the path of modernization and development. Weber had pinned great hopes on the modern bureaucracy. Based on legal rationality, the bureaucracy inculcates the same in society. Schumpeter also suggests that bureaucracy is "not an obstacle to democracy but an inevitable complement to it" just as it is to modern economic development. He says:

> ...democratic government in modern industrial society must be able to command ... The services of a well-trained bureaucracy of good standing and tradition, endowed with a strong sense of duty and a no less strong esprit de corps ... It must also be strong enough to guide and, if need be, to instruct the politicians who head the ministries. In order to be able to do this it must be in a position to evolve principles of its own and sufficiently independent to assert them. It must be a power in its own right.[12]

Do we have such a bureaucracy? What scenario is likely to emerge in such developing countries that are heading for globalization following the dictates of the WB and the IMF under circumstances where the governments are starving of funds necessary for development? The political elite is not only parochial and indulges in cheap populism but busy in making money by all means. The bureaucrats too collude with their masters in reaping a rich harvest of easy money without any qualms. Whose worry is society, then?[13]

A society does not need some external agency to run its affairs. It has inherent capability to organize itself leading further to growth and development. I am sure, if left to itself, it would grow well or even better than otherwise. But, unfortunately, both the state and the market view it conversely. According to the protagonists of the state, both the market and the society need to be regulated strictly for proper development. The economists like Krueger believe that the market follows its own rational logic which is hampered by the interventions of the government. For her, as stated earlier too, "government is the problem" that is required to be dispensed with for the free growth of the market and the economy in general. The champions of the laissez-faire policy also hold that that government is best that governs the least. Stiglitz however strikes a balance between these opposing frameworks. He does not find any of the three elements – state, market and society – dispensable. All are important in their own right and in their own place. As a matter of fact, the show proper cannot be run without all three being equal partners for an all-round balanced development.

In a developing country like ours the overarching state is ruling the roost.[14] It is under the control of such politicians who practise populist politics for parochial goals. Such an amoral state has been dictating terms and conditions to both the economy and the society. Consequently, the state and its apparatus grew out of all proportions, so much so that it has now become difficult to sustain its size. Institutions and organizations are facing closure one after another. The lack of funds is the major problem hitting them. And, this problem is a result of mismanagement of resources, material and human, and using the organization for self-promotion by the top management, of course, in collusion with their political chiefs. It is a result of these failures that it became necessary to liberalize the economy in the late 1980s, and establish a Ministry for Disinvestment in the recent past. All institutions are asking their employees to opt for the voluntary retirement scheme (VRS). These are ever ready for a golden handshake. The vacancies created due to retirement are never filled and ad-hoc, part-time and contract employment is becoming a norm with these fund-starved public institutions. The earlier indifference of officers to these institutions and the people at large has created an army of 'non-workers' who take the government job as a side-business. Corruption, suspension and then reinstatement are taken for granted in the public sector.

One can see a design behind these developments. The left intellectuals strongly criticized Nehru for mixing the economy as they were arguing that eventually state capital would help the growth and development of private capital. Over the years the state institutions have become increasingly weak that we may now see withering away on the face of globalization. With the sole exception of the security sector, both external and internal, all others are victim of freezes and cuts in their budgets. This is a pointer in the direction of privatization of all services – health, medical, education, sanitation, water supply, roads and transportation etc. – that are so very essential for the welfare of people, especially of the lower classes.

With the weakening of the government the market is raising its head more confidently than ever before. This is going to take its own toll in a developing economy. When 'everything' is thrown open to the impersonal forces of the market, how would the weak survive? Other classes too are swayed by the ruthless forces of the market that are out to exploit each and every aspect of the economy and society for profit. Both nature and culture are subjected to exploitation. The former is important in determining the nature of a society to an extent. If it is altered, the society would surely not remain the same.

To cite an example, the ideology of modernization and the market forces have induced the thrifty Punjabi farmer to clear all forests and adopt the new technology in agriculture to suck the blood out of the Mother Earth in Punjab, Madhya Pradesh and the Terai region. Fast depleting forest cover,[15] fall in the soil fertility (productivity) level and the water table are posing serious threats to the Punjab economy, which is predominantly agricultural, and its society. Dwindling economic returns from the land and rising debts are pushing farmers towards suicides.[16] Small and marginal farmers are disappearing.[17] Villages are afflicted with outmigration. The negative consequences of the green revolution and the subsequent violence in this region are glaring facts.[18] The modern industry too is violating all rules for the protection of environment. Some industries are pumping the highly toxic waste into the water table while others are throwing it out in the open and in the air. Whose worry is the present-day environment?

The component of culture here does not include culture *per se* but the whole social formation. In most of the developing countries schisms between communities and regions are getting more and more pronounced. Divisiveness, rather than consolidation, is becoming an order of the day as a consequence of rising competition in the market economy. The relations between religious, ethnic and linguistic communities are developing strains as a result of the state policy of lopsided development and partisan role. The communal riots and terrorism are also becoming state-sponsored activities in a bid to retain political power. The social and interpersonal relations too are developing strains and becoming increasingly impersonal and money-centred.

The lack of coordination between the state and the market in the context of education for youth has resulted not only in unemployment but also problems of drug and alcohol abuse that is showing a steep rise over the years.[19] The rural schools are starving of the teachers and material infrastructure whereas the urban schools are getting polarised into those for the rich and the masses. And, the elite are sending their children abroad. Recently, the upper crust of the middle class has also started aping them. This class has developed a strong sense of insecurity concerning the 'future' of their children in the prevailing context of political and social normlessness, increasing levels of corruption and unemployment, fee hikes and falling standards of education etc. They exploit every possible opportunity to send and settle their children abroad, preferably in the USA or Canada.[20] The best students of the country from the elite institutions of technology (IITs) and management (IIMs) have always set their eyes on America for prestigious jobs and higher salaries. Whose worry is, then, our society?

The women's question is another problem that is becoming serious. Not listing many items the case of female body itself as a commodity and its use for sale promotions is crassly indecent and vulgar. Exposing the female body for advertising generates luscious feelings in the minds of hitherto traditional and conservative men.[21] This 'exposure' accompanied by growing avenues of female employment and activity outside their homes owing to the market economy are making them objects of violence and violation. Rapes in educational institutions, hospitals, police stations and other public places are on the rise. The television and popular cinema are busy in exciting the basic instincts of the people to make high profit. Valentine Day celebrations in the name of becoming global are promoted by the card/gift industry even if it is a crass imitation of the western culture of dating and legitimizing eve-teasing of the bygone days.[22]

The logic of the market is to promote consumer culture. Everything is available for consumption by one who can pay for it. Has the paying capacity of majority people increased? That is surely not the case. But more and more people of the middle and upper classes are indulging in consumerism. The state too is encouraging people to do so by discouraging savings and liberalizing trade of consumer goods. Those belonging to the middle class who cannot manage on their own are helped by the financing institutions. Over the last decade every small town in Punjab has witnessed a mushroom growth of such private companies besides those of the established banks. Financing has indeed become a big business in this part of the country.

Advancing of loans only trap the innocent buyer who does not act in the capacity of an individual person. He utilizes the amount for the family in the hitherto collectivity-oriented society. Social obligations more often interfere with loan utilization that could not be used for productive purposes. That is why, once under debt, one never comes out of it in a traditional society. In Punjab, farmers are committing suicide due to debts, whereas their sons are committing the same because their wishes for consumer goods are not being fulfilled. The small farmer has been sandwiched between the state and the market.

The dowry deaths and a huge dowry are also related to the consumer culture generated by the modern market. The rise in dowry and the bride burning may be directly related to the growth and expansion of the market. In the recent past taking a bride without dowry was considered *punn da viah*, that is, a virtuous marriage. But, now, no marriage is solemnised without a heavy dowry. The problem of the rising female foeticide is also related to it. It is unfortunate that Punjab is one of the most advanced and rich states of the country, yet the sex ratio is lowest, a meagre 874 compared to 1,058 of Kerala in 2001.[23] It is distressing to note that sex ratio for 0-6 years has registered a steep fall to 793 in 2001 from 875 in 1991. On the other hand, it shows an insignificant rise from 883 in 1991 to 886 in 2001 for the seven years plus category.[24]

The market has resulted in the commodification of each object and relation in society. Marx has remarked long time ago that in capitalism all social relations, including personal family relations, will be turned into money relations. We are witnessing the same today. Brides are being burnt, wives are being exploited and daughters are being forced into prostitution. The sisters, on the other hand, are getting their brothers handcuffed in lieu of *rakhi* or *raksha bandhan* who refuse to part their share in the ancestral property. Once tied into a strong consanguineous bond are presently engaged in litigation for parental property. This precisely is the logic of the market. The brothers had always been fighting with each other but never with their sister. It is only a recent development.

Woman is no exception who in all her roles as wife, daughter, secretary and colleague has been subjected to exploitation. The market economy has brought the traditional women out into the public sphere. She brings home her own bundle of tensions besides those of her husband

and children in this competitive society. This rise in family tensions and the ensuing domestic violence are telling upon the social and physical well-being of all the family members. Altruism on the part of woman as wife and mother, characteristic of a traditional family, has been replaced by egoism in the name of identity and self-assertion.

Durkheim had suggested that the modern society must develop moral individualism. Morality, for him, "is a system of rules of action that predetermine conduct", and he identifies three essential elements, namely, the spirit of discipline, attachment to social groups and autonomy. The question of morality for him assumed greater significance in the wake of advancing secularization. Lukes writes:

> It was no good merely stripping away the religious elements in traditional beliefs and practices: Morality and religion had been "too inextricably bound together in history... for the separation to be so easily consummated". The need was to "discover the rational substitutes for those religious notions that for a long time have served as the vehicle for the most essential moral ideas". It was "not enough to cut out; we must replace".[25]

Marx also wrote in *The Holy Family*: "If enlightened self-interest is the principle of all morality, man's private interest must be made to coincide with the interest of humanity... If man is shaped by environment, his environment must be made human." He admonishes: "Thus, under capitalism, 'inhuman, sophisticated, unnatural and imaginary appetites' are encouraged, above all an obsessive need for money, so that 'all passion and all activity must be submerged in avarice'."[26]

Under the given complex of state-market relations we have become crassly individualist without developing the new morality and losing out that which formed the bedrock of Indian culture and civilization. It has happened because the 'new' institutions have failed to generate the modern ethos and have simultaneously destroyed the traditional channels of moral education. The granny's stories have been replaced by the TV soap operas, the religious institutions by the cinema houses and the market, and the moral science in the school curricula by a variety of so-called technical and modern courses. All this goes in the name of equipping the students to meet supplies to the demands of the modern market.

Last but not the least, the Indian Coffee House[27] has given way to the cyber café.[28] Once again signifying a shift from the political to the apolitical and from collectivity orientation to individualism. A coffee house promotes social interaction, interpersonal bonding, mundane politics and exchange of views thus inculcating a concern for the other so very essential for a modern society. But, a cyber café, on the other hand, isolates an individual from others in a cool or cozy environment characteristic of haute society. It draws one into one's own inner world of likes and dislikes, rights and wrongs thus reinforcing one's idiosyncrasies without ever showing a concern for the immediate neighbour, leave aside the marginalized and pauperized strata of larger population in a developing country like ours. In small towns, the way-side tea shops provided space for political discussions and debates on social issues but these too have become victims of the television and Internet culture.

The coffee house or a tea shop represents the local culture whereas the cyber café represents not the international but in fact the American culture. I have mentioned elsewhere that the so-called fusion of the local and native music in the name of globalization is in fact Michael Jackosonization of the folk and the native. And, Michael Jackson is after all an American icon.[29] Aijaz Ahmad suggests that the globalization of the cultural form has closely integrated institutions of mass culture and entertainment into the dominant American media ideologically, politically, aesthetically and in expressive form: "Part of the objective of this crusading cultural globalism is the creation of new tastes by associating them with patterns of American life and thus giving to the Indian middle classes the sense of having arrived at a global cultural scene."[30]

Notes

1. Birinder Pal Singh, 'Violence: A dominant term of discourse', *Studies in Humanities and Social Sciences*, Vol. II, No. I, 1995, p. 88.
2. Amit Bhaduri, *Macro-Economics: The Dynamics of Commodity Production*, Macmillan, New Delhi, 1986, pp. 239-40.
3. Robert Wade, *Governing the Market*, Princeton University Press, Princeton, 1990, p. 3.
4. Ibid., pp. 22-29.

5. Dipankar Gupta, *Mistaken Modernity: India Between Worlds*, Harper Collins Publishers India, New Delhi, 2000, pp. 147-48.
6. Joseph E. Stiglitz, *Globalization and Its Discontents*, W. W. Norton & Co., New York and London, 2002, p. xiii.
7. Ibid., p. ix.
8. Ibid., p. 91.
9. Ibid., p. 97.
10. Ibid., p. 47. He continues: "In practice, the draft report is often what is known as boilerplate, with whole paragraphs being borrowed from the report of one country and inserted into another. Word processors make this easier. A perhaps apocryphal story has it that on one occasion a word processor failed to do a 'search and replace,' and the name of the country from which a report had been borrowed almost in its entirety was left in a document that was circulated" (Ibid., p.47).
11. Ironically, the *World Bank Report 2000/2001: Attacking Poverty*, OUP for World Bank, 2001 has a full chapter (No. 6) on 'Making State Institutions More Responsive to Poor People', pp. 99-116. It suggests measures to strengthen institutional environment of democratic regimes especially in the developing countries.
12. Tom Bottomore, *Theories of Modern Capitalism*, Universal Book Stall, New Delhi, 1990, p. 40.
13. Contrary to the expectations of Schumpeter, the bureaucrats of modern India form the highest echelons of authority in Delhi down to the deputy commissioners in the districts are not mere spineless stooges to the politicians but also as corrupt as their political bosses. The same is the case with the police force. The police and bribery etc. are synonyms at least in the north India. The judiciary has also joined the bandwagon lately. It is sheerly amazing to notice that the harbingers of modernization and social development (bureaucracy), providers of social and physical security (police), the regulators of law and authority; and the trustees of justice (judiciary) ensuring equality and freedom to the people of India have become 'models' par excellence of corruption and immorality.
14. For a brief discussion on the nature of state in India and crises afflicting it see Birinder Pal Singh, *Violence As Political Discourse: Sikh Militancy Confronts the Indian State*, Indian Institute of Advanced Study, Shimla, 2002, pp. 96-108.
15. As per recommendations of the environmentalists at least 33 per cent area of a region must have the forest cover. But, in Punjab, it was meagre 4.19 in 1970-71 and 6.07 per cent in 2000-01, far below the minimum required. *Statistical Abstract of Punjab 2001*, Punjab Government, Chandigarh, pp. 284-85. It is also quite likely that figures too might be exaggerated. Sometimes ago, the timber trade had let loose havoc on the famous 'MP teak'. The devastation of the teak forests could

only be stalled with the intervention of the Supreme Court in the early 1990s putting complete ban on its cutting. A former Chief Minister of Himachal Pradesh had to lose office for his alleged involvement in the multicrore timber trade of *deodar* (Cederis deodara) wood. And, very recently, a Punjab Minister of Forests has also been suspended from the ministry for allegedly favouring certain contractors in the auction of Ropar forests.

16. See H.S. Shergill, *Rural Credit and Indebtedness in Punjab*, Monograph Series IV, Institute for Development and Communication, Chandigarh, 1998. It is estimated that the total debt of the Punjab farmers is Rs. 5,700.91 crores (1 crore = 10 million) out of which they owe 46.32 per cent to the commission agents only (p. 92). He writes: "These estimates indicate that the annual recurring interest charge on farmers' debt in the state comes out to Rs.1,102.78 crores – a fairly big amount in absolute terms... This burden is further highlighted when we observe that 90.42 per cent of the total cash expenditure incurred by farmers in the state on raising crops, has to be borrowed by them and they do not have any surplus savings of their own... This means crop production in Punjab has become almost completely dependent on recurring short-term crop loans" (p.69).

The problem of suicides by farmers in Punjab has been examined by the sociologists and the economists alike. Their findings suggest that increasing poverty and high indebtedness are major causes. See (a) *Punjab de pendu khetar wich atam-hatianwan: ik report* (Punjabi), Association for Democratic Rights, District Unit Patiala, October 2000; (b) K. Gopal Iyer and Mehar Singh Manick, *Suicides in Rural Punjab*, Department of Sociology, Punjab University, Chandigarh, 1999. It has been published subsequently; (c) Inderjit Singh Jeji of Masses Against State Repression, Chandigarh...

The problem of suicides amongst farmers is not only confined to the North India. Andhra Pradesh and Karnataka were also equally affected. Things have not improved since then. Parvathi Menon writes 'Driven To Dersperation' in *The Hindu*, September 14, 2003: "...the sudden escalation in suicides this year – over 200 farmers have killed themselves since April and the figure is mounting – represents an alarming new trend. It is not only that the numbers are rising sharply. From being a feature of economically backward, drought-prone regions, the suicide phenomenon is now shifting to relatively advanced agricultural regions. This would suggest the emergence of new agrarian pressures even in prosperous districts that are pulling farmers, the small and marginal among them in particular, into inextricable debt-traps.

The real crisis, ... rural indebtedness appears to be the consequence of iniquities and pressures resulting from specific *State-directed strategies* in the agricultural sector" (emphasis added).

17. Gill writes: "With the rise of development crises in agriculture, the small and marginal farmers are finding it difficult to survive. Between 1970-71 and 1980-81 large number of such holdings have disappeared... The decline is 25.3 per cent... The marginal holdings declined by 61.9 per cent and small holdings declined by 23.3 per cent." Sucha Singh Gill, 'Socio-economic Contradictions Underlying Punjab Crisis', in Gopal Singh (ed.), *Punjab: Past, Present and Future*, Ajanta, Delhi, 1994, p. 295. For a synoptic view on the problems of the Punjab economy especially in the context of the Sikh militancy, see Birinder Pal Singh, *Violence As Political Discourse*, op. cit., pp. 181-91.
18. Vandana Shiva, *The Violence of Green Revolution: Third World Agriculture, Ecology and Politics*, Other India Press, Goa, 1992.
19. The collection of revenue from excise duty on liquor alone, both country and foreign, and beer shows a staggering hike over the years: Rs.206.84m (1970-71), Rs.907.2m (1980-81), Rs.4,331.63m (1990-91) and Rs.11,935.05m (2000-01). This does not include illicit liquor, opium, poppy husk (*bhukki*), drugs etc. that are extensively consumed in the rural Punjab. Illicit distillation is very common in the villages. All along the Pakistan border illicit distillers carry country liquor in bladders on horses and ponies etc.
20. The tendency to go abroad has become very prominent over the last decade. Families after families belonging to the upper-middle class – landlords, rentiers, doctors, engineers, teachers, managers, defence services etc. – have sought immigration for the *sake of their children*.

    The case of the lower-middle class is more pitiable. They sell property or take loans to send their sons more often illegally. There are cases where a brother has married his sister and a daughter-in-law has married her father-in-law for immigration. What else devious means and methods could have been adopted by people is anybody's guess?

    The travel agencies have made fast money in sponsoring such 'rackets'. Earlier confined largely to the Doaba region of Punjab now these agencies have mushroomed in every small and big town of this region.

    Balwant Singh Ramoowalia, a former MP and president of the Lok Bhalai Party, has a list of some more than ten thousand girls that are victims of failed marriages with the NRIs. Despite all such problems – the Malta tragedy (a ship carrying about 450 passengers much beyond its capacity was drowned while illegally ferrying across the Mediterranean), legal detentions, physical and economic exploitation, failed missions and marriages – the tendency to go abroad has not declined.

    Harbhajan Mann, a famous Punjabi singer has recently made a popular film – *Ji Aayian Nun* – on this theme.

21. More than three decades ago, the vernacular press used to carry pictures of half-clad women especially in their Sunday issues to promote sales of their papers. These pictures became more lewd and luscious with the advent of colour printing. Sadly enough, coinciding with the era of 'liberalization' almost all the national dailies with a legacy of over hundred years or more have also started projecting similar stuff on their pages. And with the onset of globalization, carrying advertisements of Jockey (world class undergarments), Numero Uno (Jeans), Blackberrys and Octave Clothing, Yardley (perfumes) etc. has become a routine feature with them. Publishing half-porno shots of men and women serves the double purpose – it not only boosts their sales but also gets them revenue from advertisements. Besides such features, a prestigious daily – *The Times of India* – has started a column of jokes with double meanings and not so decent either. Earlier carried by the nation-wide edition now it is confined only to the metro edition. It hints at marking off the metropolitan culture and sensibility from its hinterland.
22. The Valentine Day (14th February) celebrations have become fashionable over the last few years only. Hardly any youngster is aware of the story of St. Valentine. For him, the sole significance of the day lies in proposing the girl of his choice with rose(s). For those having sweet hearts, this day calls for expensive gifts. For most of the first-generation urbanites and the newcomers, this day means a legitimized *chhed-chhad* or flirtation. Besides this social aspect, the political dimension is no less important. Certain political parties, like the Shiv Sena and some bands like the Bajrang Dal etc., have often taken law in their hands in damaging the shops dealing with cards and gifts for this day. Some other political parties and groups resent such moral-policing on their part thus resulting in clashes here and there.
23. *Punjab Statistical Abstract 2001*, op. cit., p. 43.
24. Ashish Bose, 2001, *India's Billion Plus People*, B.R. Publications, p. 72.
25. Steven Lukes, 1973, *Emile Durkheim: His Life and Work*, Harmondsworth, Penguin, 1988, pp. 111-12.
26. Steven Lukes, 1987, *Marxism and Morality*, Oxford and New York, Oxford University Press, p. 82.
27. The reference here is to the famous Indian Coffee House in the heart of Connaught Place, New Delhi where teachers, lawyers, doctors, political and social activists of various shades would gather in the evening to delve on the day-to-day issues of politics, economy and society. Interestingly, this intellectuals' joint was razed to ground during the days of Emergency (1975-1977). It would also be pertinent to mention that coffee houses were equally dear to Sartre and Rabindranath Tagore.
28. A modern cafe (cyber) is an obverse of the Coffee House. Samrat Choudhury and Haidar Naqvi report under the title 'The buyers aren't coming: adult magazines

take a beating as stiff competition from VCDs and the Internet lures away customers': "Now, there are at least 40 Internet cafes in Kanpur that survive on porn, according to police sources. They offer privacy in the form of special cabins where customers can see anything they want to? and (sic) the Internet has no dearth of variety.

The city's police recently raided some of these cafes with results that stunned even them. Of the 60 people arrested for watching porn, 17 were girls who were watching the sites with their boyfriends. Some of them were imitating on-screen action when they were disturbed by the police." See *Hindustan Times (Sunday)*, September 7, 2003, p. 15.

29. Birinder Pal Singh, 2002, 'Culture, Society and Violence: Emerging Issues', *IASSI Quarterly*, Vol. 20, No. 3, January-March, p. 37.
30. Aijaz Ahmad, 2002, *On Communalism and Globalization: Offensives of the Far Right*, New Delhi, Three Essays Press, p. 114.

4

Social Audit of Privatization: Emerging Interface of State, Market and Society

B.S. GHUMAN

Public sector undertakings across the globe are under scrutiny. Privatization policies have been advanced and advocated as panacea for poor performance of public enterprises. Theoretical foundations for privatization are provided by four variants of the New Right School of Thought – property rights literature, public choice theory, principal agent theory and literature on success stories of private corporate sector. The New Right School broadly argues that state involvement leads to increasing monopoly, increasing budget and suppressing of entrepreneurial behaviour, limiting choice, overproduction of unwanted services and encouragement to waste and inefficiency. The New Right School thus has forcefully advocated withdrawal of the state as a regulator as well as a producer. Deregulation and privatization, therefore, are on the top of the reform agenda of the New Right School.

In practice, impetus to privatization programme, particularly in the developing world, is given by the international bodies like the World Bank and the International Monetary Fund (IMF) under their programmes and conditionality packages. Privatization programme, initiated in the late seventies and early eighties, after making its presence felt in almost all the countries, has entered a new phase. In its initial phase, the philosophy of privatization was marketed as synonymous to efficiency, more choices, people's capitalism and boon to state exchequer. The initial results of the UK experience of privatization were so impressive that within a short span of time it became a universal policy paradigm. As privatization progressed both extensively and intensively, its negative outcomes also started surfacing, which started a debate on contribution of ownership in the performance of a firm. According to empirical evidence documented by Vicker and Yarrow (1988) and Bos (1991), ownership *per se* does not explain cent per cent variation in performance of a firm. According to these studies conducted independently (one in UK and another in Germany), along with ownership, other variables such as degree of competition, regulatory policies of the government and technological progress hold the key for performance. In India, the empirical evidence suggests that central public undertakings since the 1990s, barring a few years, have achieved commendable level of performance and often outperformed enterprises in the private sector (SCOPE, 2000 and Ghuman, 2001). Empirical evidence also suggests that in certain cases privatization has reached its limits and its ill-effects have started coming on the surface. Most appropriate example in this regard is the privatized rail service in the UK It is now a known fact that companies that took over railways in the UK did not spend sufficient funds on safety networks, the results of which are rail accidents one after the other. The ranking of railways as a safe mode of transport has suffered considerably. According to an estimate, between 70 and 80 per cent of the general public in the UK is in favour of renationalization of the railways. In case of British Railways a part of the government subsidy is diverted for paying dividend to the shareholders. If the government subsidy is withdrawn, the private companies would become loss-making companies. Recently, the UK government has decided to replace Railtrack (a private company) with a publicly owned not-for-profit Network Rail (www.guardian.co.uk).

Likewise, in the US cities after cities are fighting for deprivatization of water supply. A website (http://privatzation.home.attbi.com/page33.html) titled "Cities Going Public" lists the cities, such as Chattanooga (Tennessee), Duval, Nassau and St. Johns Counties (Florida), Huber Heights (Ohio), Pekin (Illinois), Peoria (Illinois) and Washington Court House (Ohio), which are spearheading a movement for deprivatization of water supply. Their major complaints against private firms are hike in prices, low pressure, deterioration in quality, endangered public safety and lack of infrastructure upgradation. While suggesting deprivatization of Air Canada, a letter to the Canadian Prime Minister reads: "Deprivatization is necessary to bring back efficiency, effectiveness, profitability and just plain good public management, qualities which all seem to have been lost" (http://www.grandfolkies.com/cormud.htm). Campaign against privatization got momentum in the International Conference Against Deregulation, Privatization and Labour Rights for All held in Berlin (February 22-24, 2002). The delegates of labour/trade unions and political organizations hailing from 51 countries denounced the negative impacts of privatization on workers' rights and social equity (http://www.owcinfo.org/Berlin/Conference/Final/20Statement.htm).

The denationalization of banks and telecom services has been under active consideration in a couple of countries. Above all, the sponsors of the privatization programme, namely, the World Bank and the IMF, have also started rethinking about it. In a paper titled, "Time to Rethink Privatization in Transition Economies" (Finance and Development IMF Magazine), John Nellis (Senior Manager, Private Sector Development Department, World Bank) has demonstrated empirically that results of privatization from countries such as Russia, Mongolia, Ukraine, Armenis, Georgia, Kazakhstan, the Krgyz Republic and Moldova are not encouraging. According to him, "private ownership often does not lead to restructuring (that is, making changes to position a firm to survive and thrive in competitive markets). Some partially state owned firms perform better than privatized companies. In some countries, there are few differences in performance between (wholly) state owned and privately owned firms." Poor results (stagnation and decapitalization), Nellis says, are mainly due to monopolizing the gains of privatization by the 'insiders' – managers and workers, lack of means and incentives to lead the privatized firms forward, lack of outside capital, concentration of high quality assets in the hands of the resourceful, agile and politically well connected few, lack of legal and institutional framework dealing with post-privatization issues etc.

Privatization is not under attack only on the basis of economic parameters. The negative social implications of privatization (which were not acknowledged by the theorists and practitioners of privatization) are equally pronounced and undermine the sustainability of privatization, particularly in the developing world. The objective of this paper is to conduct social audit of privatization by identifying the social implications of privatization, which are likely to impinge upon the sustainability of privatization, particularly in a developing country like India.

Methodological Issues

Methodologically, the identification and quantification of the social issues of privatization in India are very difficult on two accounts. First, there is a gestation period of the impact of privatization on society. Secondly, qualitative nature of the source of the social issues of privatization. Notwithstanding these methodological inadequacies of comprehending the relationship between privatization and society, in this study, an attempt has been made to identify social issues of privatization by combining empirical evidence available from other countries, logic, preliminary trends noticed in India and speculation. A wide spectrum of issues relating to the society constitutes social issues. In the absence of known list of social issues, this paper confines to study the effects of privatization on employment, environment, poverty and vulnerable groups, women, backward areas including border areas, socially backward classes and households.

Social Implications of Privatization

Employment Environment

In a developing country like India, generation of employment opportunities was one of the major objectives of public enterprises. Public enterprises have successfully achieved this objective. Overfulfillment of this objective in certain cases has resulted in overstaffing as well (Government of India, 2002: 33). The privatization programme, it is feared, will result in laying off staff on a large scale, particularly after the lock-in period about labour retrenchment is over. The fear is valid on three accounts. First, empirical evidence across the globe confirms it. In Arab countries and countries like Uganda and Sri Lanka, privatization has resulted in unemployment. In Uganda, about 70 per cent of the respondents in a study opined that total employment has come down as a result of privatization (Ssentamu and Mugume, 2001: 18). Secondly, the private corporate sector in India prefers to import technology from outside rather than developing indigenous technology in consonance with country's resource endowment. Empirical evidence also suggests that the technology developed in labour scarced economies is capital intensive and leads to jobless growth. Thirdly, there is no legal binding on the privatized firms to remain in business forever. In case winding of the units and selling of assets including land having prime location is more profitable vis-à-vis remaining in business, the privatized firms would prefer the former.

In the layoff process unskilled and casual workers suffer more in comparison to skilled and managerial cadre employees. It is relevant to mention here that the categories of workers likely to suffer more would not find jobs quickly in the private corporate sector due to job stagnation and emerging dominance of capital-intensive technology after liberalization. In contrast, the skilled managerial cadre employees and other top-ranking officials would not face any dislocation hardships as they are in demand in the private sector. In brief, the lower strata of workers would be hard hit by privatization. The middle and upper level employees, government officials (known as state corporate elite) having well-developed networking with private corporate sector would continue to thrive even during post-privatization phase (Jiyad, 1996).

The public enterprises in India are known as model employers on account of service conditions, working hours, industrial relations, wages, fringe benefits, provision of social infrastructure (education and health), townships, recreation centres and children education. They provide housing facilities to about 51 per cent employees. For the remaining house rent allowance is sanctioned. During the year 2000-01 public enterprises in India spent Rs. 3,79,357 crores on township maintenance and social overheads, whereas only Rs. 222.41 crores were charged from employees, thus meeting the huge deficit of Rs. 3,571.16 crores themselves (Government of India, 2002: 189). In the privatized firms, on the contrary, most of these privileges are made available on payment basis and thus would make household budgets of the workers more difficult to manage. The overall changing composition of employment structure disfavouring low-profile workers (i.e., unskilled and semi-skilled workers), non-existence of job security cushion, demand for flexible labour laws and hostile environment within privatized firms would result in workers' alienation, particularly in the absence of social security network. According to Ssentamu and Mugume, "....workers are increasingly becoming insecure and their power to organize and have dialogue with the employer has been seriously weakened" (2001: 49).

Poverty and Vulnerable Groups

Privatization in India has its origin in Structural Adjustment Programme (SAP). SAP, including privatization, has considerable adverse effects on the poor. Hike in prices, withdrawal of services from economically unviable but socially desirable areas (e.g., passenger transport from uneconomic routes), cuts in subsidies for the poor, introduction of users charges practices in social sectors like health and education, permission to private educational institutions to charge development charges in the form of high fee and official apathy towards poverty alleviation programmes are some of the outcomes of the liberalization and privatization programmes which directly hit the poor, particularly those who are the poorest of the poor. The Sri Lankan experience suggests that poverty level has worsened after privatization. In s survey conducted there in 2000, more than 50 per cent respondents were of the opinion that privatization has adversely affected poverty, cost of living and social life (Nellis, 2002). While discussing privatization and social concerns, Leipziger and Foster (n.d.) opine that privatization leads to price hikes, which make services beyond the reach of the poor. Further, the multinational corporations aiming to maximize profits are not willing to provide services to the urban slums and remote villages.

Women

In increasing gender-sensitive environment, it is essential to study privatization from gender perspective. Both theory and practice suggest that privatization in India would not be in the interest of female workforce. In India work participation rate for female is already very low (around 26 per cent). It will further go down during post-privatization phase on account of five mechanisms: labour market, price mechanism, reduction in state subsidies, relatively hostile environment for working mothers and general bias against women employment. Theoretically speaking, the prime objective of privatized firms would be the maximization of profits. This motive can be achieved by reducing cost and enhancing resources. On cost front the major constituent normally is the wage bill. The first and immediate action of privatized firm would be to reduce the manpower as well resort to wage reduction measures. In both cases, the axe would firstly fall on women and semi-skilled and unskilled workers (Jiyad, 1996). Most of these workers are on contract or ad-hoc basis engaged in activities which after privatization are either contracted out or are generally replaced from manual operation to machine operation. Women workers are normally not very active in trade union activities. In the post-privatization phase, they seem to be easy targets of labour cost reducing devices. Price hike is the most important mechanism to enhance the revenue of a firm. In post privatization phase, the environment of general rise in prices and general reduction in wages make women employment less remunerative in comparison to imputed wages for the work performed domestically.

Public enterprises, on the other hand, provide many facilities to its employees on subsidized rates such as meals, transport, medical care, accommodation and leave travel concessions. After privatization, most of the subsidies are either withdrawn or reduced. Needless to mention, for low-paid workers including women, such subsidies are big relief. In the absence of these subsidies, the jobs at lower wages become less attractive. Public enterprises are also very friendly to working mothers. They have relatively better pregnancy-related leave rules. They also provide special facilities for the convenience of working mothers like creches and preparatory schools. After privatization most of such child-friendly facilities are either closed or run on cost-effective principle. The pregnancy-related rules become more stringent after privatization. These likely developments indicate that post-privatization scenario would be relatively unfriendly to women employees. In a society like India in transition (from feudal to capitalist socio-economic system) general environment at the family as well as corporate level is against women employment. This nexus in the thinking at the family and corporate levels against women employment takes a practical shape during post-privatization phase. In the post-privatization phase, all these factors taken together compel the women workers to withdraw first from the jobs, as the opportunity cost of the working mother is really very high. Jiyad (1966) has succinctly summarized the impact of privatization on women as follows: "Combining the effects of three factors; the labour market, reduced subsidies, and higher prices a family might find out that the opportunity cost of mother going to work is really high, and therefore, the family would be better off economically if mother stays at home. This option becomes even more attractive when there is an opportunity for retirement." Limited empirical evidence from the Middle East reveals that privatization may not be in the interest of female employees (Harik and Sullivan, 1994).

Backward Areas including Border Areas

Mitigation of regional disparities is one of the leading objectives of public enterprises in India. Under this objective, considerable public enterprise investment has been made in backward states like Bihar (including Jharkhand), Orissa and Madhya Pradesh (including Chhatisgarh). In Bihar and Jharkhand, the investment of public enterprises on March 31, 2002 works out to be Rs. 25,923.18 crores, which constitute 7.02 per cent of the total. In these two states public enterprises offered employment to 3,09,000 persons, which works out to be 17.76 per cent of the total workforce in public enterprises. Madhya Pradesh and Chhatisgarh claimed 5.57 per cent of the central public enterprise investment. These undertakings offered employment to 2,21,000 persons comprising 12.69 per cent of total public enterprises employment (Government of India, 2002: 191). States like Punjab, having sensitive international border, have also in some cases received sizeable investment from public enterprises. In the post-privatization era market forces guide fresh investment. Investment prefers to go to states like Maharashtra and Gujarat having locational advantages and well-developed infrastructure. Backward states like Bihar, Jharkhand, Orissa, Madhya Pradesh, Chhatisgarh and border states like Punjab, Rajasthan, Jammu and Kashmir and cluster of seven sister states of north-east are likely to suffer on account of fresh private capital. Thus, privatization is likely to increase regional disparities resulting in many economic and social problems including social tension and secessionist movements.

Socially Backward Classes

It is not only that the public enterprises protect the interests of backward areas, these enterprises are equally friendly to socially backward classes. Under various policies and programmes, including reservation policy of the Central Government, the public enterprises are very effective instruments for protecting and promoting the interests of socially disadvantaged classes and castes. On an average, around 27 per cent of the employees of public enterprises, at present, are from Scheduled Caste and Scheduled Tribe categories (Government of India, 2002). After privatization, the benefits accruing to these socially disadvantaged groups will gradually disappear.

Households

The negative impact of privatization percolates down to the household level. The famous 'trickle-down' hypothesis though does not work effectively in the growth arena. Its working in case of negative impact of privatization at household level seems effective. In a developing country like India, there are families after families in which only one person is employed and thus dependency ratio is very high. Privatization being treated as synonymous to lay-offs would hit hard, as stated above, firstly female workers, followed by unskilled and semi-skilled workers. The single bread-earners being out of jobs have serious ramifications for family as an institution. The growing unemployment among women, unskilled and semi-skilled workers may result in high rate of dropouts, particularly that of girl students in educational institutions, reduced health care of women and the old, more family disputes, particularly relating to property relations, high divorce rate, etc. The empirical evidence from Uganda reveals that privatization has extremely impaired livelihood of many households. The following statements clearly illustrate adverse effect of privatization at household level:

> "It took me over a year to get my small package, which was after all, a mockery of the privatization process in Uganda. I was unable to pay rent to National Housing Corporation. I have now sent my family to the village

and have even failed to sell this flat for a reasonable 'goodwill'" (a household head in Buganda Road Flats).

> "Certainly, this privatization has negatively impacted on me. I am unable to send my children to a good private primary school. You can see the small house I am in, you see it yourself" (a household head in Jinja).

> "I used my small package of Ug. Sh 3.2 m to start a business which was robbed by those people in Kampala" (a household head in Kawempe).

The Ugandan study further by way of unfolding the impact of privatization at family level states: "As a result, some households have failed to raise school fees for children, meet their daily meal requirements, and even attend to health care. Even in cases where the laid off have been given their terminal benefit packages, it was revealed that it is not enough to set up sustainable self-help projects. As a result, the money is not recycled back into business but to cater for the endless family and extended family obligations" (Ssentamu and Mugume, 2001: 39). Thus, these outcomes of privatization, if taken together, would adversely affect equilibrium at household level.

Concluding Observations

Privatization as a public policy succeeded in establishing its dominance around the globe. The privatization programme started in the 70s and the early 80s has reached its limits. After experiencing initial rounds of success cases, the negative results of privatization include consistent hike in tariff rates, withdrawal or limited services for poor consumers, deterioration in quality of back-up services, no fresh investment, rather binding up in couple of cases, concentrations of benefits of privatization both during and after privatization in the hands of select rich people, etc. The negative aspects have not only been confined to the economic sphere, the social sphere is equally likely to be polluted by privatization. The significant negative implications of privatization from the societal perspective include the following:

Firstly, declining job opportunities, hitting mainly the lower strata of workers, namely, the unskilled and semi-skilled workers. The post-privatization environment is not conducive for extracting the best from the working class. The negative impact on job security, industrial relations, working conditions, social infrastructure (education and health), housing, children education allowances, etc. alienate the workers from the organizations.

Secondly, people below the poverty line suffer most on account of hike in prices, decline in subsidy and lay off.

Thirdly, the axe of privatization falls first on women. A combination of factors such as working of labour market, hike in prices, reduction in subsidies, hostile environment for working mothers and general bias against women employment compel women workers to withdraw from employment as opportunity cost of women workers, particularly working mothers, is very high.

Fourthly, people living in backward areas including border states like Punjab will also bear the brunt of privatization. In the post-privatization phase, fresh investment has very limited chances of reaching the backward areas. On the contrary, it is feared that the new owners of privatized firms may wind up these units in backward areas and maximize one-time profit by selling the assets.

Fifthly, socially backward classes/castes would also pay a heavy price of privatization. The existing privileges for these backward classes like SCs and STs would disappear in the post-privatization phase and thus depriving them the scope of social unliftment.

Lastly, family, as an institution, will also become a casualty of privatization.

References

Bos, Dieter. 1991. Privatization: A Theoretical Treatment. Oxford, Clarendon Press.

Cities Going Public: A Summary of Cities Fighting to Take Control of Their Privately Run Water SystemsHttp://privatization.home.attbi.com/page33.htmll

Ghuman, B.S. 2001. "Performance of Public Enterprises: An Assessment of India's Experience" *International Review of Public Administration.* Vol. 6, No. I, June.

Government of India. 2002. *Public Enterprises Survey-2000-2001.* Department of Public Enterprises, New Delhi, Ministry of Heavy Industries and Public Enterprises.

Hiya, Harik and Denis J. Sullivan (eds.), Privatization and liberalization in the Middle East, Valentine M.Moghadam (UNU/WIDER, Helsinki) Middle East Study Association of North America-*MESA Bulletin*. Vol. 28. No. I, July.

Jiyad, Ahmed M. 1996 "The Social Balance Sheet of Privatization in the Arab Countries. Centre for Development Studies. wvvw.fou.uib.no/fd/1996/f/712004/indez.htm

Leipziger, Danny and Vivien Foster. "Is Privatization Good for the Poor?" International Finance Corporation Publications. Issue 2.

Nellis, John. 2002. The Impact of Privatization on Labour, OECD/Republic of Turkey, October. www.iecd.org/ppt/M00037000/M00037363.ppt

Open World Conference of Workers, Berlin Conference. 2002. http://www.owcinfo.org/Berlin/Conference/Final/20Statement.htm

Ssentamu, J.Ddumba and Adam Mugume. 2001. *The Privatization Process and Its Impact on Society*. Uganda National NGO Forum Structural Adjustment Participatory Review Initiative (SAPRI).

Standing Conference of Public Enterprises. 2000. *Performance of Public and Private Sectors*, a study conducted by Centre for Industrial and Economic Research (CIER), New Delhi.

Vicker, John and George Yarrow. 1988. *Privatization: An Economic Analysis*. London, The MIT Press.

5

Social and Business Worlds: Emerging Interface

RAJESH GILL

Churchill once commented: "We build our houses and houses build us." Here, I am modifying this quotation: "we build businesses and businesses build us." This statement very aptly describes the interface between socio-cultural and business worlds, especially in the present context of globalization and market expansion. Although, there is no one-to-one relationship between the two, yet both tend to influence each other. Changes in one lead to consequent changes in the other. Global markets have brought the business world right into the forefront of societies, knowing no boundaries of space. The rationalization, which marked capitalist society, and especially its business organization, could not have been possible if appropriate ways of thought and skills had not already developed and acquired social significance over many centuries (Hughes, Sharrock and Martin, 2002). Hence, the interface between the social and business worlds has been recognized well in relevant literature on the subject.

This interface has been extensively studied and made use of by the western business schools for quite sometime now. However, there is scanty literature in Indian context. How the peculiarities of Indian culture and society have influenced the business, needs a serious study. This paper addresses to this topic. However, before going into the details, an acquaintance with 'what is business' on the one hand, and 'Indian society' on the other, must be gained.

The earlier economists conceived of the businessman and his behaviour as purely 'passive', while success in business meant rapid and intelligent adaptation to events occurring outside in an economy shaped by impersonal objective forces that were neither controlled by the businessman nor influenced by his reaction to them. The contributions of a trader, for instance, were seen as purely 'mechanical'. For Marx, the result of capitalist production is the loss by human beings of control over their own lives; in that all must obey the laws of the market, which confront them as objective, impersonal forces even though they are no more than the outcome of the activities of ordinary people (Sharrock, Hughes and Martin, 2003).

Today, a 'business' enterprise is considered as created and managed by people, and not by the forces. Economic forces set limits, create opportunities, but do not determine what a business does. The modern perspective represented most vigorously by the most renowned scholar in this field – Peter Drucker (1992) – no longer defines business only in terms of profit maximization. Business, on the other hand, has as the foremost objective of creating a customer! It is the customer who is the foundation of a business and keeps it in existence. He alone gives employment.

The two main functions of business, according to Drucker, are marketing and innovation. Elaborating on his main argument, Drucker explains that a business enterprise can exist only in an expanding economy, which considers 'change' both natural and desirable. Further, good business today demands innovation in design, product, marketing techniques, price, service to the customer, management methods and so on.

Finally, for the ultimate success of any business, future prospects and social environment are very important factors. To be specific, it is essential to keep abreast of the future changes, which are expected in the social world.

A very significant change that has happened in the business world is the perception about the role of an individual – an extremely important sociological variable. Management, according to the modern view, goes beyond simple adaptation. It, on the other hand, implies a responsibility for attempting to shape economic environment for planning, initiating and carrying through changes in that economic environment. Today's businessman has to create, innovate and transform the market trends.

I find the above change tremendously relevant because it has led to the conception of man as a rational, active and conscious actor, who instead of responding mechanically to unpredictable market situations, moulds the market forces by taking decisions. Such a realization has also led to another very important transformation in the modern world – the possibility of 'planning'. It is only recently in human history that planning has been adopted at various levels, viz., national, industry and even in a household. Hence, management theory has recognized the decisive role played by an individual in a market situation.

This realization has brought to the forefront the indispensability of formal training, business schools, etc., to acquire the expertise in business, thus bringing in the role of professional and technical skills. In the Indian situation, the rise of professionalism has emerged simultaneously along with the traditional system of family business. Hence, we find the big business houses such as the Tatas, the Birlas and others depending on the one hand on professionals like the trained managers, chartered accountants, legal experts, tax consultants, technically trained engineers etc., and on the other hand, on their own family members as decision-makers. Thus owners continue to be the decision-makers, while the professionals help run the business. It may be labelled as a case of an interface between tradition and modernity.

The Changing Socio-cultural World

The Indian society has traditionally had many distinguished characteristics, in contrast to the western societies, thereby offering a peculiar business world. Following are the salient features of Indian society, which have exercised tremendous impact upon business world:

- The importance of religion, engulfing the occupational, economic, personal and social life of an Indian. The significance of spirituality, transcendence and altruism.
- The social fabric of Indian society reflected through the *varna* and caste systems. The most relevant dimension here being the hereditary occupation.

- The joint family system, attaching a positive value with ancestral home, land, elders and social responsibilities towards not only the family but the society at large.
- A negative value attached with materialism and profit making. A renowned sociologist Max Weber (1930) has attributed the emergence of capitalism in the West to the religious ideology of Protestant Ethic and the absence of capitalism in India to the caste system.
- Theory of *karma*, rendering man as a passive being, whose survival is determined by the God Almighty. Man's conception as a creative and rational being (in purely economic sense) therefore has never characterized Indian philosophy.

The traditional society of India has undergone tremendous transformation with severe implications on its business world. The major areas having transformed may be classified as under:

The Nature of Business

A rise in professionalism, bureaucratization, largely a non-family affair, a strong profit earning motive.

One of the very strong implications of western culture on Indian society initiating with the British rule is reflected through a change in the attitude of an Indian towards business (including all profit-oriented ventures in material terms). *Artha* – one of the *purusharthas* in Indian philisophy, hierarchically below *dharma* and *moksha* – was traditionally considered only as a means to the more spiritual and transcendental ends in Hindu life. Hence, an overindulgence in the material pursuits solely for making money was accorded a negative value. Such an attitude has been blown up, thanks to the capitalistic orientation that has reached us through the West. This has completely transformed the nature of business in India – its image, its importance etc. It is no longer immoral to entertain a profit motive, rather it reflects competitiveness, innovativeness and ambition. This sort of social change has certainly made business acceptable to different sections of people thereby enlarging the scope of business in India.

The Participants in Business

Traditionally, we have always had a close association between Indian castes and business acumen. Thus, Banias were always labelled as born businessmen, inheriting the expertise from their forefathers. Further, Brahmins and other landowning castes considered it below their dignity to take up business transactions because it involved a shameless greed for money through an extensive use of dishonest mechanisms. The state of affairs has very much changed today, reflecting itself through the flooding of book stores with the tips on how to develop business acumen, how to make easy money, how to get a feel of the market, and so on. A major consequence of all this has been that almost all castes (irrespective of their traditional occupations) are trying their hands on one or the other kind of business. One finds Brahmins, Khatris, Banias, Rajputs, Jats, Ramgarhias, Sunars and others in different types of business. There is an increased trend towards entering into the business field even after securing professional degrees of Engineering MBA, MBBS and so on.

The Diversification of Business

You name an item or a service and there are people transacting in it. History has never seen such a variety of business activity as is found today. Anything you have can be marketed provided you have the business acumen. Ideas sell, products sell, services sell, parts of the body sell. Similarly, you can buy anything today with money, right from consumption items such as soaps, garments, shoes, electronics, electrical items, to specific physical features, replacement of human organs, surrogate mothers, genes and so on. This has brought the whole gamut of commodities right into the market. If one starts making a list of business activities going on in a metropolitan city of India, I am sure this is going to be endless and unimaginable.

Items which are Marketable

The transformation in Indian family has given an altogether new shape to business here. Could anyone ever think of the very basic functions of family being sold off? Today, they are available in the market provided you can pay the price. The shift from joint to the nuclear family has made life monotonous and boring – the result? One looks for diversions elsewhere

– in restaurants, discotheques, travelling and so on. The rise of such necessities has given way to novel methods of earning money.

The new socio-cultural environment has thus reinforced the modern business potentialities. It is not possible to conclude as to what really determines what? But, the interface between the business and social worlds certainly reveals important insights into the credibility of western theories of management, which need serious revision.

References

Batra, Promod and Batra, Vijay. 1995. *Management Thoughts*. New Delhi, THINK INC.

Drucker, Peter F., 1992. *Managing For The Future: The 1990s and Beyond*, Oxford, Butterworth-Heinemann Limited.

Hughes, J.A., Sharrock, W.W. and Martin, P.J., 2003, *Understanding Classical Sociology: Marx, Weber, Durkheim*. London, Sage Publications.

Olenick, Arnold J., 1989. *Managing to Have Profits, The Art of Hitting Your Target Profit*. New York, McGraw-Hill Book Company.

Sharrock, W.W., Hughes, John A. and Martin, P.J., 2003, *Understanding Modern Sociology*.

Weber, Max, 1930. *The Protestant Ethic and the Spirit of Capitalism*. Allen and Unwin.

— 1958. *The Religion of India*. The Free Press.

II

The Rural-Urban Interface

6

State, Market and Society: Issues and Interface in Rural and Urban India

S.S. BHATTI

I, like all architects, am trained to view things in a multidimensional perspective. The subject has been dealt with in this paper in four parts. Part I sets out my terms of reference by way of commonly accepted concepts of state, market and society. This brief exposition prepares the ground for discussion that forms Part II of the paper and shows where I agree or disagree with the standard concepts of state, market and society, and incorporates my views on the subject. Part III covers assessment, and highlights failures as well as the main issue that springs from the rural-urban interface. "What can be done" is outlined in Part IV, and it ends with the concluding remarks and definitive suggestions.

I
Concepts

State

State is essentially the political organization of society. It is the body politic, or more narrowly, the institutions of government. The term 'state' came to prominence in the 16th century, largely as a result of its employment by Niccolo Machiavelli in his famous book, *The Prince*. The term was also used in the phrase 'state capitalism' which, according to Leninist doctrine, is economy in which possession and management of industry are in private hands but owners are subject to extensive state controls. State capitalism is similar to what is called planned economy in capitalist countries. The primary purpose of the state is to maintain order and security. It does so by means of a system of law backed by force. The exercise of its jurisdiction is limited to a definite geographical area, but within that area the state is sovereign; that is to say, it has supreme and exclusive authority.

Welfare State

The concept of welfare state, applied to a number of liberal democratic states since World War II, involves a widening of the functions assigned to the state by individual liberalism. For the English philosopher John Locke and the early utilitarians the business of the state is confined to order and security. The state ideally should protect each individual's freedom to act as he chooses, provided he does not infringe upon the like freedom of others. This notion highlights liberty but does nothing to help those who cannot help themselves. Aid for the needy is left to the voluntary action of religious and philanthropic institutions and is not thought to be the business of the state. The welfare state has the job of ensuring the means of subsistence and basic minimum of welfare for all its members. The philosophy of the welfare state involves a more general view of state responsibility. The basic necessities of life are defined so as to include a decent measure of education, health and housing. Schemes of social insurance redistribute wealth in the interests of social justice. A welfare state has the positive function of promoting justice and welfare as well as the old negative function of protecting liberty and security.

State and the Individual

As noted before, state has both a wider meaning, the politically organized society as a whole, and a narrower one, the institutions of government. Despite the fact that several philosophical theories have been propounded from time to time, it has been natural though curiously enough, for the narrower meaning to arise. The authority of the state must be exercised through particular offices, and these come to be identified in thought with the state. Thus, Marxism and Anarchism see the state as the institutions of enforcement of rules – that is to say, the institutions of government – and as something separable from the society as a whole.

The separation of powers in democratic states helps to reduce the polarization of state and the individual. Although an individual who takes a minority view is liable to find himself at odds with the legislature, executive, and judiciary alike, the courts may nevertheless protect such an individual from an excessive exercise of power by the executive.

Attempts to counter the growth of governmental control are seen in the tendency towards decentralization achieved by increasing the scope of local and regional government. Decentralization does not, of course, limit state power, but it diffuses the exercise of that power and so gives more opportunity for the voice of individual citizens and representative groups to be heard and heeded.

Market

Market, in the most literal and immediate sense, is a place where things are bought and sold. In the modern industrial system, however, the market is not a place. It has expanded to include the whole geographical area in which sellers compete with one another for customers. Most markets consist of groups of intermediaries between the first seller of a commodity and the final buyer. There are all kinds of intermediaries – from the brokers in the great produce exchanges down to the village grocer. In general, the function of a market is to collect products from scattered sources and channel them to scattered outlets. From the point of view of the seller, dealers channel the demand for his product. From the point of view of the buyer, they bring supplies within his reach.

Origin

Markets as centres of commerce seem to have had three separate points of origin. The first was in rural fairs. A typical cultivator fed his family and paid the landlord and the moneylender from his chief crop. He had sidelines that provided salable products and he had needs that he could not satisfy at home. It was then convenient for him to go to a market where many could meet to sell and buy. The second point was in service to the landlords. Rent, essentially, was paid in grain. Even when it was translated into money, sales of grain were necessary to supply the cultivator with funds to meet his dues. Payment of rent was a one-way transaction, imposed by the landlord. In turn, the landlord used the rent to maintain his warriors, clients and artisans, and this led to the growth of towns as centres of trade and production. An urban class developed with a standard of life enabling its members to cater to each other as well as to the landlords and officials. The third, and most influential, origin of markets was in the international trade from early times merchant adventurers risked their lives and their capital in carrying the products of one region to another. The importance of international trade for the development of the market system was precisely that it was carried on by the third parties.

Nowadays, it is common to hold international fairs at which industrial products are displayed for inspection by customers, however, consists in placing orders rather than buying on the spot and carrying merchandise home. The function of the independent wholesaler, like that of the merchant, has declined as great retail business has grown to a scale whereby they can deal directly with manufacturers. But specialized exchange for primary commodities is still important.

Market vis-á-vis Social Welfare

The doctrine that the free play of individual interests in a competitive market maximizes the welfare for society as a whole, though stands demolished, has still an important influence on the formation of market ideology. The rationalization grew out of the 19th century utilitarian philosophers' Hedonistic calculus, which regarded all human life as governed by the pursuit of pleasure and avoidance of pain. This train of thought identifies pleasure with consumption, leaving out of account the whole sphere of conditions in which work is carried on and finally it sees consumption in terms of spending money. The whole economic basis of life is thus reduced to terms of commercial transactions.

The Politics of Market

The doctrine of laissez-faire is attractive in many ways. If the economy is a self-regulating mechanism and if economics is a system of scientific laws, then moral and political problems are excluded. Questions of social justice do not arise then. The function of government is to be strictly neutral between interested parties. But when people come to recognize that the market, by its very nature, is necessarily a scene of conflicting interests, every element in it becomes a moral and political problem. Thesis is distressing because one can no longer rely upon the principles of economics in order to provide safe and simple rules for finding the correct solutions. While economic affairs grow even more overtly political, at the same time commercial influences spread into new spheres. Old notions of loyalty, service and rapid technological change make it necessary for every group to defend itself against the erosion of its relative income and status. It would appear that the new capitalism, for all its benefits, may have been developing internal contradictions of its own that threaten its future stability.

Market Socialism

The secret of private enterprise (both for good and for ill) is that it is private. The manager of a capitalist concern acts as a principle and is able to use initiative and judgement. A socialist manager that is told to make profits is still an agent acting under instructions, may be somewhat less confusing and contradictory than the old multitude of targets handed down from above, but it is still arbitrary because it depends upon a system of prices fixed by decree. When the enterprise is granted the freedom to set its own prices (as in Yugoslavia), it is back to the anomalies of imperfect competition and of instability of markets.

Marketing

Marketing, in its most general definition, is the directing of the flow of goods and services from producers to consumers or users. It is not confined to any particular type of economy, since goods must be marketed in all economies and societies except perhaps the most primitive. Nor is marketing a function only of profit-oriented business. Even such service institutions as hospitals, schools and museums engage in some forms of marketing.

Marketing as a Business Function

Business, whose primary concern is the marketing of goods, usually distinguish four basic functions in their work: (1) pricing, (2) product determination, (3) distribution, and (4) promotion. More recently, a fifth function, namely, marketing research, has been added. Product determination consists of establishing the assortment of goods to be produced, as well as their qualities, and physical characteristics. Such determinations are usually made in concert with the company's manufacturing, engineering and finance departments. Promotion includes both personal selling and advertising, and is intimately related to the culture in which it is found. The provision of information is an important element in promotion, but the type and degree of selling pressure varies considerably from one country to another. Marketing research is concerned with the gathering, processing and analyzing of market information. In developing its marketing strategy a firm must determine what its best potential markets are and then select the means by which it will try to sell to them. The means are various, and the individual firm will concentrate on the specific combination (or marketing mix) that seems to yield the most successful results. Retailing and wholesaling are the two modes of selling. For thousands of years most goods were sold in market places or by peddlers. Hawkers still walk or cycle the streets of towns crying out their wares – especially those of daily use. Wholesaling consists of selling to other business firms, either for resale or for business use, usually in bulk and at less than retail prices. A wholesaler is an independent merchant operating one or more wholesale establishments. Manufacturers may engage in wholesaling through their sales branches, and retailers may also do so internally through chain store warehouses, although they are not classed as wholesalers.

Society

Society, in the social sciences, is regarded as a group of human beings bound together for self-maintenance and self-perpetuation and sharing their own institutions and culture. The concept denotes continuity and extremely complex relations. It is social life that is distinctive in the regulation of behaviour in human beings. The human animal does not have such instincts as serve to guide the behaviour of lower animals, and he is therefore more dependent upon social organization than is any other species. Institutionalized social forms are therefore assumed to play the major part in influencing human actions, and it is the task of sociology to discover how these forms operate on the person, and also how they are established, develop, elaborate, interact with one another and decay and disappear. Among the most important of such structures is the family – the subject of an important field of sociology. The peer group, the community, the economic and political orders, various voluntary associations, and special organizations such as the religious and the military, are of particular importance in this inquiry.

II
Discussion

I have given a concise account of the concepts of state, market and society, as believed to be harboured and commonly accepted by social scientists. Since I am not a qualified social scientist, in the narrow technical sense, my views of the theme are those of an outsider who sees things in a perspective few experts do because they deal with the subject as a matter of conditional reflexivity. Being a non-expert, to my experience, gives one the all important freedom to seem, assess, select and use what is offered by the experts as a routine exercise in jargon. It is in this special context that I feel I can afford to disagree with any expert's view even at the cost of annoying him. If expertise stops at the level of an acquisition of technical know-how and the skills which go with it, the 'expert knowledge' certainly fails to fulfil its basic aim of serving fellow human beings. Approaching the problem without any prejudice I will pin down concepts I cannot accept as also those I agree with. I will also let the 'issues' emerge naturally from this discussion rather than frame them as hypotheses in the very beginning. The discussion will be an attempt to unfold the 'interface' which exists among state, market and society – and is the ferment that yields through an unstoppable reaction among many varied interests the conditions in which we live.

State

I agree that the state must have emerged primarily as something over and above the society, holding the responsibility of maintaining stability and harmony among different elements of society. I also agree with the concept of a 'welfare state' which means that apart from its primary purpose of maintaining order and security, the body politic also has the job of ensuring the means of subsistence and basic minimum for all its members. Since the state is essentially the political organization of society, politics, as the art and science of government, is legitimately its chief means towards the stated ends. Thus, politics, which, in my view, is quite simply a method of ordering relations between state and society, tends to become an arena for belligerent bouts to grab power anyhow. This has indeed been the scenario in India's recent past and is now becoming uglier day by day. I therefore do not agree that the concept 'welfare state' is an improvement on the original concept of the state comprising the institutions of government whose primary task is to protect liberty and security. The innumerable scams and scandals that are being unearthed and reported by media everyday should lend support to my averment that the welfare state, at least in India, is a Wul-pher state. Incidentally, America, the only superpower in the world, has already highlighted the ugly side of politics as "manoeuvring and intriguing".

All the three organs of the Indian state – the legislature, the executive and the judiciary – are in a bad shape. The legislature largely consists of those members who have absolutely no expertise other than that of manoeuvring and intriguing which has become our national sport – for which the Lok Sabha and the Vidhan Sabhas are veritable arenas. Those who somehow outwrestle others to emerge as *Hind Kesaries* constitute the executive or the government. The judiciary, not wanting to lag behind in its contribution to the welfare state, comes up with its own brand of muscle-flexing; judicial activism, which is an ingenious method of usurping executive power, is not legitimately its own.

When the 11-member full bench of the Supreme Court of India confered on the crucial subject of appointments of judges, it was decided that the phrase "in consultation with" actually means "in concurrence with". Our judiciary scales new heights of dubious glory: it is the first in the world to invent such a novel meaning for the stated phrase (because it is something that has so far eluded all the lexicographers of the world put together).

Where does the problem lie? In my considered opinion, the problem lies with the party system of our polity. The so-called elected representatives are more loyal to their party than to the people of India.

Society

The society must have formed when people, inhabiting a certain territory, came together by the dictates of the sheer instinct for gregariousness to ensure their survival in an inhospitable environment of formidable natural elements (sun, cold, rain, floods, storms, droughts, etc.), wild animals and untamed geography. Geography determines body shape, colour and features by compulsion of adaptation to the environment. Englishman's nose is adapted to take in less cold air to maintain body temperature. Chinese slit eyes avoid the blinding glare of snow. Negro's big nose helps him breathe out fast in hot climate to keep oxygen in balance. Geography determines even our creed and philosophic outlook. Le Corbusier made sun as one of the postulates of his planning doctrine because sun is so rare in Europe. Interaction with geography (which in my view is nature's architecture) sustained over centuries ossifies into a people's thought, word and deed. India is a glorious example of what geography can do and does to the people it serves. We have all the possible climates in the country: very cold, very hot, hot and humid, arid temperature, etc. As a result, we have very different views and ways of life that we loosely call a mosaic of diverse cultures. Geography prevents us from becoming a nation, i.e., as an organic politico-social entity with one language, one culture, and similar thoughts, words and deeds. If we are together, it is more by geographic compulsions than any other single imperative. We are a network of geo-social units held together by geography as physically determined territory.

The Indian Society and Impact of Tradition

We are a tradition-bound society. Perhaps, India is the only country in the world where tradition is the single most formidable challenge to all forms of modernity. As a result, whether we know it or not, we work (if at all we do work) more by precedents than on principles. An overdose of religious injunctions has emasculated our initiative especially when we have somehow come to believe stubbornly that we are living in the entrapment of *Maya* – escape from which is our lives' chief purpose. Constantly bugged by the desire for a better life in the hereafter, we neglect what is so precious here and now. This apathy to existentialist imperatives is reinforced manifold by tropical climate. This deadly fusion of religious drugging (nurture) and lack luster lifestyle (nature) has stretched our capacity for adaptation to environment to fantastic limits.

We can live in filth without raising eyebrows. Thus, "I couldn't care less" attitude is our painstakingly acquired national trait. This trait has assumed a new form after we were freed from centuries of foreign subjugation. We indulge in all the social vices – loot, arson, cheating, swindling, rape, murder, abduction and so on – in utmost gay abandon which is at once perverted, sickly and inhuman. Religion has taught us that each one of us must work out his own salvation. Therefore, we are constantly looking for salvation rather than solutions to our daily problems. There is no concept of community or collective enterprise. It is exhibited only in its hideous form when there are stage managed communal riots.

India's Mind and Body

We have national interactionism (interactionism is the theory that mind and body act on each other) involving urban India as the mind and rural India as the body. The term 'mind' implies a well-developed faculty to which "manoeuvring and intriguing" comes naturally. It is a collective combat of 23 per cent of India's urban and 77 per cent of its rural populace. But, the beneficiary is always the urbanite. Remember the diction – mind always triumphs over matter (in this case, the body). If at all the ruralite ever gains anything, it is a small pick from the large-scale loot. This makes India the only country which is an enormous amphitheatre where a complete picture of the growth of man can be seen in all palpableness from savage to barbarian to social animal (ancient) to focal animal (Renaissance/medieval) to vocal animal (post-industrial era) to total animal (modern age of competitive market). There is a parallel growth of economy from agrarian to industrial to market, with the mode of transaction changing from kind to cash to credit card.

Since we are the very same people who constitute the state and the society, when we come to the market, we do similar things. Before dilating upon what we do to our economy, let me mention three traits. We are past masters in the art of middling, meddling and muddling. It takes us no time to transform ourselves into middlemen for bringing about reconciliation between two fighting parties. We love to poke our nose in others' affairs. We have never learnt to mind our own business, probably because we have none. And before long we are ourselves engaged in the bout. Unmatched is our genius for muddling. We can mess up anything – at lightning speed.

Economy

The term 'economy' is used in two ways: (1) the administration of the material resources of the country, and (2) a frugal and judicious expenditure of money. Propelled by the same instinct for loot, i.e., how to make a quick buck, we treat the market as crop field where manoeuvring and intriguing can be sown to yield abundance of 'unearned' money. The lure of money is so great that we are a willing victim to its multi-form exploitation. I personally think that when transaction is changed from kind to cash, this peculiar disease automatically surfaces. The 'kind' transaction in agrarian economy meant that the worker had to wait for a whole year to get his due in the form of crop he had cultivated previously. This was an uncertain matter because factors such as timely rains and favourable weather conditions were beyond anyone's control. Therefore, leaving the outcome to God's beneficence was a necessary virtue. Being resigned to fate also lowers self-esteem and dampens enthusiasm for matters mundane. But, the 'cash' transactions introduced by industrial economy changed this whole attitude. The beneficiary with cash that gave him a sense of immediate reward was suddenly awakened to the potential of personal worth. He could do what he wanted to with the money he had in hand.

The proverb "a bird in hand is better than two in bush" means a certainty is not to be thrown away for a poor chance of something better, underwent instant transaction to become: 'cash' in the hand is better than 'kind' in the future. Also, the kind of exploitation to which one is subject is possible to know (and guard against) sooner than later. The so-called contentment of the ruralite gave way to curiosity to explore the limits of his personal worth. This he could try only in an urban area. Hence, the exodus of ruralites to the towns, cities and metropolises. Oddly enough, this instant awakening of developable personal potential comes even to the utterly illiterate. But, the need to ensure his survival in an inhospitable urban situation and the urge to make a quick buck leads him to the dubious veracity of the dictum: beg, borrow or steal, and what he began to do in an innocent way becomes a preferred mode called "by hook or by crook".

Rusticity versus Sophistication

I would like a little digression here, to introduce an important concept which I have been trying to 'sell' for a long time now, without success. I have figured out that India's chief psycho-social endowment is a compounding of nine qualities: (1) innocence; (2) greedlessness; (3) sacrifice; (4) creativity; (5) camaraderie; (6) contentment; (7) innovation/improvisation; (8) religion of feeling; and (9) renunciation – not of the brand preached by the ascetics, but in the sense that one can willingly give so much as to have the minimal left for one's own survival. It is a quasi-religious, psycho-emotional mode of passive social work. Renunciation is voluntary poverty.

The attributes of rural life are: (1) the placid timelessness of village mud huts, (2) recycling of materials, (3) optimization of resources, (4) use of collective skills transmitted from generation to generation, and (5) a society founded on mutual trust and an unwritten code of conduct.

Slums as Creative Ferment

Thus, slums of India are an extension of rural genius into the urban situations. They may be described as squalid but they are certainly not without sensibility. They are indeed the ferment of adaptive creativity, which their inhabitants have brought along with them from their rural habitat to the cities. The rural migrants to cities are people with whom the urbanites have a love-hate relationship. The ruralites are there because the citizens need them and they receive their love as a tolerant sentiment grudgingly doled out. They are hated because they pollute the urban environment and are the source of many diseases. So these 'nowhere to go' people land on the cities' no man's land which is usually on the periphery. Here, they raise their hovels with utmost economy and amazing resourcefulness. Their rural background comes handy and they innovate/improvise to ensure one of the three basic human needs – shelter. Those who cannot do so right away are guests of earlier settlers, often derisively called land grabbers. Their next need is to secure a livelihood. Here too, their genius is at full play. They create many openings for themselves. They work as construction labourers, rickshaw pullers, cobblers, auto drivers, roadside servers like dyers, *dhobis*, puncture repairers and so on. Those who have acquired some skills become industrial workers. Many work in offices, shops and commercial establishments as helpers. Some are self-employed as *rehri wallahs*. Some are shoe shine boys. Others sell candies and balloons. The list is inexhaustible. The womenfolk work in households as domestic help. Young children can be found as mundus as support to a host of major occupations including those of mechanics, welders etc. These migrants are also those who move from one city to another in search of jobs. Thus, Chandigarh itself may have numerous such people from Rajasthan, Bihar, Uttar Pradesh, Himachal Pradesh and so on. It is estimated that about 40 per cent of Chandigarh's population lives in slums. To be sure, if these slum dwellers were not there to help us, we would die of hard work! At any rate, we Indians, who are lucky to inhabit the urban areas, would prefer to die than wake up from our deep slumber of constitutional lethargy into self-help activities.

Market

Thus, the market as an interface between rural and urban India becomes a curiously evolving organism of all types of interests – vested interests, vaulted interests, vaunted interests and wasted interests – for ever in ferment to make highly complex matters overly complicated. Not only does the interplay of these interests confound confusion but also provide an impetus to commercial activities. The more you lose, the more you are frustrated. The more you are frustrated, the more desperate you become. The moment that happens you plunge into a head on collision with other players in a last bid to out clever them so that you can have all the booty to yourself.

Types of Players

To the smoldering fire of many interests is added the fuel generated by four types of players: the self-employed, the self-styled, the self-serving and the self-denying. The self-employed are largely self-taught. The self-styled are always cleverly trained. The self-serving are muscle men: hooligans, intriguers. The self-denying are in drunken stupor of higher education. The self-employed are multi-tiered masses. The self-styled are the bureaucrats. The self-serving are the politicians. The self-denying constitute the so-called intelligentsia. To the last category may be added another class – the professionals, also called technocrats. I call them technobrats because they keep crying like spoilt brats, but are unable to do anything worthwhile. They think their talent is not properly recognized and patronized. When they switch over from crying to brooding, they qualify as the self-pitying class.

Qualities of Indian Masses

The nine qualities of the Indian masses, especially the rural folks migrating to urban areas, are put to the hardest test in a churning melange of formidable forces unleashed by the state, the market and the society. While their creativity and innovation/improvisation more and more come into their own, their innocence is the first casualty of an indiscriminate blitzkreig of commerce, trading and cities' cunning lifestyle. When life is driven to the brink, where death can devour one any moment, questions of morality take to the wings and existentialist imperatives urge one to secure first and foremost one's survival anyhow. An intriguing polity, a manoeuvring bureaucracy and an uncertain market aggravate one's sense of insecurity and strengthen one's convictions that greedlessness, sacrifice, comaraderie and renunciation are better preached than practised. The desperate desire to earn a quick buck meets its frustration many times until one is driven to the 'beg, borrow or steal' mode. Slums are the best place where this pragmatic dictum can be tried and developed as a survival strategy. Slums, which are products not so much of urban planning failures but of decisions taken at the highest level by those running the blighted 'welfare state', not only proliferate but also gain a secure foothold on the urban soil. The self-serving politicians could not find a better place to indulge in mass-scale exploitation of the 'have-nots'. It is their market in which they sow the seeds of future plants whereby they can grab power to have a money swindling spree for five years.

Erosion of Values

Social mores, which act as mass behaviour regulatory devices in normal situations as do's and don'ts, are constantly rehashed to mislead the society until it becomes subservient to the state and exploitable by the market. Culture comes handy as ferment for the proliferation of prejudices which the exploiters can use for spreading discontent among the people as they are forced to make a choice in favour of one political party rather than the other. Since religion is the most formidable single product of culture, it is an effective means of pandering to the baser sentiments grounded in communalism. So fundamental is the religious sentiment that when aroused people can be easily herded towards any hideous crime even on empty stomachs. Discontentment replaces contentment and everyone is driven into a maddening hurry to settle scores with everyone else. If inflammatory speeches by politicians do not work, rewards and incentives certainly do for those who are under training by their well established bosses. Whatever else may be the benefits of this kind of a covert civil war, one thing that is invariably the outcome is that the underprivileged are indeed the helpless victims.

Simplicity Complicated

As I have sketched out in the very beginning, the state, the market and the society mean different things to different people, but to a layman like me, their meanings are simple and fundamental. The state operates through politics which, to my mind, is quite simply the art and science of determining and regulating the relations between the state and the society. Market, which operates through economics, works on the relations between natural resources, production and the consumers. Society's working is studied through sociology, among other social sciences, which orders relations between man and society. Similarly, religion (functioning via theology) orders the relations between man and God. But, all these basics have been lost in the heat and dust of progress which has forced everyone to look for happiness in the acquisition of objects. Even our philosophy of life, which was originally shaped by economics, just as the kinds of society that we have were determined by geography that peoples of the world happened to inhabit since times immemorial, is rehashed into an outlook that takes care of expedient at the cost of the enduring.

America's Example

This can be best illustrated by America's example – a nation which has become the sole superpower of the world in barely two hundred years. The founding fathers decided that they would no longer be the cousins of

Europeans, and have everything that is American in origin and identity. They figured out that they needed only two things: commerce and technology. Since they started from scratch, they did not have the dead load of tradition to carry under duress. Therefore, they invented pragmatism – a philosophy or philosophic method that makes practical consequences the test of truth. Accordingly, truth was defined as "the cash value of an idea" or "truth is what sells". By contrast, we have a tradition, which is 5,000 years old, and the richest natural resources, but have little to show that we care for human life and are able to ameliorate the human condition. To justify our failings, we conveniently blame it on the ever growing population, forgetting that we have created all that mess ourselves because we are insincere, uncommitted, unaccountable, irresponsible, power blind, money hungry, mavericks!

Sub-Markets

The term 'market' covers a staggering variety of sub-markets with many which have been introduced in the modern era: telecom market, automobile market, readymade market, building materials market and so on. Many a market has been there since times immemorial, but marketing as a strategy to capture a certain market is new. Among its many strategies are the competitive rates at which the merchandise is sold, and the customer catching incentives (e.g., free gifts), allurements and advertising. Whereas the original market was to primarily cater to the people's daily needs, the modern market is by and large a profit-making enterprise selling luxury items. The necessity for market is human, and cannot be wished away, because everyone needs a host of commodities to lead a comfortable life. But its exploitation by profiteers, when left unchecked, leads to the transforming of demands into desires, leaving the theory of demand and supply gasping for a fresh breath to survive. When need is thus made greed, there is no way to stem the rot. Need has limits but greed has none. Need is physiological. Greed is psychopathic. This is a moot point that needs deep reflection. America has produced several Nobel laureates in the field of Economics. But no theory has so far been able to check inflation, which is an undue increase in quantity of money in proportion to buying power, as on an excessive issue of fiduciary money.

Thus ironically, inflation is when everyone has so much of money that there is not quite enough to buy what one wants!

Indispensability of Market

Market varies in size from a Bania's shop in the village to the focal village, block, suburban, town, city, district, metropolis, megalopolis, state, regional, interregional, national, international markets. We cannot do without market for the sake of commerce: an interchange of merchandise on a large scale between individuals or nations. Since everyone cannot produce everything necessary for leading a comfortable life, the market is indispensable. It is this single most important factor that must have led people to ask some other people to run the market for their sake. Thus, the origin of the market is akin (in my view) to the genesis of the state. Unfortunately, both have lost their original purpose in the heat and dust of so-called progress.

III
Assessment

Failure of the State

In 55 years, India, the world's largest democracy, has not been able to provide even the basic needs of society. The state, in the name of *loktantra*, is busy consolidating what I call 'feudocracy': democracy cast in the mould of feudalism (which had reached its pinnacle of glory in monarchy). Even, the Father of Nation was quite confused about it, and unwittingly gave his personal approval to feudocracy. He wanted 'Rama Rajya' to be resurrected on the soil of free India, conveniently forgetting that the state ruled by a king is feudal, and therefore incompatible with the principles of democracy which Abraham Lincoln succinctly described as "a government of the people, by the people, for the people". Democracy is self-governance that requires no ruler(s). Hence, my obstinate aversion to such terms as the ruling party and the opposition party. When it is a 'welfare state', meant for the welfare of the people, why should anyone oppose any welfare programme? But, my analysis seems to be right. The 'welfare state' is 'wul-pher' state. It is a state of thievery for an elect group of people euphemistically called *netas* (leaders). Some Prime Ministers have publicly confessed that only a token share of the money meant for the welfare of the people reaches them. The lion's share is devoured on the way by hyenas of our so-called *loktantra*.

Criteria of State's Success

The acid test of the success of the state in my view is that it has accomplished its aim of providing the basic needs of the people: *roti*, *kapda aur makan*. We know that nearly half the population of India is somehow surviving in the absence of these basic necessities. Isn't that a miracle? Those who blame the welfare state's failure on the growing population should find out how those who are abjectly hungry, undraped and shelterless reproduce themselves to embarrass the government. They may discover a new form of market for international commerce. A second measure of a developing state is that it progressively engages more and more professionals to manage the various ministries so that they can contribute to the all-round development of the nation by their expertise.

Perverted Function

With a few exceptions this second point has not occurred to our *netas*. The first part remains dreadfully unattended. Therefore, to expect people to have faith in the state is ask a drowning man not to worry because the future belongs to him. The state has perverted even its primary purpose of maintaining order and security. Characteristically, the state has given to the Indian people a disorder so that they are kept busy disentangling themselves from out of the widespread chaos, and made security a personal, highly prized, privilege: the security is now only meant for the *mantries*! I cannot understand why in a *loktantra* the representatives of the people need security against those who elect them in the first place. It seems to me that since *netas* have to go the whole hog in thievery, security (x,y,z) is their legal right – after all they themselves are the law-makers as well as the law-breakers.

Concept of Justice

Before I move on to figure out the causes of the mess that we are in and formulate the issues emerging out of the exposition, let me say a word about justice. To my experience, there is no such thing as justice. And this notion is substantiated by those who deal with the subject in reallife situations. A Union Minister of Law categorically stated that we administer law and do not dispense justice. Law is a weapon invented by the state. According to an American judge, law is an instrument in the pursuit of justice which may or may never be attained. No wonder, there are Courts of Law, never Courts of Justice.

The Society is to Blame

For all the flaws, foibles and failings of the state (and the market), I will attribute the blame to the society. The society must do lots of hard soul searching, and remove the causes that lead to such a pitiable plight. My own reckoning is that the Indian society is carrying trillions of tons of dead wood in the name of so-called rich cultural heritage, in which religion plays the most conspicuous, if dubious, role. This emphasis on an uncritical reverence of the past, when we all want to dash ahead, is like driving an automobile with one foot on the accelerator and the other on the brake. The result is a bumpy drive and a colossal waste of fuel. Since those who steer the same vehicle are different people, the polity suffers badly, but nobody cares to repair it.

Role of Intelligentsia

We, the so-called intelligentsia, have to work hard to first revive our lost virility, and then to use that power to transform the society which is estranged and has been rendered helpless, hapless and hopeless. This can be done by forming a large number of action groups who will teach the masses in rural and urban India. This programme is not merely to achieve hundred per cent literacy, but to impart education, initiative and courage to do away with what is the dead wood of tradition. The Indian society consists of two types of people: glib talkers and gullible listeners. Indians must be taught to distinguish between bad intentions, hollow promises and poor performance of the politicians, reliance on the state must be transformed into self-help initiative and self-sustaining enterprise. This is needed in three areas to begin with – education, health and the fulfillment of basic human needs. One way of doing it is to make such a plan an integral part of schools, colleges and universities, which would include all types of institutions dealing with agriculture, medicine, architecture, engineering, etc.

The Interface

The interface between the state, the market and the society is confused and mutually contradictory. Those who run the state are desperate to grab the political power by hook or by crook. Those who manage the market are in the drunken stupor of quick profiteering. Those who lead the society are engrossed in the senseless sport of moving the people backward to the world of superstitions and bigotry. The net result is the untold suffering of India's teeming millions. Although I do not agree with the Prophets of Doom, yet I am convinced that India has a bleak future unless Indians themselves as a massive psycho-social force rise to the occasion and pressurize the politicians to effect such amendments in the Constitution that would not permit country touts, hooligans and mavericks to grab power by virtue of fundamental lacunae in the *body politic*. Basic qualifications like education, experience, expertise, lower and upper age limits, etc., must be prescribed. When the government insists upon such prescriptions for its employees, why must it not apply the same criteria for those who 'form' (or is it 'deform') the government.

Rural-Urban Interface

The interface between rural and urban India is of a dubious character. The main issue is that owing to widespread illiteracy, poverty, hunger and helplessness of the rural populace, which constitutes nearly 80 per cent of the total population when we also take into account the number of the have-nots in urban India, the masses have no access to anything neither the state, nor the market, nor even the society. Within the society, such access is forbidden by the caste factor. This abomination can be driven out only by the power of right education, adequate economic independence and self-motivated individual collective initiative.

IV
What Can be Done?

To conclude, I would like to draw upon the pragmatic work of the incomparable American Richard Buckminster Fuller who, true to his convictions, said in his epoch-making book *Utopia or Oblivion* (1969): "I made a bargain with myself that I would discover the principles operative in the universe and turn them over to my fellow men." To benefit from his unique contribution, we, like him, must work hard to be functionally attuned to the structural symbiosis of science and society.

He writes: "Despite the constant increase in human population and constant decrease of materials per person, between 1900 and 1965, the number of people attaining economic and physical success – by full participation in the highest standard of living progressively developed by world industrialization – rose steadily from less than 1 per cent to 40 per cent of all living humanity. This is a personal standard of living and health superior to that ever enjoyed by a pre 20th century monarch. The 40 per cent of humanity thus surprising grown successful, despite constantly diminishing material resources per capita, can be explained only by accelerating ephemeralization."

"Ephemeralization is the doing of ever more with ever less, per given resource units of pounds, time and energy." He insists that "ephemeralization, which constantly does more with visibly less, as for instance, the one-quarter ton communications satellite outperform 1,50,000 tons of transoceanic cables – has not as yet been formally isolated, recognized, and discussed in print as such by any economists. Until economists recognize it, ephemeralization cannot be popularly comprehended and be adopted in public policy formulations."

The crucial aspect of Fuller's thesis is: "Take away the energy distributing networks and the industrial machinery from America, Russia and all the world industrialized countries, and within six months more than two billion swiftly and painfully deteriorating people will starve to death."

Concluding Remarks and Suggestions

The term 'materialism' should be replaced by 'mammonism' (i.e., worship or obsessive love of money). Since modern society has the market in focus, money has automatically become the chief determinant of social mores and political outlook. Money, being in a constant flux, perturbs our notions of permanence, which means that there is no absolute yardstick to measure what would give humans a lasting happiness. Hence, the giddy tumble from novelty to novelty that sustains the market. This has uprooted such values as loyalty, sincerity, commitment, honesty, etc. No wonder, therefore, that money turns all human institutions into industry – and commodifies culture.

Let us build more cities. If we build 40 cities of the size of Chandigarh at 25-year intervals, it will take us 1,000 years (one full millenium) to totally urbanize India. Urbanization is better than only industrialization in terms of employment prospects. And, we should ruralize our cities rather than urbanize our villages.

Reference

Encyclopaedia Britannica, 1982, Vols. 11, 16 and 17.

7

Rural-Urban Interface: The Case of an Urbanizing Village

RAJESH GILL

The urbanward migration, induced by industrial revolution, and its tremendous magnitude, prompted the scholars interested in the phenomenon, to theorize about the consequences of this process. Most of the theories of migration naturally addressed to the questions such as why people migrate from villages to towns, how do they take the decision to migrate, how do they decide about the place of destination, etc. Sociologists and anthropologists, on the other hand, have been more interested in the socio-cultural changes induced by such a process of migration, especially upon the city dwellers – both original and migrants. Such studies are preponderant and rightly so because urbanization has revolutionalized the demographic structures and social organization of large metropolitan cities that have emerged as a result of this process. But social reality is both infinite and variant. Just as all cities and towns are not alike, all rural settlements too do not generally resemble each other. Villages, which fall in a close proximity of large cities, tend to exhibit altogether different characteristics as compared to the villages located at considerable distance from a city. Such villages can neither be conceptualized as rural nor urban settlements by virtue of their peculiar experience of urbanization.

Modern cities have absolutely no resemblance with the occidental city conceptualized by scholars like Max Weber, which is both economically and politically an autonomous unit. Today, a city can just not be separated from its region (except administratively), because of an increased fluidity of the people inhabiting both in the city as well as the periphery. Studies on urbanization and urban culture will remain incomplete unless they take into account the neighbouring areas of the city it serves and in turn gets served by them.

The city-region relationship has usually been looked at from two angles. One, a city is believed to bring prosperity, development and growth in the region in which it is situated. City in this sense is generative mainly in economic terms, as conceptualized by Hoselitz (1960). The second and opposite effect of a city on its region is that a city swallows its periphery, ultimately hindering the overall development of the latter, by sucking away all its natural resources and polluting its indigenous culture. It is argued in this paper that in fact city does both: while it leads to tremendous amount of urban diffusion in its peripheral villages both in terms of economic and cultural structures, it also happens to rob the village of its age-old social fabric, traditions and cultural ethos, leaving behind a vacuum, without substituting them by the urban culture.

Although the role of a city in generating employment and uplifting the level of living of the population in the rural periphery is well documented in various empirical studies, the analysis of cities, especially the Indian, from the social perspective, is very scanty. That urbanization may trigger off a chain of social problems in its immediate periphery needs to be explored. It is in this context that a study was conducted by the present author in village Palsaura, situated in the Union Territory of Chandigarh.

This paper addresses to the following questions:

- What kind of demographic transformation has occurred in the village?
- How has the process of migration affected the village ecologically, economically and socio-culturally?
- How has the proximity to Chandigarh affected the village both positively and negatively?

The study is based upon an ethnographic account of the village, using personal interviews, group discussions, observation etc. Information was gathered personally from a sample of 200 respondents, selected by using the method of random sampling, members of the panchayat, medical practitioners in the village, Principal of the Government Primary School located in the village, Anganwadi workers, the staff at the Primary Health Centre in the village etc.

A Description of Village Palsaura

The village is located on the main road between Mohali and Chandigarh. There are some shops just on the side of the road of timber, property dealers, one private doctor and so on. Alongside, on the main road only, the Government Dispensary is located. There is an ANM, a midwife and a peon, who have been working there for a number of years and know the village in great details. In fact, they were quite helpful to me in gaining information about the village. They took me to a number of houses including those of the village Sarpanch, Pradhan and some known addicts. They also helped me in interacting with the women who had addicts in their families, when they visited the dispensary.

As one walks down the village streets, he/she finds a clean village, with shops selling daily consumption items at almost every corner of the lanes. The lanes are narrow but *pucca* brick lanes, with drains on both sides. On the whole, these are clean. Some of the houses are small while others are well renovated and give a modern look with air-conditioners and coolers.

There is a Government Primary School which looks quite nice and clean. We went inside and a lady teacher took us to the Principal, who was a pleasant woman of about 55 years of age. A girl student was sitting with her, doing some writing work. The Principal later revealed that this girl should have been in the fourth class but due to the apathy of teachers was still in the first class and was unable to cope up with even the syllabus of that class. While the girl's father, who was a carpenter, had been asked by the Principal to work at her house in return for appropriate wages, the Principal took it up as a moral responsibility to help the girl improve. She revealed that most of the children in this school were the children of labourers working in factories in Mohali and Chandigarh, rag pickers, domestic servants, class IV employees, skilled and semi-skilled workers etc. A large number of children (about 7 to 10 in each class) dropped out every year. Although parents are mostly concerned, most of the times it is the fault of the teachers who are instrumental in demotivating the children, who were weak in studies. Instead of helping them out, they usually discouraged them, in order to avoid extra work, finally getting rid of them when they dropped out. This was despite the fact that the Scheduled Caste students were getting various incentives such as free uniforms, books and stipends. Rag pickers were being given some additional financial support. Still, the quality of uniforms, note books etc. was very bad.

We moved out of the school and got into a shop where a young boy was sitting, with a telephone. He was a mechanic of electric goods and was a graduate. He had been staying there for the last eight years and was residing in the Kachi Colony just close to his shop. He told us that about ten years back, one landlord of the village rented out small plots of his farmland to migrants on rental basis. The present Kachi Colony had been inhabited thus. Later on, the land had been acquired by the UT administration and all these occupants had got entitlement to government houses. They were now being allotted one-room houses nearby for an amount of Rs. 6,000 that had to be repaid in the instalments of Rs. 52 per month. Most of the allottees had sold off their plots in black for an amount ranging between two to three lakhs. Apart from the profit motive, allottees had been disposing of their houses for the following reasons:

- they found it difficult to pay monthly installments; and
- they did not have the resources to build houses on these plots.

Many of them did not have any motivation to leave the colony and shift to a better accommodation.

Hence, people are residing in this colony for different reasons. While some have migrated here out of compulsion, i.e., affordability, others are the opportunists who do not mind staying in the dirty surroundings for sometime, provided they get highly subsidized houses. It is notable that all allottees do not readily agree to sell off the house. The ones who readily agree to do so are the people for whom the surroundings do not matter. By selling off, they are able to make easy money and enjoy life. On the other hand, there are people, especially of the salaried class, who attach a lot of importance to ownership of a house, being aware of their inability to otherwise own one by any other means, and hence, they have migrated to this colony, waiting for their allotment and then occupying the house immediately.

This small and very old village had only about 35 households at the time of inception of Chandigarh, and agriculture had been the main occupation of the residents till then. Today, the village stands most unplanned ecologically, with atleast four labour colonies having come up around it, which look just like urban slums and lie detached from the original village. The village and the colonies look absolutely different with huge buildings – both residential and commercial – and tremendous construction activity going on within the village, while the colonies have mostly *kutcha* houses, without any basic amenities. The village has four liquor shops which are always a hub of activity. This is not a village, which sends people out; instead, this is a village, which has received migrants in such huge numbers that at the time of the study, more than three-fourths of the village population consisted of migrants. There are basically three kinds of migrants in the village:

- Migrants both in formal and informal sectors, in low income category, residing in labour colonies.
- Migrants occupying the rental accommodation recently built and rented out by original residents. They include daily wagers, self-employed workers and a large number of people working as drivers, conductors etc.
- The third category of migrants include the medical practitioners and traders, who found it less expensive and more profitable to do business in the village, in view of the lower rental values of commercial property and less competition in the market here.

Migration into the village has tremendously affected the village ecologically, demographically and socio-culturally. The population of the village has increased manifold, apart from the fact that the village no longer has the typically rural homogeneity so characteristic of a traditional Indian village. Migrants in the village come from Gujarat, Rajasthan, Punjab, Haryana, Himachal Pradesh, Madhya Pradesh, Tamil Nadu and so on. Hence, the village has attained a truly heterogeneous population in terms of ethnic and regional background, language and dress, culture etc.

Agriculture no longer remains a predominant occupation of the villagers, and most of the working population are engaged in services.

As one moves from Chandigarh towards Mohali, he/she crosses village Palsaura. It now lies on both sides of the main road. It has numerous shops on both the sides, including timber merchants, *dhabas*, one new posh showroom, and outlet for electronics, private medical practitioners, automobile repair shops etc. On the left side, a huge colony named Dashmesh Colony has come up on the village land. This is inhabited by migrants mostly from Punjab, and some from other neighbouring states too. Landowners have rented out their land to these migrants, the latter having migrated from the interiors of Punjab along with their cattle, mainly buffaloes. Naturally, they are largely running dairies, fetching much higher prices in the vicinity of a city like Chandigarh. Others in the colony are working in diverse sectors as unskilled laborers, hawkers, petty shopkeepers and so on.

On the right side of the road lies the old village, totally transformed ecologically, socially, economically, culturally and demographically. According to the 1991 Census, the total area of the village is 121.81 hectares whereas the total population was 10,270.

The village had 3,289 households in all in 1991. It has one Government Primary School, one Government Dispensary and a number of private medical practitioners who have opened up clinics though most of them are not residing in the village.

The major demographic and socio-economic features of the village are shown as follows:

Table 1

Total Population of Palsaura (1991)

Total Population	*Male*	*Female*
10270	6195	4075

Table 2

Scheduled Caste Population in Palsaura (1991)

Male	*Female*	*Total*
647	526	1173

Table 3

Population of Literates in Palsaura (1991)

Male	*Female*	*Total*
1303	846	2146

The village has its workers distributed into various industrial categories in the following manner:

Table 4

*Workers in Palsaura (1991)**

I	II	III	IV	V	VI	VII	VII	IX
Culti-vator	Agri-cultural Labourer	Forestry and Mining	House-hold Industry	Manu-facturing	Cons-truction	Trade	Transport	Other Services
242	112	315	30	1076	619	806	515	757

* Workers' classification is as per the industrial classification in the Census of India.

As one enters the village, he/she finds quite a few shops inside too, within the residential areas. The lanes are made of bricks and are very clean. The drains are also quite clean. The houses are *pucca*, varying in size and structure. While some houses are very large, others are quite small, without the modern amenities such as coolers, air-conditioners etc. It shows the wide disparities within the rich on the one hand, displaying an urban lifestyle, and the poor on the other, resembling a rural neighbourhood.

Ecological Structure of the Village

The village gives a mixed feeling and looks like a rur-urban settlement. There are hardly any agricultural farms around and all one can see is the concrete buildings demarcated by brick lanes, surrounded by the labour colonies, viz., Kachi Colony, Pir Colony, Amb Colony etc. Ecologically, these colonies lie detached from the village and resemble urban slums although less congested. Most of the houses are *kutcha* while some are *pucca* too, each comprising one small room (approx. 6'x6'). No affluence is revealed through the ecology of the colonies, though the village displays affluence in the shape of big houses with all modern amenities, showrooms etc. While the interior of the village has a concentration of residential houses, the surrounding roads on all the four sides have commercial concentration, e.g., shops, private clinics etc. Most of the shops as well as houses are not very old and one can observe either renovation or construction going on at various points in the village, indicating the continuous process of migration into the village. There are four *thekas* (country liquor shops) on the periphery of the village, which are hot spots for the villagers.

Economically, the city of Chandigarh has proved to be quite generative in the sense that most of the original residents have found it very profitable to hire out accommodation to the migrants, which has been built recently by them solely for earning money, with an utter disregard for architectural planning or any sense of aesthetics. A majority of the original residents have rented out rooms with common toilets and bathrooms to migrants. The rooms measure about 7 by 7 feet, without any ventilation and fetch around 1,000 rupees a month. Some people have rented out as many as 50-100 rooms in this manner. For these residents, this is the main source of income, which is substantial, without actually making any kind of effort. In addition to residential accommodation, shops and showrooms have also been rented out to people who reside in Chandigarh and come daily for business.

What is interesting is that the colonies around the village had a very peculiar composition. These had certain people who had come here specifically to procure government accommodation at highly subsidized prices. They were quite calculating and had used their manipulative skills and farsightedness in managing to acquire a house which would not have been otherwise possible. Secondly, there were people who had migrated to the village purely for economic reasons and were not very desirous of moving out into the government houses. Such people had already been selling houses allotted to them at high premiums to the better off people, earning between two and three lakh rupees. The allotment had thus come as a boon enabling them to make easy money within which they can comfortably pursue their alcoholism, gambling, or addiction of other kinds. Such people are most likely to continue staying in the colonies, despite the rehabilitation programmes of the administration.

Caste and Occupational Structure

Initially, village Palsaura was inhabited by various castes such as Jats, Brahmins, Chamars, Ramdasias, Ramgarhias, Mazhabi Sikhs, Nais and Dhobis. These castes followed their traditional ancestral occupations. Farming was the main occupation of landowning caste, e.g., Jats. But, with the acquisition of cultivable land by the Chandigarh Administration since 1950s, farming no longer remained an attractive proposition even for traditionally cultivating castes. The Jat families of the village disclosed during the interviews that they were growing crops only for their own consumption.

Thus, both the caste and occupational structures of Palsaura have tremendously been influenced by the process of urbanization and proximity to Chandigarh.

Table 5

Caste Status of the Respondents

Caste	*Original Residents*	*Migrants*	*Total*
Jats	26	34	60
Brahmins	8	23	31
Rajputs	-	30	30
Ramgarhias	3	6	9
Khatris	1	4	5
Banias	4	16	20
Dhobis/Nais	2	8	10
Mazhbi Sikhs/	3		
Others	-	101	101
Total	48	202	250

The process of migration began in the village some 20-25 years back and is continuing unabated till date. Those who have migrated into the village belong to different states, regions, linguistic and caste groups. There are some Muslim families too which have migrated into the village, especially in the labour colonies.

Out of the 250 respondents who were interviewed, 48 were original residents of the village while 202 were migrants. Out of these original residents, a majority consisted of Jats, although there were some Jats among the migrants too, who had come to Palsaura from different districts of Punjab with an aim to improve their life chances and financial status. Others among the original residents were Brahmins, Ramgarhias, Banias and other castes (non-Punjabi), while among migrants, most of them were hailing from Uttar Pradesh, Bihar, Gujarat, Rajasthan and Tamil Nadu.

Table 6

Occupational Status and Monthly Income of Respondents

Occupation	*Monthly Income (in Rs.)*				
	20,000+	*10,000-19,999*	*5,000-9,999*	*5,000*	*Total*
Farming and rental income	24	6	9	3	42
Business	4	19	6	4	33
Government job (clerical)	2	2	7	1	12
Unskilled labour	-	-	-	27	27
Artisan	-	-	11	5	16
Factory worker	-	-	-	31	31
Rag picker	-	-	-	57	57
Others	-	-	-	32	32
Total	30	27	33	160	250

The traditional linkages between caste and occupation are still continuing in the village. Most of the Jat respondents, for instance, have been pursuing farming as their main occupation while they also received significant income from rental accommodation mainly occupied by the migrants. A large proportion of our respondents were working in menial jobs at factories, construction sites and were rag pickers. Consequently, out of the total respondents, 64 per cent had an income less than Rs. 5,000 per month while only 12 per cent of them had an income more than Rs. 20,000 per month. It may be reiterated once again that Jats and other landowning castes had considerably enhanced their economic status by renting out a large number of residential rooms to migrants.

As a sociologist, my interest was mainly in studying the social fabric that characterized this village, which neither looked like a village nor a city. Observation and informal discussions with the residents revealed that the village hardly had any close knit neighbourhood structure, or community living. The urban anonymity, so well described by scholars like Louis Wirth and others, characterized this village too. People received you with a suspicion, mistrust and similar feelings were expressed for neighbours, which was quite strange in a village. The proximity of Chandigarh had definitely brought economic prosperity to the villagers, and helped them get rid of the drudgery of agricultural labour and an uncertain income, yet the city of Chandigarh had rendered the village a place, where all kinds of anti-social activities could be carried on, in absence of the close watch of police and administration.

The village, first of all, had a terrible problem of drug addiction. There was hardly any household, even among the original residents, which did not have an addict. People, mainly male, were addicted to opium, *bhang*, *bhuki*, *zarda*, smack, alcohol, cough syrups, injectibles, painkillers, anti-depressants etc., irrespective of age, occupation, economic status, religion, caste or regional background. Young boys were taking drugs because they did not have anything to do. Those who were getting rental income were without work and hence were hooked to intoxicants. It were the women – mothers, wives and daughters – who were the worst sufferers. Addiction was rampant even in families which found it hard to survive. However, it had almost taken the shape of cultural norm, in that the usual response one received from both men and women was that everybody takes something or the other. This could be one way of justifying the act of one's husband, father or son, but it had serious sociological implications. The problem ceases to be seen as a problem if it acquires the status of a group norm, and then nobody thinks about its solution. This was also propounded by the fact that a well-organized mafia was found to be existing in the village, which helped people procure drugs in bulk, and on a regular basis. In one such case, the researcher was told how a police official, who had been hooked to drugs, would be made to beg to the peddlers in the village for his dose. Young boys from the city could be seen hiding in the fields in the village and injecting drugs into their veins. In the labour colonies, however, drug addiction was not restricted only to men, but women and small children were also consumers of intoxicants.

Another serious problem this village had been facing was the high incidence of sexually transmitted diseases (STDs). The village has already been targeted by various governmental and non-governmental organizations for creating awareness regarding STDs and AIDS. The regular visits to the labour colonies revealed that prostitution was going on unchecked, with married as well as unmarried women indulging into the business, while their husbands worked as middlemen. A few *kutcha* rooms in the colonies were being regularly hired out to youngmen normally from the city for such activities. customers in such cases were usually men from Chandigarh – young and old – who found this place safer due to the heavy surveillance in the city, especially the labour colonies in the city. It was astonishing to discover from the villagers that such sex-related business was going on within the village too, with the indulgence of women and unmarried girls from well-to-do families. These sex workers operated outside the village. During interviews, therefore, people expressed their strong reservations against commenting upon certain families, which they felt were indulging into such practices. Fellow villagers often wondered how they could amass so much wealth and luxuries in a small span of time without any regular jobs. This information was then verified on the basis of a number of respondents in the village. This phenomenon was also confirmed by the medical practitioners in the village as well as the NGOs working in the village. A kind of mistrust, indifference and suspicion thus characterized the attitude of villagers, which one would not even find in a city. This was primarily due to a very high degree of mobility, since migrants were coming and moving out in such great numbers and with such great frequency that it had become a highly fluid situation, without any vigil or policing, which is otherwise found in a city. The Village Panchayat hardly commanded much respect, with most of the respondents complaining that the Sarpanch, whoever he may be, was most of the time busy in making the best use of his official resources, both economic and administrative, while police and administration were in hand and glove with the anti-social elements.

It was astonishing to come across such glaring cases of such deviant activities going on in the village, especially because villages are known to have a high degree of collective conscience, a sense of community and cohesiveness. However, a little scratching below the surface led me to the following observations:

— The village no longer has the traditional look of a self-sufficient and close knit, agrarian community. On the contrary, it is a highly heterogeneous and commercialized village, with an increased sense of anonymity, mainly a characteristic of the urban setting. An urban-like attitude exuding an indifference and 'why bother' has emerged in the village, thus paving the way for a lack of concern for what others say.

— Among a sizeable proportion of migrants who have settled down in the village, a large number of men are employed as truck drivers. It is a well-known fact that the incidence of STDs and AIDS is very high among truck drivers who have to remain away from their families for long periods. I was told by the workers in NGOs that a large proportion of very young boys, between 10-14 years of age, were suffering from STDs. These boys had been working as helpers with the truckers and were completely oblivious of their diseases.

— A major reason for the concentration of such problems in the vicinity of a highly sophisticated city of Chandigarh is that the village Palsaura is an ideal place for such immoral activities. Locationwise, it is just two kilometers away from the city and secondly, it is a soft place, so far as police patrolling is concerned. Thirdly, a thick habitation of migrants from different walks of life has made the neighbourhoods totally anonymous. Even if neighbours suspect, instead of protesting or showing their annoyance openly, the tendency is to turn a deaf ear, ignore and close the doors one's own house. In the colonies, on the other hand, activities like prostitution or drug peddling and addiction no longer result in the raising of eyebrows since it is a normal practice, which has been accepted by the people all around.

— The glaring affluence and consumerism exhibited by the media and projected further by the city of Chandigarh has played havoc with almost all sections among the villagers. Villagers, knowing well about the implications, do not hesitate in renting out hundreds of rooms to strangers. The youth are baffled and blinded by the glamorous world and luxuries, for which they are getting money without much effort. The poor have also found short cuts to easy income, taking advantage of the location of the settlement.

Conclusion

The process of rural to urban migration has come a long way since the phenomenon of urbanization started, leading to the theorizing of the process of migration. With the blurring of boundaries between towns and villages, with the migration percolating to the peripheral villages of cities, and with the heterogenization of the peripheral villages, detailed studies of such settlements are required. An insight into the migrant population in these villages, the commercialization occurring there, the social problems haunting the village people, and the crime charts, would go a long way in evolving humane settlements – both rural and urban. By planning only urban settlements, we might run the risk of getting rural societies out of our hands, causing an irreparable damage ultimately to our society – of which both rural and urban settlements are integral parts, which are absolutely inseparable and interwoven.

References

Bailey, F.G. 1958. *Caste and the Economic Frontier*. Bombay, Oxford University Press.

Castells, Manuel. (1972) 1977. *The Urban Question*. London, Edward Arnold. Originally published as *La Question Urbaine* (Paris).

Durkheim, Emile. (1893) 1933. *The Division of Labor in Society*. Translated by George Simpson. Glencoe, Illinois, The Free Press.

Flanagan, William G.1990. *Urban Sociology: Images and Structure*. Boston, Allyn and Bacon.

Gill, Rajesh. 1991. *Social Change in Urban Periphery*. New Delhi, Allied Publishers.

Hoselitz, B.F. 1960. *Sociological Aspects of Economic Growth*. Illinois, Free Press.

Lambert, Richard D., 1962. "The Impact of Urban Society Upon Village Life" in Roy Turner (Ed.). *India's Urban Future.* Bombay, Oxford University Press.

Mumford, Lewis. 1961. *The City in History: Its Origins, Its Transformations and Its Prospects*. New York, Harcourt, Brace and World.

Rao, M.S.A. 1970. *Urbanization and Social Change: A Study of a Rural Community on a Metropolitan Fringe*. New Delhi, Orient Longmans Ltd.

Redfield, Robert and M. B. Singer. 1954. "Cultural Role of Cities", *Economic Development and Cultural Change*. Vol. 3, 53-74.

Simmel, Georg. (1905) 1950. 'The Metropolis and Mental Life'. In *The Sociology of Georg Simmel*, edited by Kurt H. Wolf, 409-24. New York, The Free Press.

Venkatarayappa, K.N. 1973. *Rural Society and Social Change*. Bombay,.

Weber, Max. (1905) 1958. 'The City'. In *The City*, translated and edited by Don Martindale and Gertrud Neuwirth, 63-89. Glencoe, Illinois, The Free Press.

Wirth, Louis. 1938. "Urbanism as a Way of Life", *American Journal of Sociology*. Vol. 44, 1-24.

III

Emerging Gender Images and Family Ties

8

Commodification of Women in the Economy of a 'Market Culture': A Critique of Women's Representation in Popular Media

ANU CELLY

The quintessential market is everywhere around us. Like the coils of a knot, it hold us in an iron grip or what W.B. Yeats has called the 'widening gyre', holding our existence to ransom at the hands of a culture that is irrevocably guided by the dictate of a market economy. In the name of liberalization, the flood gates of mindless consumerism have unleashed anew, the instincts of avarice and materialism to inveigle us into living beyond our means, lending to all our moves and deeds, the ethics of profitable transaction as the ultimate objective. Be it a marriage proposition or an act of devotion, a Booker-winning novel or a chart-buster music video, a populist newspaper or an avant-garde movie, a sanctimonious teleserial or a children's magazine, a pseudo-religious sermon or a political manifesto, every facet of our life and every nuance of our experience cannot remain untouched by the nexus between commercialization and commodification.

Dimock (1986: 123) analyzes the brutality of the 'marketplace' in a Marxist-humanist vein when she says: "As controlling logic, a mode of human conduct and association, the marketplace is everywhere and nowhere, ubiquitous and invisible". Everything sells in today's world, right from ideas to gimmicks, from identity to spirituality, from software to sexuality and amidst this blitzkrieg of a culture mesmerized by the mirage of happiness, expansion and progress through financial aggrandizement, what is lost is the sanctity of the self and a relationship of joy and fulfilment and of a holistic approach to the values and ideals attendant on humanism.

The market personifies forces of capitalism in alliance with urbanization and industrialization and thrives on the coalition between class, gender formulations, patriarchy and politics, breeding determinism in our value system and a disproportionate distribution of wealth and status between men and women, between the privileged and underprivileged. Even as the upper and upper-middle classes place a premium on exigencies of wealth, luxury and display, it is pertinent to examine what it means to be a woman or a 'feminine type' amidst a money system that is inimical to growth, a sadly defective system of grooming that encourages farcical appearance at the expense of reality and gives to the mind no objects worth of its prowess, even while accustoming human faculties to the sense of its own superficial and trivial nature. Amidst an abundance of leisure-class values, wherein civil society and its places of inhabitation have been reduced to a muddle of misapplied ornament over a thin shell of utility, what has surfaced is a surfeit of gorging love for pleasure, a cultivation of factitious aesthetic insouciance and a coming together of sexism and financial profit-making as the predominant forces in the dynamics of what has been called the 'economics of sex-gender system'. To employ a cantankerous metaphor, a certain class of women have been reduced to being 'objects of circulation' or as items of transaction, even as the popular media purports to make of them a conduit to commercial relations, while masculinist supremacist economic values makes of men the primary beneficiaries in the dynamics of exchange and traffic.

One does not need to be inordinately perceptive in dissecting the (con)text of women's (re)presentation in popular media. Feminist criticism, itself, is no longer relegated simply to the written text and social activism. It has come into a pro-active mode of interface with all forms of media – newspapers, journalistic writings, films, video and advertisements. One can no longer afford to turn away from these mediums as these appropriate a much larger space in our lives than they did in the past. Popular media may be considered as a site of plural signification, in its rôle as a vibrant and dynamic medium for effectuating social change, a signpost of cultural values and as a receptacle of dominant ideologies. Popular media has a conscious and self-referential relationship to questions of ideology, politics, culture, identity, representation and, of course, aesthetics, all of which are involved in a tenuous link with technology.

This paper attempts to focus on the commodification of women in popular culture at the behest of vested interests propelled by economic and political concerns. Whether in movies or TV serials, advertisements or music videos, novels or media reports, the Satis, Parvatis and Madonnas of today's world have been packaged and resold as highly remunerative role models, icons and art d' objects, unjustifiably far removed from the challenging and uplifting graph of women's actual lives.[1] The image of women in popular media, as a mere spectacle or an object of dominant cultural discourses, needs to be analyzed, just as one needs to decode the dissonance and discrepancy inherent to the representation of women's position therein. Annette Kuhn considers the representation of women's position, whether through cinematic, literary, journalistic media, as the site of a gendered narrative:

> Representation sets in play certain relations of power through which, among other things, discourse around sexual difference and subjects and for those discourses are originally produced... Representation participates in the various relations of power with which we are surrounded and in which we are always in one way or another implicated. Representation can be understood, then, as a form of regulation.[2]

In popular Hindi cinema, the pace of evolution seems to have taken on a reverse gear and the representation of women's image has been successively typecast, wherewith an entire range of regressive role models, right from the sorry figure of the mother to the submissive though harassed daughter-in-law, to the rebellious and conniving sister to the seductive mistress to the Machiavellian vamp are presented on a platter, catering to the taste of the cross-section of elite and maverick masses. They are supposed to lap up a sumptuous feast of titillation, moral upliftment, ethical outrage and righteous self-glorification – all rolled into one. The identity politics inherent to the stereotyping of women's image makes it mandatory for her to be a perfect combination of certain typical traits and idiosyncrasies used in an oft-repeated pattern of mythical iconography. Quite often, especially in parallel cinema, the 'image' derived from the social categorization womanhood frees itself from the 'icon' which has remained encased in a mould of superimposed ideology, to assume shades of defiant though often aborted shades of self-representation.

A semiotic and psychoanalytic approach to the representation in popular cinema reveals that the image of women is not wholly congruent with the reality of women's life and conduct outside the cinema hall; on the contrary, woman functions as a 'sign' within the definitive parameter of myth, custom and ritual. The functional allocation for such a 'sign' as per the view of Roland Barthes is to remain active as the signifier of an ideology which will denude it of all its denotative meaning, in order to invest it with purely connotative dimensions. Claire Johnston makes a succinct analysis of myth as a patina for the exercise of the 'political unconscious' beneath the cinematic production and circulation of women's image, when she says: "Myth, as a form of speech or discourse, represents the major means in which women have been used in cinema: myth transmits and transforms the ideal of sexism and renders it invisible – when it is made visible it evaporates – and therefore natural."

Day in and day out, the so-called women-oriented TV serials continue to invade our sensibilities as well as living rooms with an ideology that is avowedly patriarchal and smacks of prejudiced gender formulations. The mould of femininity, especially in Ekta Kapoor's chart-busting TV serials, is fashioned along traits which range in between extremes of perverted malice to self-eroding stoicism, pernicious aggression to defeatist humility, vituperative villainy to misplaced idealism. The middle path of normalcy is simply missing in these serials. And so are the real-life aspects of sensitivity and courage, strength and piety, sturdy willpower and mature altruism found abundantly among our womenfolk. Aiming at an intermingling of the old cultural tradition of a *pativrata* woman with a modern go-getter who believes in herself, most of these TV serials try to create the image of a new woman in the garb of a traditional one. The portrayal of a woman a la Parvati in *Kahaani Ghar Ghar Ki* or Tulsi in *Saas Bhi Kabhi Bahu Thi,* who is completely flawless and has to undergo a rigorous prosecution in lieu of her perfected adherence to the norms that have been set for the Bhartiya Naari stereotype, is much in keeping with the packaging of an agenda of *Hindutva* that has been propagating through the scriptures and now through serials, a whole lot of orthodox values and masculinist ideals governed irrevocably by the market forces, for the Sitas and Satis among the Indian women.

Besides being unrealistic and retrogressive, such serials are also nihilistic to the extent that they tarnish the image of women and destabilize family relationships in the course of rustling up popular appeal to a stratified section of bored middle class housewives. Rarely do they offer any progressive roles to women and hardly ever do they portray women characters standing up to fight against a brand of oppression and injustice that is not perpetrated by women themselves. Most of the serials portray women whose essence is matrimony and motherhood or on the flip side guile and gossip-mongering. In the name of a complete sell-out to Indian values, women are portrayed as being irredeemably stoic and self-effacing and the only avenue of independent, self-affirmative choice open to women is that of gross villainy and conniving vanity.

On the other hand, tens and thousands of women in India die untimely deaths each year either through dowry immolation or through female feticides simply because they are not boys and so presumably a source of financial burden for the family, who wants to do away with the huge cost of getting them married, without making an effort to make them financially independent. As per a straightforward assertion of Mala Sen, "it is a complete cycle of violence and oppression – from birth to death – and women themselves seem to have helped perpetuate this practice in the name of religion and tradition. Many have seen their own lives as not worth living, and have tried to spare their daughters from a similar fate"(2001: 51). Female infanticide has become a big business across cities, towns and villages with unscrupulous doctors making large fortunes. Not only this, even the enforced act of *sati*, in our country, has not been spared from being taken up as a lucrative business adding to the coffers of Roopkanwars' in-laws and to that of the state government.

When one takes into consideration the art of selling wares on the television, what catches our attention is the enticing world of advertisements which defeat our logic and dupe our reason into an inadvertent obeisance to the 'diktat' of our needs and desires. More often than not, such advertisements appear like a personification of our dreams and a catalyst for our fanciful illusions, transporting us with startling immediacy to the 'utopia' of wishful indulgence, wherein all our curtailed yearnings seem to reach fruition. Be it the gleaming gold of a luxury car or the shining white of wall paint emulsion, the contours of our imagination are etched with the colourful and spell-binding signposts to prosperity and well-being, comfort and respectability. No longer does a diamond bracelet or a dishwasher appear like a superfluous or improbable possession to us, as our mind becomes attuned to a barrage of 'mediaspeak' which is as incredibly inviting as the moon is to a child looking askance at the configuration of his palpable fantasies. The influx of 'multinationals' via electronic gadgetry into our living rooms and kitchens has brought with it a trap for the human vulnerability to fall a prey to the maladies of materialism and mindless consumerism.

The facets of women's image in popular advertisements, more often than not, employ a 'reductionist aesthetic' (Felski, 1989), reinforcing repressive ideological concerns in juxtaposition with essentializing images of women, since the art and craft of representation has a role to play in the perpetuation of and resistance to power relations. The reinforcement of repressive and essentialist image of womanhood in popular advertisements takes us back to a realm "where bikers ride" over the curvaceous body of a female, literally and figuratively the LML motorcycle of invincible virility and where a Bajaj mobike is celebrated as a 'male' because its a power-driven vehicle. The 'body politic' of masculinistic assumption, then, seeks to reduce woman to a suppliant receiver, the silent stillness of whose sensuous and supine form deserves to be codified and predominated upon. Indeed, there are ads galore where women have been allegorized as cars, in a position of interchangeable proximity to 'vehicles' of desire, meant to be driven at will. The prerogative of creation, possession and protection a la Pygmalion is always invested with the male, while the woman a la Galatea, is to be imaged as a finished product which is malleable enough to mould itself to presumptuous injunctions.

Advertisements that are less subtle and more prolific in confiscating the potential of meaningful tasks from women, at large, tend to focus on women's involvement in self-edification through means of artifice. All kinds of cosmetic companies, including those that organize beauty pageants, purport to fetishize woman as an object d'art meant to assume completion only through the normative gaze of the male. The woman allows herself to be converted from the dusky earthiness of an unattractive persona to the 'fair and lovely' visage of a *persona non grata* whose destiny to be an airhostess or a wife is to be decided ultimately by the condescending male. Be it a bathing soap or a moisturizer, a perfume or a nail varnish, the 'target' groups of women are assumed to be creatures of vanity constantly seeking to be rewarded by the men in the family.

Rarely do the ad film makers betray the need for an egalitarian harmony as the essence of power relationships and the need for striking a balance in the respective allotment of their roles and duties. It is always the newly-wedded *bahu* trying out the effectiveness of the *bartan* bar sounding sanctimoniously the sublime bliss of standardized domesticity. Why is it that only the women characters, presumably handpicked from the mainstream of our middle class society, are shown as taking pride in having washed the dirty linen of their in-laws with a 'tidal' and 'surf-like' whiteness, so that the menfolk in their family, quite ironically, may walk away with a 'clear' conscience. The 'Wheel' or the 'Whirlpool' of fate does not spare them from the grinding threat of reprisal to be inflicted by the husband and by implication from the entire society, if they fail in the stricture of lending unalloyed brightness to clothes soiled with worldly tasks, including a construction project or a job interview assigned to men. Invariably, the male figure is depicted to be in charge, right from the bedroom to the battle ground as the woman's identity and contribution to society is fashioned around the demonstration of her bodily features and domestic labour. Stevie Jackson's analysis may be considered within the wider context of a sociological critique of women's domestic work being a non-lucrative labour: "Women's domestic work is undertaken as a personal service to a male head of the household. He effectively appropriates her own person and the labor she embodies, so that the work that she does is potentially limitless and depends on his requirements . . . a man realizes the value of domestic labor he has appropriated when he exchanges his labour power – which his wife's work has produced – for a wage .which controls. This ...is the main mechanism of exploitation within the patriarchal mode of production".[3]

Undoubtedly, women's sexuality or even the agonizing drudgery of their fruitless labour is to be controlled and regulated according to the strictures of an acquisitive patriarchal mode of economy. Even in the 'nestle' of her 'kamasutra' relationship with man, the woman has to be branded as a passive receiver, acted upon by the phallocentric assertions of unmistakable male authority. According to Lisa Adkins, "one example of what might be regarded as women's non-market and non-cash nexus labor market work is the sexual labor that many women tourist workers are required to perform. In such cases, sexual labor is not formally incorporated into an exchange relationship, nor is it cash nexus or simply market orientated. But while this work may be regarded as 'traditional' (in that it does not bring with it monetary reward, power or status) it also does not bring with it the potential for labor market creativity, for instance the ability to create labor market, but rather leads to specific forms of appropriation – in this instance the appropriation of sexuality".

For long has patriarchy disguised itself as a capitalist in the relations of our production and productivity, as women continue to be the source of surplus though superfluous value in our homes and in our economy.[4] Women are often ascribed with 'non-material' work – housework, child care, emotional burden and other modes of non-reflexive production. The aesthetics of representation is sublimated at the altar of celluloid glamorization, fuelling a volley of questions regarding the relationship between the use of popular art and mass media for the propagation and imposition of socio-political ideology. This also leads one to interrogate how the cultural ethos of a nation may be perverted for the financial aggrandizement of a few multinationals.

As the advertisements continue to flaunt the image of woman as a monolithic apotheosis of 'femininity,' an icon of romanticized or denigrated ideals, perforce, one ponders on the extent to which these correspond with the real features of women's character and conduct. Media representations of women, whether in documentary, advertisement, parallel or popular cinema, have become a central concern in the present phase of feminism in order to explore the process which converts women into "signifiers in an ideology" (Pollock, 1990).[5] Cinematic images which conceptualize women as an archetype or an artifact, need to be decoded rather than to be lapped up, with a level of 'consciousness-raising' in our perspective. We need to define our responses to the most potent and wide-reaching impact of the media-generated sub-text that has increasingly become an apparatus for hegemonic interventions on the nature of identity and agency.

For women to register a meaningful presence in the cross-current of our public and private life, popular media has to work towards a transformative vision, even through the intensely effective means of advertising, for breeding a positive cultural ethos and for constructive socio-economic space leading to the expansion of human interest at large. Unless we are weary of the ways in which popular media is used for re-inscribing capitalist, market-oriented and patriarchal supremacist values, we will continue to perpetuate the normative structures of representation as tools for the utilization of women as the exotic 'other' in the discourse on life. Unless we take cognizance of the manner in which the culture of consumerism is packaged at the expense of commercializing womanhood in popular media, we may well nigh fall into the trap set up by the engineers of sexual and cultural politics.

Notes

1. Madonna, more than any other pop star embodies the new post feminist heroine in her heady combination of an irresistible brand of seductiveness and alluring innocence: but, in her gutsy sort of independence and self-ordained life, she defies the ideological caricature of the 'Material Girl' that is often used to encapsulate her within deterministic formulations. For an extended critique of her image, see Ann Kaplan at random.
2. In terms of psychoanalysis, one may resort to the view that makes use of feminist theories of representation to mark the limit of the image in the political image of sexual and racial 'other'. Representation always conveys more than it intends and is never totalizing. The 'excess' meaning conveyed by representation creates a supplement that makes multiple and resistant readings possible. To put it in the words of Peggy Phelan: "Despite this excess, representation produces ruptures and gaps; it fails to reproduce the real exactly. Precisely because of representa-

tion's supplemental excess and its failure to be totalizing, close readings of the logic of representation can produce psychic resistance and, possibly, political change (1993: 13).

3. It would be pertinent to take into account the view of Lisa Adkins when she asserts: "Whilst woman may be key in the construction of community, the products of this work – a sense of identity and belonging may not be accessible to women because this work is performed in relations of appropriation. Put another way, women cannot claim ownership and mobilize the product of their work as resources because they themselves do not own their labour through which it is constituted in the first instance" (1998: 42).
4. The interlocking pattern of stark material inequalities and material oppression faced by women, is explicated by Stevie Jackson, thus: "The challenge for feminist social theory today is to analyze the localized contexts of women's everyday existence and the meanings women give to their lives without losing sight of structural pattern of domination and subordination… it ever was and remains necessary to grapple with the complexities of a post colonial world, the intersections of gender, ethnicity and nationality. The material foundations and consequences of institutionalized racism, the heritage of centuries of labour, are atleast as important as culturally constituted difference" (28).
5. There is no doubt that visual representation poses certain vital problems both for feminist thinking and for feminist politics. Literature, art and feminist criticism together can help create new perceptions and new needs, rather than reflecting passively on the already constituted images and needs. The dialectical relationship between audience and text ought to encompass the particular relation of the same to the social and historical contexts in which it is produced and received. In the same vein, feminist literature ought to be instrumental in its enabling function as "a critique of values and as a source of positive fictions of female identity, while simultaneously insisting that feminist literature, like feminism itself, must be viewed not in isolation, but in relation to the social and ideological conditions within which it emerges and against which it defines itself" (Felski, 1989: 182).
6. The interlocking pattern of stark material oppression faced by women, is explicated by Stevie Jackson, thus: "The challenge for feminist social theory today is to analyze the localized contexts of women's everyday existence and the meanings women give to their lives without losing sight of structural pattern of domination and subordination… it ever was and remains necessary to grapple with the complexities of a post colonial world, the intersections of gender, ethnicity and nationality. The material foundations and consequences of institutionalized racism, the heritage of centuries of labour, are atleast as important as culturally constituted difference" (28).

7. There is no doubt that visual representation poses certain vital problems both for feminist thinking and for feminist politics. Literature, and feminist criticism together can help create new perceptions and new needs, rather than reflecting passively on the already constituted images and needs. The dialectical relationship between audience and text ought to encompass the particular relation of the same to the social and historical contexts in which it is produced and received. In the same vein, feminist literature ought to be instrumental in its enabling function as "a critique of values and as a source of positive fictions of female identity, while simultaneously insisting that feminist literature, like feminism itself, must be viewed not in isolation, but in relation to the social and ideological conditions within which it emerges and against which it defines itself" (Felski, 1989: 182).

References

Adkins, Lisa. 1998 "Feminist Theory and Economic Change." *Contemporary Feminist theories.* Ed. Stevie Jackson and Jackie. Edinburgh: Edinburgh University Press.

Dimock, Wai Chee. 1986. *Debasing Exchange: Edith Wharton's The House of Mirth.* Edith Wharton. (Ed). Harold Bloom. New York: Chelsea House of Publishers.

Felski, Rita. 1989. "The Dialectic of 'Feminism' and 'Aesthetics'." Beyond Feminist Aesthetics: Feminist Literature and Social Changes, 175-82. London: Radius.

Kaplan, Ann E. "Whose Imaginary: The Televisual Apparatus, The female Body and Textual Strategies in Select Rock Videos on MTV." *Female Spectators Looking at Film and Television*. E. Deirdre Pribram, 132-55. London: Verso, 1988.

Phelan, Peggy. 1993. "Broken Symmetries: Memory, Sight, Love." *Unmarked: The Politics of Performance,* 1-33. London: Routledge,

Pollock, Griselda. 1990. "Missing Women: Rethinking Early Thoughts on Images of Women." The Critical Image, *Essays on Contemporary Photography*. Ed. Carol Squiers, 202-16. London; Lawrence and Wishart.

Sen, Mala, 2001. *Death by fire: Sati, Dowry Death and Female Infanticide in Modern India.* New Delhi, Penguin Books.

9

Market and Mandira

SUDIP MINHAS

More than a year ago, television in India witnessed a silent revolution which if not ignored altogether had very few people sitting up and noticing it to write about. The Sony Max television channel had not only usurped the relay of a cricket tournament (the ICC World Championship) what was till then considered the preserve of sports channels like Star Sports and ESPN but also did the unthinkable by introducing a woman on the panel of cricket experts. Ruby Bhatia's misadventure was soon forgotten but then came the World Cup – the ultimate spectacle. The television channel persisted with the same format but with a different presenter – Mandira Bedi. She clicked by the same age-old formula – she generated controversies, curiosity and naturally the TRP rankings jumped. She had an Indian face, a quizzical look, great clothes and a range of sentimental emotions. And, naturally, this time around, the channel attracted a lot of attention, mostly for non-cricketing reasons. The general reaction was: what is a woman doing on a cricket show? After all, this is a man's show. One of the great bastions of male control. Her very presence was disconcerting, most of all to her co-panellists. Ridicule replaced shock – more and more was being written about her. Her dress had to be modified once the channel realized that the ratings and especially women viewers had abandoned the show. All in all, this show did make people sit up and notice.

This paper is an exploration of some vital questions regarding structures of media representations being challenged and realigned within the present globalization scenario. To begin with, there is an important question of woman as an image/spectacle. Then, there is the aspect of her becoming the site of meaning production, which ultimately also becomes the means of resistance to naturalization. Whether this resistance is possible at the level of authorship or viewer will also take into consideration the multiplicity of gazes that television makes possible. I wish to deconstruct the episode in an effort to demystify the male control of cricket and its attendant knowledge.

In the present situation, when the television occupies the personal space as different from the public space of the cinema, its effects cannot be seen only in the sense of its projection of the culture. The dynamics of the television viewing has an inbuilt self-reflexivity. Its pervasive intrusion makes it a political and an ideological tool. The images on the television tend to be taken as more normative than in the cinema, though the techniques employed are largely the same. Women theorists or the critically aware thinkers respond to such intrusive media in three different ways. One is the most straightforward but least active, i.e., censorship; second is the strategy of practices of representations and finally the strategy of critical practice.[1] The last two strategies are by nature active agencies though again the last one is a practice of active political mediation and change.

This practice of generating an active aesthetic response to media and image is a result of understanding the role of the spectator as the space where meanings are produced rather than simply consumed. The meanings are produced not merely as self-sufficient acts between the viewer and the image but it is an outcome of a discursive practice. I would like to consider the cultural products as participants in a particular discourse and these certainly do not exist in isolation.

The subject of the female spectator is also very relevant since for a longtime she was marked by an absence. Then, the idea of sexual representations, identities and readings is created from different and disparate perspectives within the presentation. Within the text, the woman as a symbol exists at different levels at the same time. Sometimes, as a sexual object, as a consumer or signifier of modernity, rebellious sexuality and more importantly within the Indian context as a signifier of religious and cultural traditions. All these competing, sometimes contradictory discourses, make the attempts to construct wholeness a very fragmenting tasks. Within these shifting processes of meaning construction the Indian female spectator reworks the subjectivity from a stable position to one of a process.

She explores the myriad ways in which the image of a woman is figured, addressed, positioned and formed. Simultaneously, she is also hoping to locate her position outside the patriarchal constructions of the femininity as the 'other'. This is an acceptance that the identity is always dependent on the "relation to systems of sexual positioning," but there is a need to discover the ways in which women can reposition themselves in relation to the "discourses of popular representations". This ultimately remains the task of the critical practice that I mentioned earlier.

Mary Ann Doane, in her book *The Desire to Desire: The Woman's Film of the 1940s*, writes that the female gaze is also incited towards the feminine object. The understanding of the female viewers that there is the decidedly narcissistic identification with the image rather than the narrative movement explains the Sony TV's attempt at trying to bring in the female viewer with the help of the designer Mandira Bedi. As we shall see below, such constructions of female viewing are fundamentally problematic. It also brings into focus the question of desire and sexuality but within this programmme it is again riddled with the problematics of its form.

The other major area of feminist visual theory takes a critical view of the silence of the woman in media. From Laura Mulvey onwards one major concern of the feminists has been the woman without a voice. If we see the history of film and television representations, it is hard to disagree with Mulvey that the women have been silent. In fact, if we look at her argument of a contradiction about the way women have been supposed to be given the voice in the melodramas, it becomes clear that this is also not an unproblematic area. The argument that I take later on in the essay deals with the voice and an image inherently unstable. Therefore, it is within these structures that this image and the voice prove unstable for the patriarchal form of the programme.

Before I come back to the main argument of Mandira and cricket, I wish to briefly talk about the game as a cultural form in the Indian context. After *Lagaan* the question of cricket and its colonial heritage has been inducted into the popular linguistic as well as social memory. As Arjun Appadurai, while tracing the history of cricket in India in his essay on "The Decolonization of Indian Cricket", says: "the game was a quintessentially masculine activity, and it expressed the codes that were expected to govern all masculine behaviour: sportsmanship, a sense of fair play, thorough control over the expression of strong sentiments by players on the field, subordination of personal sentiments and interests to those of the group, unquestioned loyalty to the team."[2] It adhered to the Victorian morality and the values of the Victorian upperclass. In its first explorations of the game Indian men considered it as an experiment with the mysteries of the British Empire. It was an exploration of the power which separated the 'them' from the 'us'.

The indigeniszation of the game involved a process of democratization through the use of the vernacular in media. Both All India Radio and Doordarshan were largely responsible for getting the common man into the fold of cricket-speaking fraternity. What it still could not achieve or perhaps did not deem it worthwhile to include was women amongst their listeners or viewers. The viewership and the viewer time were also split on gender lines. Cricket was a man's sport. The British Victorian hegemony of using technical terms in impeccable English was reinvented by the multinational TV channels like Star Sports and ESPN. What it did was to effectively alienate the woman as a spectator. Women's participation was reduced to constructing cricketers as icons of female desire. The game was well and truly left to men. They knew the game because they had become members of the physical activity at some point of their life; therefore, they enjoyed the viewing and the spectacle at the experiential level. The commentators made sure that this high level of involvement was maintained. The cricketing jargon in a complex manner heightened this physical experience of the viewer. A bouncer, a flipper, a skidder and endless other cricketing terms percolated down to young boys.

Mandira Bedi's *Extraa Innings* was expectedly a breach of this code of conduct. She dressed differently and almost provocatively, she confessed her ignorance of the game (a sacrilege considering cricket is religion in India), but importantly it also confirmed what Indian men had to say – "women don't know a darn thing about cricket". She giggled and bit her lip; she expressed emotions on stage when she had to be an almost objective commentator. She most painfully reflected the viewer. In psychological terms she represented the split. The outrage now we understand was genuine.

She was introduced by the TV channel because they understood the dynamics of the market which had forced on them a segment of viewers largely ignored by the cricketing media until then, i.e., women. Female viewers had been responsible for a revolution in the prime-time slot. It made better economic sense to include women as viewers – the patriarchal hegemony had to be challenged or at least realigned. Women did indeed walk into the living rooms and appreciated Mandira's/Ritu Kumar's wardrobe.

I come back to the important question of what is it that this show has done which can be viewed positively. My argument is that the Mandira factor was a disruptive device which has fore grounded the insecurities of the male viewer. As Jacqueline Rose says of that the "sexuality lies less in the content of what is seen than in the subjectivity of the viewer, in the relationship between what is looked at ... the relationship between viewer and scene is always one of fracture, partial identification, pleasure and distrust."[3] According to Freud, our identities as male or female, our understanding of realities, our construction of the image we consider perfect or flawed are all fantasies. Such visual representations, which disrupt the structures of normalization, unsettle our certainties.

This disruption does not take place at the level of the viewer; the whole structure of the show is replete with fissures and contradictions. First, Mandira's image as a sexually attractive woman could not be successfully used as a means of attracting female viewers. The strategy was later modified. Second, as the name suggests, the show was not only about the game. It was being fashioned on the great Indian film tradition (a whole series of spoofs on the Hindi films were used as a publicity campaign – *Deewana Bana De*). Then, the contradictions generated at the level of discussions – with panellists including ex-cricketers and Mandira at centre stage asking rather than commentating. All of these add to a viewing laden with conflicts and constantly escaping the fixed image which generates naturalization. Identities are disrupted when the viewer, instead of participating in the common knowledge of cricket with the panel experts, is interrupted by simple, sometimes inane questions of Mandira – like Tony Greig barely concealing his irritation said "for heavens sake ask a sensible question Mandira". A sensible question in this case would have been one with more confusing jargon, the kind associated with some sports which are elitist in nature and unlike hockey or soccer which have relatively simple processes. Athletics and some field sports can be explained midway as one winning for the moment but cricket is very unlike such a sport where the 'glorious uncertainties' encourage panel discussions, arguments and comments. Coming back to Greig's comment what the great cricketer and expert forgot was his job description. In fact, he was there to answer such questions from the unheard viewer. But cricketing public in India has a multidimensional aspect, best reflected in the polls that were conducted and the very large numbers who scored the hits. On the other hand, there are a myriad of uninitiated (women among them), who had to understand the nuances of a game which boasted of technicalities at every stage.

Now, the structural pattern of this programme attempts to bring together two genres which are contradictory in nature. One is a panel discussion show which is the reality show and the other is a genre of the film which is in the realm of the 'imaginary'. This pattern elaborates and explains my argument that the disruptions that are visible are a result of the reinvention or the breaking up of traditional structures. A talk show primarily rests on an intellectual activity and in this programme it is the physical act (game) which is incorporated in the intellectual. The woman who is also positioned in the centre works against this traditional structure. She is an object/visual/spectacle counteracting against the action. Then, the medium of the film is also an unsettling element. From the 'imaginary' to the question of the 'real' the question which operates here is "can this be taken as reality?" The package then reveals the deliberate form of the pastiche. It is certainly a very postmodern attempt at recycling the older genre of sports commentating. According to Frederick Jameson, "whereas modernist texts often took a particular critical position vis-à-vis earlier textual modals, ridiculing specific stances or attitudes in them, or offering a sympathetic, comic perspective on them, postmodernist works tend to use pastiche, a mode that lacks any clear positioning with regard to what it shows, or toward earlier texts that are used."[4] It becomes very difficult therefore to understand her (Mandira) position as one in which she is seen simply as a sex object or is pastiching the earlier models available in the films.

If the programme is preceded by the series of spoofs on the films, it brings into focus the kind of seductive control the films and cricket have over the Indian masses. But, my interest is more focused on the way this show itself tries to blend together some elements of the films. The dress, as mentioned earlier, carries its cinematic codes. The dress also embodies the dominant ideologies as obviously what sells depends on what is consumed. But these codes are decoded at various levels. What can be termed as the multiplicity of the gazes within the television. But then within this it becomes exceedingly difficult to know who is looking? If the look is displaced and decentred in the television, does it make it any easier to fix the meanings? My answer is certainly no. It is because of this that the possibilities of reinterpretation exist. Precisely because of the element of the pastiche in the programme that it (programme) can move out of the monolithic sports show structure. And once out in the undefined space it offers both resistance and pleasure. As E. Ann Kaplan suggests:

> The new postmodern universe, however with its celebration of the look, surfaces, textures, the self-as-commodity, produces an array of images/representations/simulacra that co-opts any possible critical position by the very incorporation of what were previously 'dissenting' images; this makes difficult the process of foregrounding or exposing gender issues that feminist filmmakers have used. As a cultural mode, postmodernism would eliminate gender difference as a significant category, just as it sweeps aside other polarities.[5]

Mandira's centre position in the panel in a neatly arranged semi-circle disturbs the centre-margin relationship. The cricketing knowledge and the power it yields, was received from the curves of the panel and the centre was continually displaced metaphorically. Media representations cannot be taken simply as a working out of reality situations even if they are from the "reality/sports shows". "Representations are not merely reflections of reality, whether 'true' or distorted, but are rather the product of an active process of selecting and presenting, of structuring and shaping, of *making things mean* – of what came to be termed a 'signifying practice'."[6] Nevertheless, the physically centred position that she occupied did manage to create ripples that have reached beyond tele-consumption into academic/journalistic debates.

A very vital question that still remains unanswered is that whether it is possible for women/feminists to take pleasure in visual representation. At this stage, it would be pertinent to have a look at Laura Mulvey's formulations about scopophilia or the pleasures of watching in cinema, in her very famous essay, *Visual Pleasure and Narrative Cinema.*

The cinema satisfies a primordial wish for pleasurable looking, but it also goes further, developing scopophilia in its narcissistic aspect. The conventions of mainstream film focus attention on the human form. Scale, space, stories are all anthropomorphic. Here, curiosity and the wish to look intermingle with a fascination with likeness and recognition: the human face, the human body, the relationship between the human form and its surroundings, the visible presence of the person in the world. Jacques Lacan has described how the moment when a child recognizes its own image in the mirror is crucial for the constitution of the ego. Several aspects of this analysis are relevant here. The mirror phase occurs at a time when children's physical ambitions outstrip their motor capacity, with the result that their recognition of themselves is joyous in that they imagine their mirror image to be more complete, more perfect than they experience in their own body. Recognition is thus overlaid with miss recognition: the image recognized is conceived as the reflected body of the self, but it's miscegenation as superior projects this body outside itself as an ideal ego, the alienating subject which, reintrojected as an ego ideal, prepares the way for identification with others in the future. This mirror moment predates language for the child.[7]

According to her, it is this fascination with the image which is used by the producers, of course it is done on the level of the unconscious. When the image of the presenter on the show brings in sexuality where otherwise it does not exist, the contradictions are then sought to be assimilated in an effort to make the show popular amongst women. But, as the show progressed, it was soon realized that the spectators' reactions are not only culture-specific but also erratic. The proposition of Mulvey's argument cannot be therefore taken as the ultimate explanation. In the Indian context women are equally fearful of sexuality. Their understanding of this sexuality as a spectacle conjures up more negative images. The contradictions also lie in the fact that the spectacle and the narrative are mutually antithetical to each other. This can be understood from the aspect that most of the theory that is constructed depends on the Hollywood films.

The positions that are available to feminism would necessarily take into account two aspects: one censorship and the other critical practice. The former is a highly problematic strategy because it would mean obliterating a presence and also because every censor will create a desire for it. The other is a more appropriate strategy of critical practice. To raise the consciousness of men and women by which to understand and resist the ways, they are positioned by broad social forces and discourses. This resistance is possible with defamiliarization of the normative, which I think is achieved to a great extent by the structural form of the show. The demystification of the jargon and therefore a resistance to the power associated with that knowledge. This leads to the democratization of a sport which, despite its concerted effort at decolonization and indianization, continued to exercise its control over membership rights or exclusivity to men. Another important factor that the discerning female viewer will notice is the ways in which such disruptions and resistance will force realignments which, if not change things drastically, will inevitably bring about realizations or possibilities of difference. One admirable feature of Mandira's presentation I would like to mention is that despite ridicule and being written off, she withstood her ground with a dignity far exceeding those of her fellow panelists.

The other question is what did her clothes signify? After all, it is undeniable that her dresses attracted a lot of attention from both males as well as females for different reasons. As Shobha De says that women were watching *Extraa Innings* to check Ritu Kumar's styles and that they (women) were still less interested in what the cricket czars had to say about the game because after a point cricket commentary is repetitive. It proves Mandira's point that she was "an entertainment VJ" on a cricket show. But I think the crucial point is that whether the voyeuristic male gaze was also responsible for the criticism that she invited? It is clear that such a dress on any other show would not have invited similar responses.

Clothes and sartorial structures have predefined codes which have been fairly well debated and discussed by Claude Levi Strauss. But, in postmodern times, the element of pastiche and experimentation in the style of clothing has foregrounded an important aspect of social resistance. The anarchism of punk fashion, for instance, politically repudiates social order and discipline as well as normative style and taste, employing a distinctive pastiche for purposes of communal and individual liberation. Similarly, Vietnam-era bra burning and the widespread renunciation of cosmetics among certain feminists attest to committed politics of dress, as do certain innovative practices of retro fashion. As these different examples suggest, the politics of dress among marginalized groups more or less demands of cultural criticism symptomatic conjunctural analysis attentive to the nuanced motions, both local and global, of hegemony and resistance. Clothing is not free from intricate political entanglements at all moments and levels. Yet to dress politically does not mean simply to don a military uniform. To elude current fashion is to escape the reigning symbolic order, which depends on stability and coherence. Contestation through imaginative dress challenges class and gender demarcations, opening spaces for rearticulating subjectivity. Successfully to transform hegemonic dress codes is to win not just a style skirmish but a cultural battle. Sony Max made a clear break from the dress codes of other channels which even introduced neck ties with their logos. But even on Sony it was Mandira and her dresses which challenged and denaturalized a sports channel's sartorial structure (what with all the finery and jewels). Sometimes, the converse of feminist dressing can also become a political instrument like in the case of Mandira dressing up.

Cricket, which started its journey to India as a means of colonial hegemony and strictly followed codes, was incorporated into the nationalistic mainstream by subverting these very codes of conduct. But if we analyze cricket in the present times when media dictates the rules of the game, it is becoming increasingly patriarchal in its outlook. The same codes of Victorian morality mixed curiously with street smart aggressiveness have alienated women. The male bonding best represented by great Indian team huddle, wives and girlfriends off limits, and finally the shirt waving Indian captain at the Lords have not been the best advertisement for women to join the bandwagon. In such a scenario Mandira and her brave effort cannot be underplayed, I say, even if it is motivated by the forces of market.

Notes

1. Sandra Kemp and Judith Squires, "Visualities," *Feminisms*, Oxford: Oxford University Press, 1997, pp.385-386.
2. Arjun Appadurai, "The Decolonization of Indian Cricket" in *Modernity at Large: Cultural Dimensions of Globalization,* University of Minnesota Press, 1996,
3. Jacqueline Rose, "Sexuality in the Field of Vision," *Feminisms*, edited by Sandra Kemp and Judith Squires, Oxford: Oxford University Press, 1997, p.388.
4. E. Ann Kaplan, "Whose Imaginary? The Televisual Apparatus, the Female Body and Textual Strategies in Select Rock Videos on MTV," in *Feminisms,* edited by Sandra Kemp and Judith Squires, Oxford: Oxford University Press, 1997, p. 413.
5. Ibid., p. 422.
6. Sue Thornham, "Feminists Media and Film Theory," in *Contemporary Feminist Theories,* edited by Stevi Jackson and Jackie Jones, New York: New York University Press, 1998, p. 215.
7. Laura Mulvey, "Visual Pleasure and Narrative Cinema," in *Feminisms*, edited by Robyn Warhol and Diane Price Herndl, New Jersey: Rutgers University Press, 1997, p. 441.

10

Rape: Socio-Economic Perspective and Its Legal Regulation

MADHURIMA AND PEEYUSHI DIWAN JAIN

As we have entered the new millennium, the rights and status of women in society have gained paramount importance worldwide among policy makers and civil society alike. Meanwhile, the integration of women to the mainstream development process has pushed women's issues from the private sphere of life to the public. However, the question remains whether the process has helped to reduce repression against women or opened up new avenues for exploitation. While domestic violence against women has always been a general feature of the social structure of both rich and poor nations, women's increased participation in outside activities has endangered her external security as well. Incidents of rape, gang rape, acid throwing, sexual harassment and violence at the workplace, eve teasing and the like, have not only increased recently, but have also turned much more ominous. According to Vishwanathan (2002), today, there is a double resonance of violence against women in the male gaze. On the one hand, there is the voyeuristic or pornographic male gaze which eats or consumes the woman. On the other hand, there is the covert gaze where men feel threatened by the diminishing 'exclusivity' of public spaces since women are taking over more and more spaces that belonged to men's.

Further, the declining sex ratio, due to advancement in technology, is another factor related to gender-based violence. We already know that gender-based violence is deeply associated with the existing patriarchal social structure, which is also manifested and reproduced in the legal system of the nation-states. Nevertheless, the recent upsurge in gender-based violence poses the question as to whether the increase is only a demonstration of the existing patriarchal social structure or whether other factors too are at place.

In this paper, an attempt is made to highlight what are these factors. The paper also aims to focus on the role of the law-enforcing agencies vis-à-vis women security. It also looks into the existing legal framework and makes probable suggestions for revision/enactment of new law.

Rape is undoubtedly the most direct breach of choice a woman can face. Sexual assault removes any semblance of control a woman has over when, where and with whom she will have sex. Rape gives men the ability to 'undo' in a single act, all the freedom and autonomy women's rights activists have fought so hard to guarantee.

As women move out of traditional sanctuary of home at all levels and at all places, they get exposed to man's lust. Sex-related offences take place everywhere in streets, parks, fields, railway coaches, platforms, hospitals, police stations, women's homes and even inside the family. In the rapacious greed of man, women of all ages are raped – whether babes in cradle, old woman on verge of dying, young woman, married, unmarried, pregnant – all are susceptible to this crime.[1]

Military histories rarely refer to rape. For example, the rape of an estimated 2,00,000 Bengali women during the war of independence from Pakistan had come to light as part of the competing diplomacies of war, illustrating the viciousness of the conqueror or the innocence of the conquered. When war is over, rape is comfortably filed away as a mere and inevitable 'by-product', a matter of poor discipline, the inevitable bad behaviour of soldiers and briefly "out of control". Similarly, at the time of ethnic conflicts, it is reported as raping the enemies' women – the enemy in this formulation being the male combatant and he seemingly all-male nation or religious or ethnic group. The victim is male, humiliated and emasculated by having failed as both warrior and protector. Women are targets of abuse at the same time that their existence and subjectivity are completely denied.

Whilst there is far less research conducted internationally on rape than other forms of violence against women, nonetheless, the number of studies is not inconsiderable. Statistics around the world suggest that rape is an all too common reality in the lives of women and girls. In the United States, for example, six well-designed studies suggest that between one in five and one in seven American women have been the victims of rape. According to one estimate, in India, every 54 minutes, there is a rape. There were 374 reported rape cases in Delhi in 2000 which makes it the most unsafe metro, followed by Mumbai (124), Kolkata (35) and Chennai (24). A non-governmental organization "War Against Rape (WAR)" reported that in Pakistan at least eight women are criminally raped every 24 hours, more than two of them by gang and more then five of them are minors.

Sexual violence, and rape in particular, is considered the most dramatically underreported crime (American Medical Association, 1995). The most common reasons for not reporting rape include:

- Not naming the event as rape oneself.
- Fear of disbelief and blame.
- Distrust of the police/courts.
- Fear of the court process and public disclosure.
- Fear of family/friends knowing.
- Fear of further attack/intimidation.
- Threats by offender/his family or friends.
- Divided loyalty in cases involving current intimates and family members.

Those who report have strong informal network support. Several studies have shown that friends are the most likely people to be told, and if they strongly communicate that what happened was not woman's fault, this increases reporting (Schwartz, 1997). In addition to violating a woman's biological integrity, rape can have serious consequences for her reproductive health. Along with physical injury and emotional trauma, rape survivors also run the risk of being pregnant or contacting STDs including AIDS. The impact of rape is multiplied and becomes sexual enslavement when it is institutionalized as forced prostitution or linked with the threat, fear and/or reality of pregnancy. The expressed intent to make woman pregnant is an additional form of psychological torture; the goal of impregnation leads to imprisoning woman and raping her until she is pregnant; the fact of pregnancy, whether aborted or not, continues the initial torture in a most intimate and invasive form; and the fact of bearing the child of rape, whether placed for adoption or not, has a potentially lifelong impact on the woman, on her liberty and on her place in the community. In India, rape as a form of violence, can beget more violence due to stigma surrounding loss of virginity in unwed girls. In some of the Muslim countries the strain of rape is so great that victims are sometimes killed by family members who believe they are cleansing the family honour. In a study of women murdered in Alexandria, Egypt, 47 per cent were victims of rape who had been killed by a relative.

Explanations of Sexual Violence Against Women

Explanations of violence against women have usually suggested that its cause lies within the personalities and social backgrounds of individuals who commit violence. But, the empirical data on women as victims indicate that the causes of violence lie not in the characteristics of offenders but in the social status of their victims. This is not to say that women are responsible of the violence committed against them. Contrararily, it locates the causes of violence within the political and economic status of women in society. Theoretical explanations of rape can be broadly categorized into four groups:

- Psychological theories
- Sub-culture of violence theory
- The gender socialization theory
- The economic theory

Psychological Explanation of Rape

Psychological theories of rape look to individual characteristics of personality, maladjustment and psychosexual development as the origins of men's motivation of rape. However, empirically, it is difficult to establish the personality differences between men who rape and those who do not (Albin, 1977). Further, this explanation is based on biased sample as rapists tend to be both class-based and race-based. The suggestion in the psychological studies that only abnormal men rape thus carries an implicit class and race bias that defines these men as deviant and psychologically deranged. At the same time, such studies underemphasize the causal contribution of the social environment to the occurrence of rape.

Sub-Culture of Violence

A second theory of the causes of rape comes from the sub-culture of violence perspective in criminology. Adopted from Wolfgang and Feracuti (1967), the sub-culture of violence theory claims that violence is a cultural way of life in the working class and black communities; thus its members comes to take violence for granted, and it becomes a routine feature of everyday life. This theory blames the presumed pathological culture of these people for violent behaviour.

Critics of this perspective point out that violence is equally extensive in the dominant culture; it is just more easily hidden or legitimized as appropriately masculine behaviour. The sub-culture of violence theory gives an inadequate explanation of violence against women because it does not explain why violence is also symptomatic of the dominant culture.

Gender Socialization as a Cause of Rape

Feminists have suggested that the causes of rape can be traced to the dominant culture and its emphasis on masculinity as a learned pattern of aggression and domination. Men who rape see sexual aggressiveness as legitimate. Further, various institutional factors such as the family, peer group, religion and the media may promote sex-role stereotypes by teaching or reinforcing female and male role imbalances. Men who rape thus do not think that they have done anything wrong. According to the perspective of gender socialization theory, rape occurs because men have learnt that forcing women to have sex is legitimate and normal behaviour. This perspective is inadequate without an understanding of how the cultural concepts of masculinity and feminity emerge from the status of women and men in the society.

Rape and Economic Status of Women

Rape alienates a woman from her own body and destroys her sense of security. Rape is an expression of male domination and misogyny a vehicle for terrorizing and subordinating women. It is the manifestation of the historically unequal power relations between man and woman. When a woman is perceived as a weak creature apart from an object of gratification of a man's sexual needs, the crimes like rape and sexual harassment become the symbol of the masculinity for the perpetrator. Further, the use of women as sexual objects in advertising reduces their sexuality to a commodity. Moreover, images of violence against women in advertising and the popular media legitimate violent behaviour against women and reiterate their status as sexual objects. To become an object is to become a piece of property and this status dehumanizes women and makes them an object for male violence.

Also, the fact that most rapists do not believe that they have done anything wrong shows that violence against women carries some degree of legitimacy within the society. It is the victims who are ostracized. Those who are perceived as the least valuable in the society are more likely to be raped. This fact explains why refugee women, migrant workers, destitute women, women in detention, women with disabilities and women in situations of armed conflict are the most frequent victims of rape. Cross-cultural evidence discloses that the level of violence against women is lowest in those societies where women have the most social, political economic autonomy (Fried, 1975). In patriarchal societies, where men rule women, women lose their autonomy and are encouraged to be dependent on men. Research on rape victims shows that women who are not identified as belonging to a man (i.e., women who are alone in public, single, divorced, separated, or living with non-family members) are most victimized by rape.

Violence against women is based on the economic and political powerlessness of women in patriarchal societies. In order to stop violence against women, it is thus essential that they are liberated from oppressive social and economic relations. In sum, violence against women is supported through the institutions of society. Cultural institutions ideologically promote violence against women; patriarchal social institutions encourage violence against women; criminal justice institutions minimize or cover up violence against women; legal institutions resist radical change in policies to protect women from violence.

Thus, the above mentioned explanations help us to report that rape is a unique crime for the following reasons:

- It is not just a physical assault, but a violation of personal intimate and psychological boundaries.
- It is surrounded by persistent cultural myths and stereotypes.
- It is overwhelmingly a gendered crime, committed by men predominantly against women and girls but also on some boys and other men.
- The perpetrator is in the majority of cases someone the victim knows, thus the crime involves betrayal of trust.
- Victimization often results in potent and debilitating self-blame.
- It carries particular health risks and consequences such as STDs, involuntary pregnancy and HIV infection.
- The process of reporting the crime and any legal case are often experienced as a form of re-victimization.

Legal Regulations

The governments all over the world have always been aware of this phenomenon and almost all the countries have laws to deal with this crime. In our country we have substantive as well as procedural laws dealing with this crime. The former is contained in Sections 375 and 376 of the Indian Penal Code (IPC) which was enacted in the year 1860. The procedural law pertaining to this offence contained in Indian Evidence Act (Section 114) and Code of Criminal Procedure (Section 327). Consent is the vital element to constitute rape. But, if consent is obtained by putting her in some sort of undue pressure or duress, it would cease to be full consent, and further, administration of some intoxicants vitiates free consent.

Another feature is that mere penetration of male organ is enough. To constitute rape 'satisfying sex' is not the mere ingredient. Ejaculation or orgasm is not necessary.[2]

In the legal context rape can be classified as:

- Ordinary rape
- Constructive rape
- Custodial rape
- Aggravated form of rape

Ordinary rape would fall within the ambit of Section 375 – first and secondly[3], constructive rape would fall in the ambit of Section 375 –

thirdly to sixthly.[4] The meaning of word 'constructive' is inferential, i.e., which could be deduced or interpreted. At one point, we say consent or rather absence of it is the vital element of rape and a bare reading of Section 375 thirdly to sixthly entails consent but an inference can be clearly drawn from this reading that consent is not free and hence we call it constructive rape.

The third form is custodial rape. The provisions of the same are contained is Section 376 (2) (a), (b), (c), (d)[5] where there is a breach of trust. Custody implies trust and when the custodian himself becomes perpetrator, then it is a breach of trust.

Aggravated form of rape is contained in Section 376 (2) (e), (f), (g).[6] A mere reading makes it clear why we call it an aggravated form of rape.

There is another aspect of this form, that is, rapes committed on women during wars, communal or other riots and in such other abnormal situations. These types of rapes ought to be brought under the purview of violation of human rights and must be made part of our legislation.

The punishment for ordinary rape and constructive rape is contained in Section 376(1), which is for a period not less than 7 years but extendable to 10 years or life and also fine. Punishment for custodial and aggravated rape is for a period of not less than 10 years but extendable to life imprisonment. There is a proviso to both that court can award a punishment for a period less than the minimum prescribed period for adequate and special reasons to be mentioned in the judgment. These reasons have to be strong and not frivolous.[7] It is submitted here that if rape is followed by murder, then as, per rule, capital punishment ought to be awarded. Though, in our criminal jurisprudence, capital punishment can be awarded in rarest of rare cases, therefore, rape followed by murder ought to fall within rarest of rare cases.

If we trace the development of rape jurisprudence in our country, then *Tukaram versus State of Maharashtra* (Mathura case)[8] is the watershed case. It led to many changes and major amendments were made in the IPC, Code of Criminal Procedure and Evidence Act in 1983. Section 376 A-D has added another dimension to this concept. It deals with cases where a woman consents to have sex with her superior officer when he exercises undue pressure on her. She succumbs to pressure and consents.

Though it is strictly speaking not rape but nonetheless it has been made punishable, because element of free consent is absent in these cases.

Now, judicial trend, especially of higher judiciary, is in favour of victims. Earlier, character or rather allegation of loose character was a valid defence for rape. Defence would invariably try to prove that woman asked for it. Happily, this trend has changed and raping a prostitute is as grave a crime as raping any other woman.[9]

Section 114-A of Evidence Act raises a presumption in favour of woman that if she alleges that she was raped in the custody, it would be presumed that she was raped and the custodian would have to rebut the presumption.

Further, rape is seldom committed in public gaze, so to find corroborative evidence or evidence of some of the persons except the victim is difficult. Now, courts are holding that corroboration of victim's statement is not essential.[10]

Medical examination is an essential evidence. Earliest possible medical examination could lead to solid evidence. Woman has a right to get herself medically examined in a hospital even without a police report.[11] Court is now awarding compensation to victims. Though compensation can never revert or restore a woman's honour but it may act as balm or may be utilized for medical purposes. In fact, the Supreme Court has directed Government of India to constitute a Criminal Injuries Compensation Board to furnish compensation to victims.[12]

Conclusion

We have had laws on this aspect since a long time. But, the problem continues to persist rather in greater amplitude. In the contemporary world, where woman has come out and is trying to be economically independent in the society which is still patriarchal, this problem continues unchecked. As discussed earlier, the foremost reason is that more often this crime goes unreported. A society which is obsessed with virginity and chastity, a case of sexual assault or rape brings more disrepute and humiliation to the victim rather than the culprit. Faulty investigation, sloppy prosecution, prolonged trials and low conviction rate are some important reasons causing discouragement among the victims of crime.

In view of these facts, it becomes clear that the most essential thing to free the society from this most heinous crime is to simplify time-consuming legal process so that justice is seen to have been done for both the victims and the accused. Further, there is a need to change the mindset of the society to essence a general regard for the dignity of woman. It is also essential to dispel the myth that rape has anything to do with the chastity of the victim. Chastity lies in the mind and soul and not in the body which has accidentally been a victim of a sexual assault. In fact, the notion of the physical base of the chastity is based on patriarchal and feudal values transmitted from generation to generation. Rectification of such types of the defective social vision would go a long way in psychological rehabilitation of the victim as also in exposing the perpetrators before the law and the society.

Notes

1. Paras Diwan, "Law Relating to Dowry, Dowry Deaths, Bride Burning, Rape and Related Offences II Ed., p. vii.
2. See *Madan Gopal v. Naval, J.T.* 1992 (3) SC 270.
3. A man is said to commit rape who except in the case hereinafter excepted, has sexual intercourse with a woman under circumstances falling under any of the six following descriptions:
   First – Against her will.
   Secondly – Without her consent.
4. Thirdly – With her consent, when her consent has been obtained by putting her or any person in whom she is interested in fear of death or of hurt.
   Fourthly – With her consent when the man knows that he is not her husband, and that her consent is given because she believes he is other man to whom she is or believes herself to be lawfully married.
   Fifthly – With her consent, when at the time of giving her consent by reason of unsoundness of mind or intoxication or administration by him: personally or through another of stupefying or understand the nature and consequences of that

to which she gives consent.

Sixthly – With or without her convent, when she is under sixteen years of age.

5. Section 376 (2): Whoever
   (a) being a police officer commits rape;
      (i) within the limits of the police station to which he is appointed; or
      (ii) in the premises of any station house whether or not situated in the police station to which he is appointed; or
      (iii) on a woman in his custody or in the custody of a police officer subordinate to him; or

   (b) being a public servant takes advantage of his official position and commits rape on a woman in his custody as such public servant or in the custody of a public servant subordinate to him;

   (c) being on the management or staff of jail remand home or other place of custody established by or under any law for the time being in force or a women's or children's institution, takes advantage of his official position and commits rape on any inmate of such jail, remand home, place or institution; or

   (d) being on the management or staff of the hospital, takes advantage of his official position and commits rape on a woman in that hospital.

6. Section 376 (2): Whoever
   (e) commits rape on a woman knowing her to be pregnant, or
   (f) commits rape on a woman when she is under 12 years of age, and
   (g) commits gang rape.
7. *Madan Gopal v. Naval, J.T.*1992 (3) 270; *State of Karnataka v. Krishnappa*, AIR 2000 SC 1470.
8. AIR 1979 SC 185.
9. *State of Maharashtra v. Madhuker, JT* (1990) 4 SC 169; *Milind Ambadas Mahaske v. State of Maharashtra*, 1998 Cr LJ 1357; *Joseph v. State of Kerala*, AIR 2000 SC 1608.
10. *Madan Gopal v. Naval, JT* 1992(3) SC 270; *Kalyan Singh v. State of Rajasthan*, AIR 1952 SC 54; *State of Maharashtra v. Chandraprakash Kewalchand* Jain, AIR 1990 SC 658.
11. *State of Andhra Pradesh v. Maryare*, 2000 (3) RCR (Crl) 24 (SC).
12. *Chairman, Railway Board v. Chandrima Das*, 2000 (1) RCR 303.

References

Albin, R. 1977. 'Review Essay: Psychological Studies of Rape' *Signs*, '3, Winter 423-435.

Fried, I.E. 1975. *Women and Men*, New York, Holt, Rinehart and Winston.

Schwartz, M. 1997. *Researching Sexual Violence against Women*, Newbury Park, Sage.

Vishwanathan, Shiv. 2002. 'The Male Gaze', *Sunday Times of India*, December 8, 2002.

Wolfgang, M. and F. Feracuti. 1967. *The Sub-Culture of Violence*. London, Tavistock.

11

State, Women and Governance: The Indian Case

RAJESH GILL

Empowerment of women has little meaning unless it involves them in the decision-making process. More so, since the democratic and secular India endeavours to provide the necessary conditions for greater participation of women in different realms of life. Constitutionally and legally, equality of opportunity is guaranteed, and discrimination on any ascriptive grounds is prohibited. Yet, in reality, women's participation in decision-making at all levels – national to local – is abysmally low. However, this is not the only cause for concern. A more important issue is that even when women participate in the decision-making bodies as people's representatives, they mostly remain passive players rather than assuming an active role in the process. It is now time to probe into such issues and identify the ways through which an effective participation of women into political bodies can be ensured.

The present paper makes an effort in this direction. Implementation of the 74th Constitution Amendment Act is a major – in fact a radical – step to empower women with a significant role in the urban local bodies like nagar panchayats, municipalities and municipal corporations. How far the reservation for women in urban local bodies has produced desirable results? What are the major hindrances in the way of women's effective participation in the decision-making process? And, what should now be done to ensure a meaningful participation of women in the elected urban bodies? The paper has tried to address to these questions on the basis of empirical work done earlier on urban local bodies, with special focus on women representatives.

The paper has three-fold objectives. First, it attempts to describe the factual situation regarding the experiences of women representatives in urban local bodies (ULBs). Secondly, it identifies the prominent issues confronted in the achievement of women's political empowerment. Finally, measures are suggested to ensure an effective and meaningful enforcement of women's participation in the decision-making process.

The studies on which this discussion is based were conducted soon after the municipal elections, since the implementation of the 74th Constitution Amendment Act. The incumbents were new and the municipal bodies thus formed were the first of their kind. Time span is important because for women this was the first and a novel experience. Also, their men (husbands, sons, brothers or uncles) looked at them with a complete lack of trust as effective councillors. In fact, in one of the interviews, the son of a councillor said: "Husbands in fact are the trainers who prepare the women for their future roles". Initially, most of the women lacked both the confidence as well as a clear conception of the roles they were expected to perform. The situation must have improved by now as the feedback from rural panchayats has shown. In one such analysis of the cases of women panchayat members, this research has highlighted both success stories and stories of failure, but certainly, women panchas, especially the dalits, had gained tremendous confidence and competence over time. When we interviewed the male counterparts in local administration, especially the Commissioners, Municipal Corporations (CMCs), the response immediately became indifferent and apathetic the moment we asked them about their reaction towards women councillors. It was extremely difficult to elicit information from these men because of a very stiff mindset, perceiving women representatives in Municipal Corporations with distrust, casualness and disapproval.

Women councillors in Punjab during interviews, except a few, were not very forthcoming, not because of an unwillingness on their part to respond, but primarily because they neither possessed the information on various aspects of the 74th Constitution Amendment Act, nor had they any opinion on issues confronting them as councillors. The situation was much better in Chandigarh, where a majority of women councillors were quite forthcoming in sharing their experiences as councillors. Even those enjoying the support of political parties, were articulate enough to bring forth their viewpoints, except two Scheduled Caste women who were illiterate and were most of the time being represented by their husbands. So far as the CMCs were concerned, the communication generally got blocked the moment the issue of women councillors was brought for discussion. It seemed as if for them this issue was non-existent, unnecessarily being attached so much of centrality.

Factual Situation

Women elected to the urban local bodies are far from a homogeneous group. They range from completely uneducated to highly educated, poorest to the most affluent, housewives to the professionally qualified, and so on. Each of these attributes plays a significant role in their perception of their newly attained role, their commitment towards it, their effectiveness, and so on. Also, these women had a varied age structure. While most of the women councillors in Punjab were affiliated to one or the other political party, only three had a direct affiliation. Others were associated with a party through their husbands, followed by fathers-in-law, brothers and fathers. This has significant implications as reflected through our interaction with them. These women had confusion writ large on their face, mainly because they had been pushed into the roles they were not prepared for and moreover, they were hardly permitted to function on their own. They would turn towards their husbands for every small query. Inheriting a political position by a woman need not be taken to criticize the provision of reservation, as is normally being done. If the same inheritance has worked for men for centuries, why to make an issue out it in the case of women?

An important observation, emerging out of both the rural and urban local bodies so far studied, is that the provision for the rotation of reserved constituencies often goes against the women incumbents. Women councillors, just like the women panchas, initially assume their role hesitatingly, lacking both confidence and a clear understanding of the new role. By the time they acquire confidence, commitment and an identity of their own, not only is their term over, but their chances of being elected from the same constituency once again get remote, since it may no longer be a reserved constituency the next time. The emphasis of political parties being on the constituency, she may never get a second chance as to the male aspirants waiting for the last five years take charge. This problem can be solved if more and more women contest elections and enter the field on their own, and not as representatives of their male counterparts.

Most of our women respondents were found to be only remotely interested in the functioning of the municipal corporations in Punjab, and came to the office only for a meeting. These meetings too were attended more often by their husbands, who as we were intimated by an official in Chandigarh Municipal Corporation, had to be physically pushed out of the meeting hall. The whole experience of women's empowerment – whether economic, psychological or political – so far has indicated that this exercise involves the total society. Many a times, the whole issue is taken as if it touches only the women. In fact, it touches, or rather 'pinches' men even more. Empowering the women simply means withdrawing power from men. Even, the case studies of women NGOs, which can be termed as success stories, show that women in these NGOs had carried their men along. Hence, it is a gender issue involving both men as well as women. It was observed in this study that men as bureaucrats, officials and subordinate staff were highly non-cooperative. Women councillors, due to the callous attitude of these employees, often had to face a lot of embarrassment, when encountered by their constituencies.

For a moment, let us go back to the objectives of the 74th Constitution Amendment Act, particularly an expectation inherent in it, that with reservation provisions, issues relating to women and child development and those relating to the poor will come up for discussion much more frequently in the municipal corporations, and a programmatic shift towards these issues would take place. This expectation has hardly been realized mainly due to various reasons. The assumption that women representatives will take up joint issues is ill-founded. Given their diverse composition, clubbed with political affiliations, issues relating to women and children have often taken a back seat. In both Punjab as well as

Chandigarh, more often than the women from different political parties, it is the women from the same party, who are at daggers drawn. The past experience shows that the candidature of a woman for the post of Mayor has more often been opposed by other women of the same political party, making it even easier for men to grab the post. The fact is that divisions within the women incumbents have done them greater harm, often pushing back the women-based agenda. Studies from panchayats too reveal that the women panchas or Pradhans, who have made a wonderful performance, are those having garnered the support of fellow women in the village. Given the age-old patriarchal structures, and monopolized authority of men in politics, women, in order to be effective, will have to have lots of women at their back, irrespective of age, caste, income and so on. As a consequence of political interests ruling the women, just like their male counterparts, issues relating to women and child development often sink to the ground.

A second reason why women's issues get buried underneath is that even the male colleagues, belonging to the same party, having supported the woman candidate during elections, never allow her to gain prominence either within the party or the municipal corporation, thus causing tremendous frustration among women councillors, especially those committed and efficient ones. For instance, the Chandigarh Municipal Corporation has, during the last four years, witnessed maximum infighting within the ruling party, over issues such as election of Mayor, and nomination to important assignments. Issues therefore get sacrificed in favour of wasteful political gimmicks. In line with the experience of panchayats, this analysis also shows that as far as women's issues are concerned, SC women councillors are much more effective as compared to their upper caste counterparts. The reason is that low caste women who also happen to be poor in most cases, find it very convenient to approach a woman councillor belonging to their own status and convince her about their problems. These councillors too were found to be taking up such issues in various committee meetings.

With the constitutional provision for women constituencies, the politically active men naturally look upon women contestants close to them. They find their wives/daughters etc. as the most eligible candidates for various reasons. One, it ensures that the political centre does remain within the family. Two, after winning elections, political mileage is practically enjoyed by the male member. Thirdly, it helps the man in preserving his ties with the political party, not allowing anybody else to hijack the political gains. Finally, the seat is secured for the next election when the constituency is no longer reserved and the man can himself encash upon the last term. Had it not been for these reasons, the husband would never have digested even the thought of pushing the wife into political field – a public front, forbidden for her. Thanks to the 74th Constitution Amendment Act, which has forced men to expose their womenfolk to political decision-making.

Though most of these women initially were confused, hesitant and ineffective, lacking any interest in the role, they have been found to have shed all inhibitions and assume an active participation over time. For instance, the study of Chandigarh Municipal Corporation undertook an appraisal of two male constituencies, female constituencies (general) and SC women constituencies each, in order to gauge the difference in their performance, from people's perspective. Assessment of the councillor's role mainly depended upon two factors – accessibility of the councillor and people of the constituency. People liked a councillor if he/she was easily accessible to them at times of need. In this regard, it was notable that SC councillors were more popular among the people mainly because of their easy accessibility. Similarly, people in the affluent constituencies had extremely high expectations out of their councillors. This became a strong reason for their being mostly dissatisfied. The personality traits of the woman councillor also went a long way in winning the confidence of people. For instance, women who were articulate, communicative and effective, were believed to be more resourceful by the people. Such incumbents had very bright chances of getting re-elected. In short, people looked for similar characteristics in their woman representative as in the case of any male incumbent.

Women councillors in Punjab were found to be mostly silent spectators as compared to their counterparts in Chandigarh. The patriarchal structure of Punjab, also reflected through the panchayats, is mainly responsible for such a trend, which certainly would change with time. We need serious studies on the association between the cultural ethos of a region with an effective participation of women in public life. On the contrary, women incumbents in Chandigarh Municipal Corporation were quite vocal and effective, although the practice of nominated councillors was not favoured by most of them. These nominated members could never win over the trust of elected ones. One of the spokespersons of ruling political party in Chandigarh Municipal Corporation reported that "given such an experience, we will see to it that in the next Municipal Corporationn nominated councillors are our own people, providing us support rather than opposition".

Challenges Faced by Women Representatives

Following are the challenges faced by women representatives:

— At the moment, having secured reservation for themselves in various political bodies – local as well as national – women do not have to rejoice, because they face enormous challenges ahead. They have to overcome attitudinal, institutional, cultural, structural and social barriers which have grown over centuries.

— An extremely antagonistic attitude of not only the males but even the females among bureaucrats, superiors, subordinates, friends, family members and public at large, against the women as competent candidates for decision-makers. Such a negative attitude came uniformly from the administrators, members of municipal bodies etc.

— Misuse of constitutional provision by the politicians, mainly men, to retain the political power within the family by first making female relatives contest elections and then forcing them to act as dummies, thus tarnishing the public image of women incumbents in public eye.

— Repeatedly calling politics "a dirty game", suitable only for men (as if dirt could only pollute women and not men), and keeping educated, competent and articulate women out of the fray.

— A complete politicization of the whole issue, with serious repercussions on reserved constituencies. For instance, it may not be possible to successfully contest without a political backing. Even if you get elected without a political tag, it may not be feasible to effectively participate subsequently.

— Politicization of municipal bodies not only up to elections, but more so afterwards, when the taking up of issues, getting financial aid, receiving public support – everything depends upon your political affiliation. In this political manoeuvring gender issues have invariably got buried underneath, dividing the women from within.

— The gravest hurdle in the way of women's empowerment is, as observed by the Committee on the Status of Women in India, "the large masses of women continue to lack spokespersons who understand their special problems and are committed to their removal in the respective bodies of the state".

— It is going to be a much more difficult and challenging task for women to rise to high levels of political office, get into existing patriarchal structures, stay on and be effective. This is true mainly because women's empowerment and participation is a political question, linked to changes in power relations. Contemporary history indicates that in defining identities or values that have to be preserved, it is the perceptions of male political leaders that rule the day.

— It must be admitted that even when placed in the highest political offices, women have not been able to change the lives of the mass of women. Gender sensitivity has to be brought not only among men but also women – to negate the damage that has been done through centuries.

— A major hurdle facing women today relates to the efforts on the part of vested interests to bifurcate women on the basis of religion, caste etc.

Suggestions for Future

It is not sufficient to know that thousands of women have entered these decision-making bodies, we also need to investigate as to who among them have been effective and why and also who have failed and why. Longitudinal studies on these women could provide us very insightful information on their experiences, performance and limitations. My experience has shown that irrespective of whether she was forced by her male relatives or friends, to jump into the political field, confidence and efficiency of a woman representative get strengthened over time. The consequence of this has mostly been a stronger and politically ambitious woman emerging in the end. But, she must definitely not be left to the mercy of men around her, who may use her according to their convenience. The social structural barriers need to be identified and removed for a meaningful and fearless participation of women in public life.

Further, it is not possible to club all women councillors in a single category. Their performance differs tremendously in terms of caste status, political backing, economic and educational status, personality traits and male support. The success stories of women councillors need to be probed and publicized in order to give them a moral boost.

It is not sufficient to provide training to these women representatives, but it is high time to evaluate such training programmes conducted by both governmental as well as – non governmental organizations. The feedback received during these sessions must be recorded and harnessed for further improvement. Having seen the urban local bodies work under the 74th Constitution Amendment Act for more than a term now, there is a need to build a data base on the kind of jobs women councillors in different urban bodies have been assigned. For example, which committees are they made members of? This is essential so that these bodies too do not become gendered.

There is an urgent need to attract educated, independent and committed women to the role of councillors. Municipal bodies are the local level reflections of national democratic scenario, suffering from similar kinds of political gimmicks, politicization and so on. Just as in the case of panchayats, urban local bodies too can witness the corruption and patriarchy being challenged by competent women representatives. Media also needs to play a positive role in highlighting the constructive role played by women representatives in various local bodies. This can go a long way in stimulating women take up the challenging role more courageously. Media must stop glorifying every example of a weak councillor, thus damaging another woman struggling hard to come on equal terms with her male counterpart.

Political parties have also been fielding women candidates only conditionally, because their interests are long term. Studies however confirm that even if these parties field their women candidates out of compulsion, these women in the process become politically ambitious, often aspiring for another term, whether political bosses like it or not. It needs to be investigated as to what happens to such women who may become sores in the eyes of not only the party concerned but also their own menfolk. Women in such situations need to be provided all kinds of support.

The past experience of women representatives in urban local bodies calls for the following steps in order to ensure their effective and meaningful participation:

— Educated, enlightened, articulate and competent women must enter the field.

— Women incumbents must not allow politicians to bifurcate them in the name of caste or religion, thus diluting the whole issue of their political empowerment.

— Entry of women into decision-making bodies must be acquired as a matter of right and not as an act of generosity.

— Women must counter the propaganda that politics is not a woman's cup of tea.

— Women bodies must field their own candidates not only in reserved constituencies, but also in general ones, irrespective of religion, caste etc.

— Concrete steps must be taken individually and collectively to change the public opinion in favour of women representatives. Women's recognition as efficient professionals, managers, teachers and now decision-makers must be strengthened.

Challenges will keep on multiplying but the best thing would be to face them, understand them and solve them, rather than pushing them under the carpet. The war has hardly been won with the constitutional amendment; the real war has just begun. We need to learn from the experiences of women representatives at different levels of urban local bodies, in order to enable the amendment achieve what it has been intended to achieve.

References

Gill, Rajesh. 2003. 'Political Empowerment of Women: Lessons from Municipal Corporations of Punjab and Chandigarh' in M.S. Gill, *Punjab Society: Perspectives and Challenges,* New Delhi, Concept Publishing Company.

— 1999. 'Seventy-Fourth Constitution Amendment and Political Empowerment of Women in Punjab: A Study in Urban Governance', *Urban India,* Vol. XIX No.1.

— 1998. 'Women in Local Governments – Experiences in Municipal Corporations of Punjab', in *Urban Governance in Punjab: A Study in the Context of the Constitution* (74th Constitution Amendment) Act, 1992 *Institute of Social Sciences*, New Delhi.

— 1998. 'Women in Local Governments', *Man & Development,* Vol. XX (2).

12

Market, Media and Gender in Globalized Punjab

RAJESH GILL

India, like all other countries in the world, is already undergoing in the process of globalization. The experience is multifaceted, multidimensional and diverse, with the economic, political and cultural arenas getting globalized simultaneously. One can say that India is a part of the global village, although it will be more so once the WTO comes into force within the next two years. Although the process of globalization was initiated long ago, the last few years have witnessed unprecedented transformation in the fields of agriculture, communication and information technology, culture, education and so on, making it look almost like a revolution.

This paper intends to focus upon the globalization of culture, particularly gender relations. The relationship is peculiar because culture never absorbs any impact passively. On the contrary, it always reacts in a specific manner and perhaps this is the reason that the thesis of homogenization, popularly treated as a necessary concomitant of globalization, has confronted rigorous rejection, both in developing and the developed nations of the world. It is indeed extremely interesting to look at the interface between globalization and culture because the two interplay reciprocally, not always in a predictable manner, and making the whole process culture-specific.

At the same time, however, it is most difficult to make an assessment of the impact of globalization on culture. Firstly, because, it is methodologically impossible to identify its indicators. Secondly, the assessment is heavily based upon value judgements, since cultural change cannot be objectified or quantified. Thirdly, changes in various cultural items are far from consistent, or unidimensional, making it often extremely difficult to pinpoint the direction in which change is happening. Hence, it is a difficult terrain, though worth trying. Again, culture includes so many elements, viz., language, customs, norms, mannerism, ways of dressing, eating etc. In the present paper, the focus is mainly upon gender relations, which are governed by the prevailing ideology in a society.

Let us start our discussion with the assumptions underlying globalization, which though theoretically, were expected to result into specific impact, both in the developed and the developing societies. It promised the celebration of human rights, especially the rights of the weaker sex, calling to question the patriarchal ideology in its entirety. The era of globalization thus paved the way for women's movement and gender justice, leading to a consciously evolved distinction between gender-blind policies of the yesteryears and the gender-aware policies of today. The assumption was that such a positive transformation would be faster if accompanied by economic growth and technological advancement.

No doubt, these expectations got reflected through various policies of the Indian State since independence. Gender justice was ensured, mainly theoretically, both through constitutional and legislative structures, projecting a gender-wise just society as an ideal future. The question that is being addressed in the present paper is whether all these sincere intentions translated into policies have successfully removed the imbalances between gender relations perpetuating through centuries in India, particularly Punjab? The answer to this query is that all this has had an effect only at a superficial level, hardly putting a dent in the age-old systems of patriarchy, both in the private as well as the public domains.

This author is fully aware that things have tremendously improved in favour of women in India. For example, ideologically, our society celebrates gender equality, so that most of the policies initiated by the Indian State have increasingly turned out to be gender aware. But, this is also true that so much insistence upon gender equality, particularly women's rights, cannot be solely attributed to endogenous sources, because the issue has been on the global agenda for quite sometime now. Since our cultural preferences too have been travelling largely from the global powers, we, as a nation, just could not afford to keep the gender issue out of the agenda – political, economic, ideological and social. Hence, it is more western, and therefore, more modern to talk in favour of gender equality, especially in the public discourses.

The second positive effect of globalization on gender issue has been that technological advancement, urbanization and modern education have pulled women out of the private domain directly into the public domain. Women are certainly more visible, especially in modern metropolitan cities, driving cars, shopping, working both in private and public sectors, participating in the beauty pageants with an ever-increasing vigour and enthusiasm. Watching them on the ramp, sashaying and displaying their physical and mental skills makes one wonder if they still suffer from any kind of social discrimination. Such an aggressive visibility of women in public domain sounds quite optimistic, as regards the future of India is concerned. But, the question is what about the private domain? While gender equality remains the top agenda at the macro level, what are the experiences of these women in their mundane life, is a question to be probed into.

Women today have an effective visibility even in traditionally male-dominated areas, such as professionals, elected representatives in rural and urban local bodies, bureaucracy and so on. Women make their presence felt as lawyers, teachers, police officers, managers, receptionists, doctors and so on. This is true in Punjab too, which happens to be one of the most economically prosperous states of India. Recently, a beauty contest was held in Punjab, where Miss World Punjaban was chosen. The contest had many interesting sub-titles on the lines of international competitions, such as *'Lum Slumi Gutt'* and so on. For a moment, one is forced to believe that things have really improved in a state like Punjab, which has had a strong tradition of celebrating patriarchy more rigorously in the public domain. One is, therefore, forced to ask: "have the stereotypes changed in favour of women in Punjab?" Before jumping to any conclusion, let us first look at the following facts with regard to contemporary Punjab:

- The state has around 2.4 crores of total population.
- It has about 34 per cent urban population.
- Punjab has 17 districts and 72 tehsils, 157 towns, 12,729 villages and 12,369 panchayats.
- There are 14 class I (one lakh plus) and two million plus (metropolitan) cities in Punjab.
- The state enjoys the status of being one among the states with a high per capita income.
- It is one of the most agriculturally developed states.

Along with these attributes, Punjab also is a state with the following characteristics:

- A highly patriarchal society.
- An alarmingly declining sex ratio – from 882 in 1991 to 874 in 2001.
- 0-6 age group, from 875 in 1991 to 793 in 2001.
- A very low participation of women in the labor force.
- A society with a strong preference for sons at the cost of daughters.
- A highly consumerist society, posing most serious challenge to the rural Punjab.
- An increasing degree of disenchantment, especially among rural youth, with the farming as an occupation, and a strong urge to earn lots of money, quickly and with ease.
- An extremely addicted society, especially the rural youth, with devastating effects on family ties, status of women etc.
- A society indulging into a naked display of wealth on marriages, often pushing the middle class farmers to suicides, ultimately severely damaging the dignity of women.

I shall focus only on the problem areas and not the achievements, because these need to be immediately addressed.

Society in Punjab, primarily rural agrarian, like other such societies, is highly patriarchal. Punjabi society has all through supported an extremely patriarchal social structure – depicted by folk tales, folk songs, proverbs, customs etc. Sikhism, which is known for its forward-looking character in terms of both caste practices and women's status, too failed to hit the patriarchal structure in Punjab. Instead, various movements of

Sikhism like Singh Sabha movement prescribed the same role to a woman as was suggested in Hinduism, i.e., of a 'pativrata'. The high caste reformers of various hues in Punjab tried to protect their high born status and social privilege by controlling women's sexuality (Malhotra, 2002).

As early as in 1851, the prevalence of female infanticide among the Bedis of Dera Baba Nanak was brought to the notice of British authorities. Finally, the practice was found to be widely prevalent in Punjab, especially among the upper castes, like Rajputs, Khatris, Aroras, Brahmans and even among Muslims and Jats (Montgomery, 1853). According to a scholar, Hindu women, on losing a female infant, would, by the practice, take her body into the jungle and place it in a sitting position under a tree. The next day, they would visit that place again and if the body had been pulled by animals towards the home, it signalled the arrival of another female child, but if the body had been pulled away from home, it meant that a male child would be born next (PNQ, 1884). Such historical accounts clearly bring out the fact that preference for a son in Punjab is not a novel phenomenon, it has existed here for centuries. In the 19th century Punjab, as in any other patriarchal society, procreation of male progeny has always been the most important duty demanded of women.

A woman, who could not attain motherhood, invited the worst social rejection, which often was unbearable. Such a woman would indulge into multiple types of witchcraft. One such practice was that such a woman would try to capture the spirit of a recently dead young man in her wombs by cooking rice pudding on the place of his cremation during night. The soul of a body, which was half burnt, was considered to be most fruitful since at that point of time, its soul was said to be trying to free itself (Malhotra, 2002).

Having had such a past, the society in Punjab continues, in the present age of women's empowerment, to instil in its women an extremely strong urge to give birth to son or sons, in order to earn social prestige and a dominant status in the family, besides becoming a favourite with her husband and his family. It is this urge that makes today's educated, liberated women of Punjab go in for sex determination tests and subsequently undergo termination of pregnancy in case it is a girl, not once, not twice, but multiple number of times, even at the cost of their life and health – both mental and physical.

Have we started blessing a newly-wed would-be mother as "May God bless you with a beautiful daughter", without getting a blow from her in laws? Certainly not! I am sure, somebody giving such a blessing is likely to get you a big blow, since it would be taken as a curse, the worst that could be given to a mother. Since one is likely to have one or two children only, atleast one must be a boy. People say that things have changed today. Have we started distributing *ladoos* over the birth of a girlchild? In fact, if a person celebrates the birth of a daughter, he is ridiculed by the people, who claim that such a gesture would invite more daughters. The fact remains that everybody wants to have a son – rich or poor, educated or uneducated, rural or urban, and so on. The question that needs to be posed here is why is it so? It could be answered asking another question: Has a daughter stopped being a liability for the father?

This is the basic issue that needs to be pondered over. As long as a daughter continues to be a liability to her parents, she would never be welcome into the family. Her arrival is most likely to cause pain, frustration and depression to the parents, because she needs to be protected both at home and outside, from strangers as well as acquaintances, from childhood till youth; and then she has to be married into another family, along with a huge expenditure on her dowry. She is thus not only a financial, but even a psychological and social liability. The liability does not end with her marriage, it extends beyond, till the end. A daughter carries on her back the extremely heavy burden of 'family prestige', which needs to be protected at any cost.

There has always been a strong effort in Punjab, more so among the upper castes, to keep a strict vigil upon women, particularly young daughters and daughters-in-law. This emanated from the belief that the 'purity' of a woman's womb determined the purity of a caste. In the words of Das (1990), "women were the 'gateways' to the caste system, for as reproducers they were crucial to the caste maintaining their ritual status".

Is it no longer necessary for the father of an educated, employed daughter to worry about her dowry? Can we answer this question in "YES"? If not, things have really gone worse. The questions that need to be asked are:"With so much of economic development, with the coming up of Punjabi women into the limelight as entrepreneurs, farmers, police officers, writers, scholars and administrators, why is it that the girl in a village of Punjab still finds it hard to experience an independent identity of her own? Why does she always bow down to the pressures of her family to marry and unknown NRI, so that her uneducated brothers can migrate abroad and taste better quality of life? Why it is still a curse to be a girl's father, undergoing tremendous agony and pain in bringing her up, providing her with education and then marrying her off on the terms and conditions dictated absolutely by the groom's family?"

The reasons for the problems are many. In fact, any social reality is too complex to be squeezed to a simple one to one explanation.

1. Patriarchy, instead of getting weakened, has in fact strengthened its hold over the Punjabi society and modern technology has significantly contributed to it. For example, technology has made it possible for the parents-to-be, now, to choose the sex of one's child before birth. Technology can be put to better use today to practice patriarchy, relegating the modern ideals of equality and human rights to the background.
2. Media has greatly served in feeding the patriarchal structure in many ways as under:
    - Commodifying the culture, particularly women. There are umpteen number of advertisements and commercials celebrating the traditional feminine image of woman. Popular culture too projects the Punjabi girl as physically liberated, westernized, giving a damn to the *desi* culture, but at the same time, dancing to the tunes of *desi* guy, the same rustic Punjabi boy exuding the same old masculinity all over. Does the Punjabi music of contemporary times project Punjabi woman? Who are these girls who are depicted in the popular culture? Which class do they belong to? Do the girls of Punjab identify themselves with these girls on the small screen? These are some of the questions worth picking up. While watching the Punjabi pop songs, one is stuck by the centrality of the male lead singer, surrounded by accessories, mainly westernized, scantily clad girls, clinging to the guy, shadowed completely

under his identity. Aren't they becoming the reference model for the girls in Punjab?

- Commercialization of woman's body has been tremendously popular, particularly in Punjab. It is very common during the elections for contestants to engage very young girls perform with scanty clothes in villages, in order to pull large crowds at the election rallies. These girls are watched by the patriarchs of Punjab with lustful eyes and insatiable greed, the same men who refuse to give even a minimum amount of freedom to their own women at home. These live performances by adolescent girls on titillating numbers have become an integral part of social ceremonies like not only marriages, but even the house warming, turban tying etc. While the guests hurriedly attend the actual ceremonies, they wait impatiently for the zinda dance or rain dance by these girls. It seems that the more such events gain prominence, the more these same men push their own women back home into the interiors of their homes, into the private domain.
- There has been a tremendous effort towards the glorification of woman's body, especially through the beauty contests. As a result, every girl visualizes herself only as a pound of flesh. The commercials have further led to a terrible complex among girls not so good looking, and in order to overcome this complex, they often indulge into all kinds of senseless acts, just to be noticed. According to a popular advertisement, a professionally qualified girl, because of her dark complexion, fails to attract a good match for matrimony, thus causing a great pain and frustration to her father. Then, one fine day, she discovers 'Fair and Lovely' cream which makes her fair, thus fetching her a handsome husband, ending the woes of her father. Thus, a girl at any cost has to be good looking, not for her own sake, but to keep her father happy too.

3. The highly consumerist culture has eaten up whatever good even the most patriarchal culture Punjab had. For instance, the value of being a daughter, shared commonly by the kinsmen, neighbours and the village at large, is no longer visible. Marriages are just like parties,

where you go to have fun and enjoy, with little empathy with the family. In old times, when the relatives and friends went to attend a girl's wedding, they would consider her as their own daughter, empathizing completely with the parents of the bride. Today, the bride's father has not only to cater to the fancies and whims of the boy's side, but his own too, with the same level of formality, extravaganza and glamour.

- In order to consume more, you have to have more money. Hence, the rural youth, fascinated by the urban-based television serials, films, and city life, crave for lots and lots of money quickly, and they have started hating the extremely hard and filthy life, a peasant has to lead in a village setting. Accompanied by lack of quality education, proper guidance and glittering city culture, these boys are either getting hooked to drugs, or selling whatever little land their fathers had, to bring out music albums, which bring them on televisions often without much success, or force their parents to spend exorbitant amounts enabling them to immigrate abroad, just to run away from the drudgery of farm or other kinds of labour. This is a small mirror reflection of the contemporary Punjab.
- One of the greatest blows that has hit the status of women everywhere, particularly Punjab, is the glorification of the ceremony of marriage, with an ever-increasing expenditure. And, this has made daughters a massive liability for the parents. If earlier the girl who was usually only a little educated, non-earning, totally dependant, was to be given some essential household items as a compensation, in the shape of dowry, whereas today, the same girl, who is normally much more educated than the boy, earning and economically independent and capable of taking care of the young and the old in her husband's family, has to be given not only the essential items (branded ones), but also the luxuries like car, microwaves, and so on. The dowry list has gone longish. Who says it has shrunk?

4. The NRI marriages in Punjab have forced the State Police Department to open a separate cell to deal with such cases, which run today in thousands. The stories of these girls are heartrending.

The greatest fact to be worried over is, that despite all this, parents of a marriageable girl in Punjab eagerly search for NRI boys through newspapers etc. Why? One major reason is that the cost of marriage is reduced and the recurring costs also are less. But, at what cost? Actually, the fact is that marrying a daughter is much more important than whether she is happily married or not. In our society, a marriageable daughter at home is the greatest stigma, which is hard to be digested by the father, who in such a situation often finds himself helpless. And, finally, he ends up giving her hand to somebody, compromising many things.

5. The rural Punjab is reeling under a severe problem of drug addiction among the rural youth and it has already acquired an alarming proportion. According to a recent study by WHO, every third male and every tenth female student in the state has had drugs on some pretext or on one occasion or the other. Another survey in Punjab has indicated the highest prevalence of drug abuse in the age group of 16 to 25 years as 53 per cent of the males and 48 per cent of the females were reported to be prone to drug addiction (*The Tribune*, 2001). An opinion survey conducted by Punjab Agricultural University revealed that about three-fourths of the rural male adults were habitual drug takers in about 23 per cent of the villages (Singh, Gupta and Jindal, 2000).

Punjab is a state that has had the dubious record of enjoying a high per capita income and agricultural development, along with a constantly declining sex ratio. Various explanations are being put forth such as a high incidence of sex determination tests, followed by female foeticide, negligence of girlchild, denial of proper care and nutrition to her, and so on. All this has resulted into the phenomenon of 'missing girlchild syndrome' in Punjab. Despite its economic prosperity, Punjab continues to have a low level of female participation in labour force. Further, last few years have witnessed a continuous exodus of girls to foreign countries arranged by their parents, in exchange for the migration of her brother(s) abroad, where there are better job prospects. As a result of rampant menace of drug addiction among the Punjabi youth, especially in rural areas, coupled with increased employment among them, there is an increased incidence of well-educated young girls being married off to illiterate or semi-literate boys, out of fatigue and helplessness. Even, the much talked about and shocking incidents of farmers' suicides in Punjab have been largely attributed to the inability of peasants to meet the exorbitant expenditure to be incurred upon the marriages of their daughters. Such helplessness had often driven parents towards an acute state of indebtedness, out of which they could just not come out given their meagre resources.

The Government of Punjab declared the year 2003 as the Women's Year. One really wonders as to how come that all of a sudden the patriarchal society of India in general, and Punjab in particular, has become so sensitive about the women's issue. I strongly believe that the credit largely goes to the globalization of the women's issue, which has forced societies, especially the less developed, to introspect their social systems in terms of gender discrimination. Punjab is so much worried about its all-time low sex ratio, not so much because of its love for the fair sex, but mainly because of the watchful eyes of the global agencies, which are a deciding force in the progressive future of the state. Thanks to globalization and the concept of global village, today, any incident of gender discrimination, be it in panchayat, or bureaucracy, or even private domain, is capable of getting flashed on television screens, newspapers and magazines and even the Internet all over the globe in no time. An unintended consequence of this has been that at least ideologically, it is extremely difficult for any individual, organization or government to publicly vow for patriarchy.

A second positive impact of technological advancement, information revolution and education has been that a much larger proportion of women have found space in the public domain, which was earlier denied to them. The visibility of women has certainly increased, especially in cities. One gets struck by a predominant presence of women on roads driving two wheelers and cars, in government and private offices occupying positions at almost all levels, and in erstwhile male-dominated professions. The Indian women have in the recent past made themselves most visible at the international beauty pageants, winning the most coveted titles consecutively. Punjabi women have managed to reach the centre stage in almost all realms, e.g., films, police, literature, academics, and so on.

The recent past has also seen an increasing number of women in economically, politically and administratively prestigious positions. The

73rd and 74th Constitution Amendment Acts have pushed a large number of women into panchayats and urban local bodies. In Punjab, quite a few women have ventured into farming as a full-time job on their own and they have produced successful stories, which have received sufficient coverage by media. All these developments indicate tremendous change, favouring women, especially in a state like Punjab, where patriarchy has survived very strongly for centuries. Historical accounts show that male control over the female body was considered essential for maintaining the purity of caste in Punjab. The restriction of woman's world within the four walls of home was actually imposed in order to check her exposure to the outside world, guarding against her sexual impulses.

Given all these advances in gender context, the question remains as to whether all these changes have succeeded in making a dent in the age-old patriarchy in Punjab. As mentioned earlier, my argument is that these changes have only resulted in changes at a superficial level, without touching the real issue. I present the following arguments in support of my thesis.

Punjab, despite all the hullabaloo of globalization, has experienced a declining sex ratio, despite the consistent propaganda against female infanticide and foeticide. The patriarchal ideology in the state has continued to reflect itself through the low workforce participation by women. Recent history of Punjab, especially the Doaba region, has witnessed a forced exodus of young girls through marriage to foreign countries, in exchange of the migration of their unemployed brothers. Also, it is very common for highly educated girls to get married to low educated boys, because of the hassles involved in match making.

Women's status in Punjab suffered a terrible setback during terrorism and militancy, which once again pushed them into the background and causing much harm to their physical, psychological and cultural well-being. An empirical study, conducted by the Institute for Development and Communication, on the victims of militancy in Punjab reveals how the period of militancy resulted into adverse impact on women's health, reduced their mobility in public spaces, impinged upon the childhood of girls, led to early marriage, imposed code of conduct on them, had them sexually abused and led to their victimization, which was totally invisible (IDC, 1998). The militant movement in Punjab, according to this study, made the patriarchal structures even harsher, abandoning hundreds of women who had been affiliated to militants, or had been sexually assaulted by them. While the society glorified and celebrated the male victims, it stigmatized women victims, thus writing a black chapter in the history of Punjab so far as the women were concerned.

With the passage of many years since then, has the situation in Punjab improved? Let us start with the question: has the public attitude in Punjab changed towards a daughter? What is the response of the family, the neighbourhood and the society at large at the time of the birth of a girlchild? Normally, the relatives, on hearing the news, would ask the child's family, "Didn't you get the sex determination test conducted?" Then follows the consolation, "Don't worry, it will be a son next time. But don't forget to get the test done." When a test determination test is conducted, the medical expert, in case of a male foetus remarks, "Get ready for *ladoos*." On the birth of a son, it is common to distribute *ladoos*. So *ladoos* are associated with a male child. If things have changed, even the birth of a girl should be followed by *ladoos*. But, the fact is that if someone is innovative to indulge in such an act, the comment comes: "Such a fool, you know, if you distribute *ladoos* on the birth of a girl, many more will follow." Just imagine a newly married girl being blessed by someone like this: "May God bless you with a beautiful daughter!" The person is sure to get a big blow from the parents-in-law of the girl (or perhaps even by her own parents). All this makes one feel that things have not probably changed too much.

The most striking impact of globalization has been seen on the popular culture of Punjab. The whole of music industry has been revolutionalized. Young boys belonging to rural peasant families have forced their parents to sell their land, raise money and produce audio as well as video albums, of Punjabi songs, popularly known as Punjabi Pop. While these men can boast of globalizing the Punjabi language through these songs, all over the world, Punjabi girls are certainly getting globalized in the process. Invariably, the overriding theme in these songs is based upon one male singer and dozens of girls, most westernized or Americanized, in scanty clothes, without a speck of Punjabiat of which the main male singer seems so proud of. These girls are nothing more than accessories to the visual, assisting the singer divert the attention of audience from his shabby voice towards more pleasant looking dames. The point is that you are able to get such talented, beautiful models, to fill the space and render the albums saleable.

Punjab has made girls visible not merely on television but it has also to its credit the increased visibility of the fair sex live on the stage shows. It is common to find very young, usually adolescent girls, scantily clad in western outfits, dancing to the tune of popular numbers on marriages, other social functions and, most importantly, in election rallies, in order to woo the audience. During elections, both parliamentary as well as the assemblies, these girl artists are abused by the contestants, normally very respectable and seasoned citizens, to gather crowds before they themselves arrive on the scene. One wonders, are these the same Punjabi men who are so particular that their daughters, sisters or wives must not go out in public alone, unescorted by a male, without covering their head and without inviting the gaze of men around? How can these men enjoy watching others' daughters exposing themselves just to amuse the men? If this is not patriarchy, then what else is this? It is my firm belief that the more there exist such 'other girls', the more women will be pushed back in the private domain and there is little hope for their liberation thus.

In medieval times it is said that daughters were not welcomed because they symbolized huge investment, a great liability, both financial and social. Avoidable expenditure was to be made on her, knowing fully well that she is of no use to her parents in their old age, since she would be leaving them one day. People say that things have changed. As we discussed in the beginning, girls in Punjab have made inroads into the public domain. The question is, have they ceased to be a liability to their parents today? The answer can definitely not be yes!

References

Das, Veena. 1976. 'Masks and Faces: An Essay on Punjabi Kinship', *Contributions to Indian Sociology*. Vol. 10., No.I.

— 1990. 'Indian Women: Work, Power and Status,' in B.R. Nanda (ed.), *Indian Women: From Purdah to Modernity*. New Delhi.

Pilot Study on *Victims of Militancy,* Institute for Development and Communication, Chandigarh, 1998.

Malhotra, Anshu. 2002. *Gender, Caste and Religious Identities: Restructuring Class in Colonial Punjab.* New Delhi, Oxford University Press.

Montgomery, R. 1853. *Minute on the Infanticide in the Punjab.* Lahore, OIOC.

Punjab Notes and Queries, 1884, Quoted in Malhotra 2002. *Gender, Caste and Religious Identities*, pp. 50-51.

Singh, S., Gupta, A.K. and Jindal, B.R. 2000. *Menace of Drug Abuse in Punjab: An Opinion Survey* (quoted in IDC 2001. Substance Abuse in Punjab).

— 2001. 'Who Alarmed at Rise in Drug Addiction', *The Tribune*, May 13.

13

State, Market and Gender in India

KUMOOL ABBI

This paper attempts to explicate the relationship between state, market and gender in India. It takes into account the developmental role of the state and biases inherent in it, which has made the developmental process highly gendered and male centric. Even, when the ostensible aim is the empowerment of or amelioration of the social situation of women, the intended or not so intended built-in administrative biases end up receiving only cosmetic benefits if at all. The paper though primarily relies upon secondary sources and reviews of significant studies on selected issues mainly centring on Punjab and North India, yet, wherever considered relevant and necessary, also refers to studies carried out elsewhere. However, before attempting a review of studies, it may be in order to refer briefly to changes in the state vision of development from time to time.

In this connection, as Mary E. John points out, "it is crucial to notice that globalization, liberalization and programme of structural adjustment are by no means the sole forces redirecting contemporary agendas. Rather, a multiplicity of emergent phenomena and realignments characterize the present" (John, 1996). John goes on to list among these phenomena the Mandal and Ayodhya, changing status of region-specific development, shift since the 1980s from the restrictive frame of 'woman and development' to 'gender and development', problematizing development itself as an issue, World Bank Report (1981) stressing women's role as efficient economic actors and managers, Shramshakti Report (1988) highlighting women's extreme vulnerability in the informal sector, the Draft Country Paper on the Fourth Women's Conference held in Beijing in 1995, issues of violence, war, terrorism linked to women as victims or otherwise as sufferers, increasing withdrawal of state from welfare and growing reliance on NGOs, critical studies of academic and researchers, women's movements and pressure groups (see also Choudhary, 2003; Jackson and Pearson, 1998).

All this makes clear that the role of the state is intertwined with a variety of other actors and needs a much wider canvas than provided by the limited scope of this paper.

Capitalism, State and Gendered Inequality

The nexus between state, capitalism and gendered inequality, both social and sexual, has been theorized in a number of ways. The most popular approach has been the Marxist approach, which undertakes to understand the relation between the family and capitalism, the complete degradation of women's productive role, the trivialization of women's domestic work and its invisibility and discrimination meted out to women in terms of wage differentials. Another approach which has become popular is that set forth by the socialist feminists who feel that 'Marxist' categories, like 'capital', are sex-blind and need to integrate other aspects and viewpoints to be completely effective. To make their point, two approaches have been popularized:

(1) The dual system theory, which argues that patriarchy and capitalism are "distinct forms of social relations and interests" (Tong, 1989), whose interaction leads to the oppression of women. This attempt largely consists of combining "a non-materialist account of patriarchy with materialist accounts of capitalism". Among the prominent exponents were included Mitchell, who perceived patriarchy as an ideological onslaught, which could only come to end when its bio-social and ideological aspects changed, while Hartman views patriarchy "as a structure of relations in society that has a very material base in men's historical control over women's labour power". This control is exercised

by controlling women's access to important economic resources, controlling female sexuality and reproduction. (2) *The unified systems theory* attempts to make an analysis of capitalism and patriarchy with one concept. The major proponents of this theory were Young and Jagger. Young felt the need for "a division of labour analysis to understand this interconnection and explain to us gender-based capitalism". She called capitalism a patriarchy and felt that "the marginalization of women and thereby their functioning as a secondary labour force is an essential and fundamental characteristic of capitalism". She also felt the gender bias of capitalism was reflected through "unequal wages, sexual harassment, uncompensated domestic work and the pernicious dynamics of public private split" (cited in Tong, 1989). Similarly, Jaggar, in her book *Feminist Politics and Human Nature* found 'alienation' to be a unifying concept to understand the nexus between capitalism and patriarchy. Jagger found this alienation in respect to a woman's own body, and herself, from the product of her reproductive labour, and from the process of her reproductive labour and finally an alienation of women from their own intellectual capacities (quoted in Tong, 1989).

This analysis is largely beneficial for an understanding of patriarchy in the capitalist centres where capitalism has firmly entrenched itself and has almost become a way of life. However, an interesting aspect to know would be the impact of capitalism on 'capitalist peripheral areas', i.e., places of subsistence economy with their different production, social and cultural structures. The manner in which capitalism has sucked in these areas into the global markets, eroded their autonomy and shifted the emphasis of production from use values to exchange values, is a matter of interest.

Mies (1989) has tried to understand the penetration of capitalism through a variety of concepts which refer to (a) the gradual erosion of material base of women's subsistence production, by their exclusion from circulation of commodities; (b) gradual polarization and inequality between the sexes leading to wage labour being performed by men and women in charge of subsistence household production; and (c) the coming about of an acute polarization of classes in the rural areas.

Thus, all these changes come about with capitalism engulfing all the economies to further its accumulation and concentration. As put forward by Rosa Luxemburg, "capitalist accumulation is not possible without existence of non-capitalist strata" (quoted in Mies, 1989). A realization of surplus value is possible only if means of consumption and production produced over and above the requirements, can be sold to non-capitalist strata and countries, the subsistence peasants and colonies.

Industry

In the field of industry this penetration has been felt in the sphere of subsistence economies or household economies engaged in small-scale production. Most of the Third World countries are the base for labour-intensive and export-oriented industries, which is the source of employment to a large section of female workforce, specially in the sphere of electronics, garments and textiles. As has been pointed out by many scholars, what has been realized is that the 'social construction' of female labour is different from that of male labour. Patriarchy, one of the most important cultural and social norms governing distribution within households, assigns the burden of reproductive work to women. On the other hand, the forces of capitalism, which are central to current restructuring, make certain demands of female labour. The same forces of capitalism have assigned to the household a central place in human resource production in order to meet the demand for specific kinds of human capital. Hence, today, both patriarchy and capitalism together compound the emphasis upon women's role in the production of human resources within the household (Ranadive, 2000). In the domain outside home, the 'feminization of labour' has been recorded as one consequence of economic restructuring. This has been seen in four ways: (i) an increase in the female participation rate relative to men; (ii) substitution of men by women who take over jobs traditionally handled by men; (iii) increase in women's involvement in invisible work (family labour and home work); and (iv) the changing character of industrial work on the basis of new technology and managerial strategies whereby work is decentralized, low paid, irregular with part time or labour contracts, that is increasingly like women's work but which is not necessarily done by women (Chhachhi and Pittin, 1996).

A large number of studies have shown that the modern industrial and agricultural sectors, which are based on capital-intensive technology, have pushed women into the low wage sector of the economy where they form the bulk of the unskilled labour in the Indian context. Further, the influence of economic differentiation, caste structure and the nature of the family interaction with one another has worked towards the formation of female workforce. The crucial role played by class-caste correlation gets sharpened with the impact of the macro policies for growth based on top-down planning which particularly has affected women by marginalizing their economic contribution and overlooking the economic activities that they perform (Kak, 1994) Here, the crucial documentation of women's invisible work becomes significant (Kak, 1994), particularly the focus on time as a measure (Jain, 1996) as well as the complexity of tasks performed in the household.

Similarly, in India, a large capital-intensive pattern of development was undertaken, which implied an emphasis on the policy of impact substitution, thus not leading to a large-scale absorption of women in the labour force. But women became important pivots in the sphere of the household industries: lace making, garments, *beedi* making, handicrafts etc., which due to popular demand became geared for exports and in this process were caught in the web of the global market. Capitalist penetration in this home-based work implied erosion of the autonomy of the women workers increasing their exploitation and making more invisible, their already hidden work.

Essentially, "the comparative advantage of women's disadvantage" explained the reason for their status as the preferred labour force of these industries. "They needed a cheap labour force to cut down on their costs and they needed a 'flexible' labour force, which could be drawn, and expelled from, employment in response to changing level of demand" (Kabeer, 2000). Other factors, like manual dexity, easier employment, easier exploitation and easier retrenchment, were crucial for the employment of women. Coinciding with this planning was the "deliberate promotion of various cultural practices in the workplace by employees in the attempts to extract maximum profit from female workforce" (Lim, 1978; Aarufin, 1983; Mather, 1985). While other studies too have explained the policy of recruitment of women in terms of "patriarchal traditions which allowed the smooth transfer of their submission to patriarchal authority from the family patriarch to the capitalist patriarch" (Safa, 1990; Salaff, 1981) The whole industry is organized into an interlocking chain. Companies provide threads to stockists who pass them on to the middlemen. The middlemen then give it to the lace makers and pay wages to them.

Mies (1989) has conducted an extensive study on how women are exploited in the household industry. This study was conducted on the lace makers of Narsapur in the West Godavari district which has nearly 1,50,000 women engaged in the lace industry. A sudden spurt in export orders is revealed from the fact that in 1970 lace goods worth about $ 1 to 1.5 million was exported to Australia, West Germany, Italy, Denmark, Sweden which Britain jumped up to $ 8 million in 1977. The work performed by women is largely based on the 'putting out' system where the producers are women but the agents, traders, exploiters, i.e., windows to the outside world, are men. The lace making process has become a part of the household and includes the work of women, including old women, children etc.

Zarina Bhatty (1987), in a study of *beedi* workers in Allahabad (U.P.) finds that despite its invisibility the *beedi* industry employs largely women workers, who are paid meagre wages and 75 per cent of the total workers are below the poverty line. Moreover, women account for a major part of the household income. In a household, with a total annual income not exceeding Rs. 300, 86 per cent of the income was contributed by women. Households, with an income between Rs. 500 and Rs.750, 95 per cent of the income was contributed by women, whereas between Rs.750 and Rs.1,000, 79 per cent was contributed by women and between Rs. 1,000 and Rs. 1,500, 77 per cent contributed by women, thus Indicating the major economic role of women performed as part of their household chores – a necessity which leads to a greater exploitation in the hands of middlemen etc.

Another important study relates to women workers in the garment industry in Delhi, which has geared itself to export orientation. Thus, establishing a link between largely small manufacturing and global markets, the study conducted by Rao and Husain (1987) reveals the creating of a large number for small workplaces and the process of sub-contracting, largely reflected the 'putting out' system, which also links the household (housewife) in her home to the world market. The garment industry employs approximately 1,00,000 workers, out of which 25 per cent are women. Largely work to be done is sub-contracted through agents and payments made on the basis of piece rates. The need for this employment among a large number of women reveals their potential for exploration, which is shown in the meagre rates paid out to them. For cutwork the rate ranged from Re. 0.50 to Rs. 2.00 per piece. In a total day's work the earnings being only one-fourth of the minimum wages, whereas for embroidery the piece rate was Rs. 15 a piece, needing almost six-and-a-half hours of labour, and the payment averaging to Rs. 4.61 for an eight-hour day. For crochet work, the rates are extremely low, varying from Rs. 2 to Rs. 6 for rosettes and Rs. 11 for a blouse. For tracing, a woman could earn about Rs. 100 per month, even in the process of button stitching the rates range from Re. 0.75 to Re.1 for 100 buttons.

All these statistics show how this work which requires such a lot of skill and hard work is grossly undervalued in the unorganized workforce, where dealing with an abstract employer is pliable to exploitation, while the exporters themselves are gaining on account of very low labour costs.

Another important study conducted by Husain on capitalist penetration in the handicrafts industry of Bangladesh is also indicative of the role of capitalism in an economic sector, which had a history of women participating in production activities but their work had an element of invisibility. However, in the last decade or so, their invisibility in work has increased due to organization of cooperatives etc., for the development of export promotion. A consequence of that has been the need for quality control of rigid division of labour according sex. She has apprehended that cooperatives, which are largely multi-class in character with management in the stands of the elite, would eventually lead to the erosion of interests of producers to that of exploiters (cited in Singh, 1986).

All these studies reveal the manner in which women, who constitute a large, unorganized labour force, are drawn into the capitalist system, especially in relation to small-scale industries for export promotion. As these industries do not require a strong infrastructural base in relation to investment in terms of capital, location, premises, machinery, permanent wage labour etc., this kind of industrial activity rests itself on a nexus of sub-contracts, through which it sucks on and exploits the labour of women. Thus, even in respect of the industries, women fail to have greater interaction with the outside world. The women's interaction becomes more limited and retreats into the household, while the products of their labour are handled by a greater variety of men, from the local agent to the export marketer.

Agriculture

Agriculture, in the form of capitalist penetration, arrived through the Green Revolution during the mid-1960s, which, through its system of efficient production mix, got reflected in the selection of HYV seeds, use of high quality fertilizers, pesticides and large requirements of water revolutionalized farming and farm techniques leading to a big break from product for use to production for the market. The effect of the Green Revolution has been seen in the change of cropping pattern from a variety of crops produced earlier to largely mono-cultures (rice and wheat), introduction of double cropping, leading to high yields and more crops for sale. However, this also resulted in a large number of changes in the socio-economic structure of the village. The introduction of production for sale implied growth of capitalist production relations based on a relationship of cash and a breaking of all other traditional forms of interaction between the landlord and his workers based on relations of reciprocity and exchange (Gill, 1988; Chaddha and Bhalla, 1983).

Similarly, a lot of controversy has been generated in relation to the trickle-down effect of the Green Revolution. While it has proved beneficial to the big and middle farmers, its repercussions for small and marginal farmers have been more controversial, who, it is felt, are increasingly being marginalized and have joined the ranks of the agricultural proletariat. This reflected in the agricultural statistics on Punjab through the decline of operational holdings from 13,75,382 hectares in 1970-71 to 10,27,127 in 1980-81 – a decline of about 25.3 per cent. The marginal holdings declined by 69.9 per cent and small ones by 23.3 per cent (Gill, 1988). Reflecting a tendency of their pauperization, another study by Bhalla (1989) reflects that by 1980-81, 24 per cent of small farmers and 31.5 per cent of marginal farmers fell below poverty line, indicating a growing tendency for wage work. Similarly, the average size of landholdings decreased from 3.81 hectares in 1980-81 to 3.77 hectares in 1985-86 and to 3.61 hectares in 1990-91.

It put emphasis on a provide mix which brought about successful results. While the ploughing of the field required the tractor, not the plough, the harvesting required the combine and not the sickle thus, implying a heavy dependence of men on this hi-tech knowledge from outside the domains of their village, from outside the resource of their traditional knowledge to ignorant seekers in a world linked in the global market.

Thus, in the village structure, since most of the outside work was performed by the men, this task too was entrusted to them. The transmission of knowledge about the secret of the HYV became a man-to-man affair. It was also necessary because the supervisory personnel happened to be men as well. Thus, it can be seen that knowledge and information about agriculture and its activity was an important factor, which created the first chism between both men and women in the rural structure – a factor which took alarming proportions in an area with a strong patriarchal structure. Hence, it can be said that the new technology favoured the men for it opened their horizons and interactions into a wider world. It meant a close interaction with the market in relation to the buying and selling of produce, the purchase of fertilizers, pesticides, etc., interaction with government personnel for loans, hiring of tractors, threshers, combines, payment of electricity bills, etc. – all making the entire process male-centered, thus leading to a certain extent to the withdrawal of women from agricultural process in general. A factor not only affecting the agricultural labourers including landless, marginal and small peasant women, but also medium and large farm householders, where it enforced the *purdah* ideology and a growing consumerism.

As it has been seen, a sudden increase in production brought about a large cash income, which sought its diversification in consumerism. In the Green Revolution areas, especially in the North (Punjab, Haryana), it resulted in a spirit of consumer durables for the farmers – Maruti cars, to begin with Ceilo, Zen, Lancers, television, tape recorders, VCR's, VCDs, gas, ovens, microwaves, mixies, grinders and even electric butter churners, thus creating an active consumer culture where status became closely linked to lifestyle.

It also meant a grown dependence of women on the menfolk for cash incomes. The comforts provided to them tended to largely eroded their autonomy and freedom of movement, confining them to their homes giving them the brand of useless consumers who had nothing to contribute except their presence at home reflecting the status of men. Thus, a very important consequence of the Green Revolution has been the emphasis on the domestic role of women, who are seen as being the pride of the house, rather than active beings meant to do and in control of an assortment of tasks. Their vital link with production reduced to gains from it in terms of consumer durables. Thus, the shift from the *chullah* to the dining table indicates not so much an improvement or mobility but a confinement to values which are largely alien to the village structure. The activity of the women, which spread across a long working day, including an assessment of tasks – both inside and outside their domain – has been confined in wards with male patronage.

However, this retreat into domesticity has meant a general endorsement of these values as a symbol of high class (Abbi, 2003). Thus, a growing feeling about the role of the women as being meant to adorn the home has gained importance. A corollary to that being a conscious attempt to look down upon women's work, specially those relating to production and other subsidiary activities, is also prominent. Thus, in order to reach the level of upper class women who cook with the gas stove, comes the urgent need for cash income, for status measured in relation to women's activity at home. In almost all Green Revolution areas, there comes a cut off point even among the smaller and marginal and landless households when the women voluntarily give up work and proclaim that they are being looked after by their husbands.

The Green Revolution and capitalist penetration have come not only as an economic package but as an ideology as well bringing in attitudes that look down upon manual work which provided the basic substance and power to the women in the household while upholding middle class values, white-collar workers etc., which acquire the education of women, training and other skills. However, it is not so much her own independent position, as the cultural ethos surrounding it and being reinforced which remain a stumbling blocks for women either way.

Thus, this leads to the gradual feeling of women being treated as a dispensable commodity, who have no value, except that of being unproductive consumers. It is this which leads to increase in dowry and other discrimination a point which will be elaborated later. As Shiva (1988) has articulated, "violence of nature, which seems intrinsic to the dominant development model, is also associated with violence to women who depend on nature for drawing sustenance for themselves, their families, their societies".

In areas where capitalist penetration has taken place, resulting in an increase in the standard of living, making inroads into market economy etc., there has been seen an urgent need for cash income. The pressure for which seriously comes on the women agriculturists who have to work to make both ends meet. As has been observed, the Green Revolution with mechanization has displaced a large agriculture workforce, which performed the traditional agricultural work. This has also had its effect on the most marginalized segment i.e., women, who, suffering from the impact of mono-culture, have lost a large number of their specialized tasks and uses from agricultural waste which provided them subsistence. Picking cotton, process of shaving off already beaten rice, to glean the grains etc., thus reducing the specialized tasks performed by women and creating competition with large labour force of men. What has resulted instead is the masculinization of modern chemical-intensive and mechanized capital-intensive agriculture and the feminization of traditional subsistence food production which feeds the bulk of the rural poor (Shiva, 1988).

However, despite the dichotomy between the two, the growth of a large agriculture labour force is a telling commentary on the lack of access of women to land and land use. As Agarwal (1986) has found out, the percentage of women agricultural labourers rose from 25.6 per cent to 49 per cent during 1961-71. Mies also endorses the point working on the same data. She argues that female cultivators dropped by 52 per cent between 1961 and 1971, the number of female agricultural labourers rose by 43 per cent, whereas until 1961, the proportion of women among cultivators had been between 1961 and 1971 a mere 135 women to a thousand men. Even, the female ratio among agricultural labourers between 1961 and 1971 had dropped from 819 women per 1,000 men to only 498 women which is a decline of about 40 per cent (Shiva, 1988; Agarwal 1986).

Along with the increase in proportion of agricultural labourers women also face the problem of discriminating wage differentials. As Analyzed by Agarwal (1986) for the period from 1964-65 to 1974-75, while, at the all-India level, the differentials declined, the state-wise breaking revealed an interesting picture. The male-female differentials increased in Punjab, West Bengal, Bihar and Orissa. However, the pioneer of the Green Revolution – Punjab – excelled in wage differentials, the ratio being 2.58 to the male earnings. According to Bhalla (1989), wage for cotton picking fell from 100 in 1961 to 86 in 1977.

A detailed analysis of the Green Revolution and its impact on women workers is relevant in order to understand the sexual inequality brought about by capitalist penetration. In India, the Green Revolution made its impact on Punjab, Haryana and parts of Tamil Naidu, especially Thanjavur district. Sen (1987), who made a comparative study of both the places, found certain similarities and differences regarding both. While there is a similarity in relation to conditions of work, wage differentials and tasks to be performed, the difference observed was in relation to conditions of landholding and landlessness in the two regions, which provided the basis for a differential impact of the Green Revolution. Traditionally, in the northern region, due to a large number of factors, viz., cultural, social, village exogamy, kinship, impact of Islamic culture etc., women traditionally did less of the fieldwork. They performed a variety of tasks relating to levelling the fields, watering them, transplanting rice dropping seeds, weeding, harvesting, gleaning the fields, picking cotton, plucking corn and millet etc. However, due to factors mentioned above, there is a certain specificity of the women workforce in Punjab.

(a) Punjab, with its high level of prosperity and most advanced agricultural region, has the lowest participation rate of female labour force in the country, i.e., 1.67 per cent in 1971 and 3.09 per cent in 1981. While for 1991 women main workers account for a mere 4.35 per cent, while 93.59 men.

(b) Percentage of female workers in Punjab is twice as high in urban areas as in rural areas whereas in other states rural rates are higher.

(c) In Punjab, cultivators and agricultural labourers are a little over one-fifth of the all-India average distribution of female workers. On the other hand, female other workers are the highest in Punjab (84.34%) as compared to all-India (26.09%) (other workers), followed by Assam (68.34%) and Kerala (47.01%). Similarly, for 1991, 93.59 per cent marginal workers are women as compared to 6.41 per cent men.

(d) Majority of rural women are concentrated in agricultural household and non-household industries, which are non-paying, whereas the urban majority are in other areas.

(e) Unfavourable attitude of people in sending unmarried girls to work, both in rural and urban areas and the highest percentage among gainfully employed women (rural 60.38%, urban 56.79%) consists of married women.

(f) In terms of their total proportion to the total female population, the widowed and divorced separately are much more strongly represented than married and never married in Punjab. The widows in total population are 5.53 per cent as compared to 14.90 per cent representation in workforce. Similarly, divorced and separated together are 0.04 per cent in total population whereas they are 0.23 per cent in the workforce. These facts are important in understanding different values and perceptions to women's work (Singh, 1984; Sandhu, 1976; PHDR, 2001).

A detailed study by Sen (1998) on female agricultural labour force in Haryana brings out a large number of hidden factors, reflected in the status of other workers in Punjab, whose work largely is counted as invisible. The study, based on three regions of Haryana on criterion of their being forward and backward, observed significant differences in the next most advanced regions comes from households whose main income is cultivation. Thus, these data reveal the extent of displacement of small farmers and the desire for cash incomes.

In both the overall wage employment of women and in employment of women from it, women form only 8.5 per cent of agricultural labourers in the most backward regions, while they account for 15-16 per cent in the two advanced high technology regions. The data largely confined to permanent and regular casual labour.

The reason for this high number is attributed to the exhaustion of male labour in agriculturally advanced regions paving the way for absorption of women, while in the backward regions men still continue to perform most of the major tasks. Another important point of reference relates to the fact that in most of the backward regions over 81 per cent of female labourers come from landless labour households and only 18.7 per cent from households whose main income source is cultivation, i.e., small farming households, while, on the contrary, 38.9 per cent of all regular female labour in the most advanced regions and 49 per cent in the composition of the labour force was strongly affected by the new technology.

Bhalla (1989) found that Green Revolution in Haryana has almost reversed the relative importance of permanent and regular labourers. The highest proportion of permanent to regular casual labourers was found in most advanced Green Revolution areas in 1972-73. Thus, in this hierarchy of labourers beginning from permanent and regular to several and seasonal. Women labourers come at the bottom of ladder and are largely seasonal.

This is largely due to the fact that works and tasks performed by women have been mechanized, e.g., wheat threshing, corn shelling, sugarcane crushing, sowing and weeding etc. Hence, the option for female labour is limited to traditional tasks and seasonal labour at the time of harvest largely in family teams. Moreover, as pointed out by Bhalla (1989), female labour is largely absorbed by small farms where task of hiring male labour is high. Hence, female labour gets compensated on the other hand by hiring done by big farmers, as family teams or for specific tasks. Thus, the study from Haryana points to the facts that there is a large agricultural labour force of women, women are at the bottom of choice preference for hiring, wage differences continue to be high between sexes, women are hired for specific tasks and only so when availability of a large class of male agricultural labour is not available.

The discriminated meted out to women in the employment front has its repercussions on attitude towards women, girlchild, marriage, dowry etc. The sex ratios for the states of Punjab and Haryana in 2001 were the lowest in the country, i.e., 874 and 861, respectively. Similarly, the gender discrimination in relation to access to food and health care is sharpest in the northwestern states (Haryana/Punjab) and the least in the south. Agarwal (1986) also connects the fact that FLP (proportion of female workers in specified female population) and female marriage costs act both independently and interactively on the extent of discrimination against female children in the family.

In this context, the northern states are characterized by lower FLP rates, a higher incidence of dowry, greater intra-household discrimination against female children and lower female survival (to male) chances than male children (Agarwal, 1986). Studies of Das Gupta (1987), Basu (1991), Punjab Health Department (1991) and Wyon and Gordon (1971) have pointed to differential allocation of food, health, nutrition and medical care to girls leading to their neglect (Kaur, 2003).

Studies of UNFPA based on data generated by National Family Health Survey have pointed out that female foeticide accounts for a significant part of the decline in fertility and the increase in small family norm achieved in Punjab and Haryana (Kaur, 2003). As it has been elaborated, "the sex ratio of the state from 1991-2000 has registered a decline of 8 points as compared to the national average which has increased by 6 points" (Kaur, 2003). This also points to a very important aspect which is happening in the context of women: the adherence to small family norm which has led to lessening of their reproductive span, which leaves them comprehensively free of child care responsibilities and leads to emptiness, breaking the chain between production and reproduction (Abbi, 2003). Linked with this is the crucial decline in child sex ratio in Punjab from 875 to 793 (decline of 83 points), followed by Haryana from 879 to 820 (59 points), Himachal from 951 to 897 (54 points) and Chandigarh from 899 to 845 (Kaur, 2003; PHDR, 2001). Of the fifty-five districts in the country that have less than 900 girls per 1,000 boys, 28 districts are in Haryana and Punjab. While, of the 10 districts with lowest sex ratio, seven belong to Punjab (PHDR, 2001). A comparison of the (1990) HDI (Human Development Index) with the GDI (Gender-related Development index) shows five states with the highest differentials: Haryana (24.3%), Punjab (19.8%), Uttar Pradesh (15.9%), Bihar (13.6%) and West Bengal (13.1) (PHDR, 2001).

This indicates a growing discrimination against women. This has its repercussion on a very high rate of dowry in the state which has assumed alarming proportions in combination with the consumer culture becoming strongly embedded. Giving a Maruti Zen for a wedding is an indication of a man's status and his love for his daughter; the cost of vehicle and type increasing with prosperity. However, this is not followed by a consequent inheritance of property by women. Shiva (1988) also associates this issue with the growing violence against women in these states and relates it to the general aggravation of violence in Punjab, pointing to the invisible consequences of the Green Revolution.

However, while accepting the view that with agricultural development, a withdrawal of women has taken place in the northwestern regions, except for work during paddy and wheat season and couple of other particular tasks, women are not involved in the direct production process. However, this withdrawal should not be taken only in the category of agricultural and population statistics. For a large category of invisible work, subsumed under the category of domestic work, is in fact performed by women, in order to supplement their cash incomes.

This relates to dairying, including the complete process of looking after buffaloes, feeding and milking them, delivering the milk for sale, maintaining herds of goats and sheep, cleaning and storing the grain, grinding corn, making cowdung cakes, sifting cotton, making quilts – all attempts by women to better their lot but all within the territorial and cultural domains of their village. Thanjavur, with its rice revolution, however, presents a much simpler picture of pauperization. The area reflects a concentration of large landholders and householders operating small farms. Area specialized in wet paddy cultivation had women (non-Brahmin) working in fields or family farmers, as agricultural labourers, sowing, transplanting, weeding, applying cow dung, green manure, harvesting, threshing etc. The land reforms provided some land to rich farmers owning 15-20 acres and to poor owing 0.02 - 0.03 acre. The district showed an increase in proportion of agricultural labourers from 52 per cent to 65 per cent between 1952 and 1976.

The farmers, including the small farmers, adopted the new technology in a big way. However, the HYV seed did not develop well. It had a number of problems: it is too short stemmed to withstand flooding, it matures early, it is susceptible to more pests and diseases, and problem of water control etc., thus creating problems of cost benefit to the small farmer.

Apart from that a large amount of tenant eviction has taken place leading to a large number of women taking to work as coolies, etc., especially those who previously worked on family farms. The decline of 'Panniyal' – a system of bonded labour – and sudden spurt of capitalism resulted in a large surplus available labour force. As pointed out by Gough, there is now so much surplus population in agriculture that male coolies are hired to do work sometimes traditionally done by women. For women, decline of 'Panniyal' status has led tremendous impact in relation to the looking after their hygiene, nutrition, health care etc. They also face discrimination relating to wages. In 1976, on the average, male agricultural labourers were paid Rs. 6 per day while women between Rs. 3.50 and Rs. 4, thus proving the thesis that with a generation of a large labour force, available to out compete, the women no longer do the same kinds of tasks which they earlier performed. Thus, both Punjab and Haryana and Thanjuvar reflect the changes in the rural social structure after the Green Revolution but the difference between the two lies in the kind of contribution that women's wage employment makes to the small farming household and in the extent to which reserve of unemployed labourers acts to push women out of employment (Shiva, 1988; Agarwal, 1986).

Conclusion

This paper has highlighted the complex role of the state in the context of deepening integration of India's economy with the WTO-linked regime of globalization, a major feature of which is not only an increasing free flow of commodities and finance but also of social and cultural influences. Linked to this has been a growing increase in economic disparities and a undue spread/dissemination of consumerist lifestyle. Wherein women's role as consumers, their preoccupation with the domestic status and enhancing activities, have greatly increased, to the neglect of their role as producer. The paper has also highlighted the complex ramifications of this shift in emphasis of gender relations.

References

Abbi, Kumool. 2003. 'Rural Development and Women: Visibility, Changing Lifestyle and Invisible Hands' in M.S. Gill (ed.), *Punjab Society: Prospects and Challenges*, New Delhi, Concept Publishers.

Abbi, B. L. and Kesar Singh. 1997. *Post-Green Revolution Rural Punjab: A Profile of Economic and Socio-Cultural Change (1965-1995)*. CRRID: Chandigarh.

Agarwal, Bina. 1998. 'Who Sows Who Reaps?' Women and Land Rights in India', *Journal of Peasant Studies*, Vol. 15, No. 4, pp. 531-581.

— 1989. 'Rural Women, Poverty and Natural Resources: Sustenance, Sustainability and struggle for Change', *EPW*, Vol. XXIV, No. 43 PWS – 46-WS 65

— 1988. 'Neither Sustenance nor Sustainability: Agricultural Strategies, Ecological Degradation and Indian Women in Poverty', in Bina Agarwal (ed.), *Structures of Patriarchy: State, Community and Household in Modernizing Asia*. New Delhi, Sage Publications.

— 1986. 'Women, Poverty and Agricultural Growth in India', *Journal of Peasant Studies*. Vol.13, No.4, July.

Andrea Menefee Singh and Anita Kelles,Vitanened. 1987. *Women in Home - Based Production*, New Delhi, Sage Publishers.

Beneria, Lourdes. (ed.). 1982. *Women and Development*. New York, Prager Publications.

Bhalla, G.S. and Chaddha, G.K. 1983. *Green Revolution and the Small Peasant: A Study of Income Distribution among Punjab Cultivators*, New Delhi, Concept Publishers.

Bhalla, Sheila. 1989. 'Technological Change and Women Workers: Evidence from Expansionary Phase in Haryana Agriculture' *EPW*, Vol. XXIV, No. 43, PWS 67-WS89.

Brita, Brandtzaeg. 1979. 'Women, Food and Technology: A Case of India', *EPW*, Vol. 14, No. 47, pp. 1921-24.

Cecile, Jacbson and Ruth Pearson (eds.). 1998. *Feminist Visions of Development: Gender Analysis and Policy*. London, Routledge,

Chand, R., Sidhu, D.S. and Kaul, J.L. 1985. 'Impact of Agricultural Modernisation and Labour Use Pattern in Punjab with Special Reference to Women Labour', *Indian Journal of Agricutural Economics*, Vol. XL No. 3, pp. 252-59.

Chaudhri, Maitreyee. 2003 'Gender in the Making of the Indian Nation-State', in Sharmila Rege (ed.), *Sociology of Gender: The Challenge of Feminist Sociological Knowledge*, New Delhi, Sage Publishers.

Chhachhi, A. and R. Pittin. (eds.) 1996. *Confronting State, Capital and Patriarchy: Women Organising in the Process of Industrialization*. Macmillan (with ISS), Hague, Basingtoke.

Choudhary, Prem. 1994, *The Veiled Women. Shifting Gender Equations in Rural Haryana, 1880-1990*. Delhi, Oxford University Press.

Dak, T.M., and Sharma, M.L. (eds.). 1988, 'Social Framework of Female Labour Participation in Rural Section' in *Women and Work in Indian Society*, New Delhi, Manohar Publication.

Das Gupta, Monica. 1987. 'Selective Discrimination Against Female Children in Rural Punjab, India', *Population and Development Review*. March 13, Vol. I, pp. 77-100.

Gill, S.S. 1988. 'Contradiction of Punjab Model of Growth', *EPW*, Cot. 15, p. 2167.

Jain, Devaki. 1996. 'Valuing Work: Time as Measure', *EPW*, October 26, 1996, WS 46-56.

Johl, S.S. 1988. 'Future of Agriculture in Punjab'. CRRID, Chandigarh.

John, Mary E. 1996. 'Gender and Development in India, 1970s-1990s: Some Reflections on the Constituent Role of Contexts'. *EPW*, November 23, pp. 3071-3077.

Kabeer, Naila. 2001. *Bangladeshi Woman Workers and Labour Market Decisions: The Power to Choose*. Vistaar, New Delhi.

Kak, Shakti. 1994. *Subsistence Economics and Women Work. A Case Study of India.* NML New Delhi, Number XLVII.

Kaur, Malkit. 2003. 'Socio-Cultural Correlates of Low Sex-Ratio in Punjab' in M.S.Gill (ed.) *Punjab Society: Prospects and Challenges*. New Delhi, Concept Publishing Company.

Kaur, Rupinder. 1988. Female Work Participation: Caste, Class and Gender Analysis in Rural Indian Punjab' *International Journal of Punjab Studies*, Vol 5, No. 1

Krishnamurty, J. (ed.) 1989. *Women in Colonial India: Essays on Survival, Work and the State*. New Delhi, Oxford University Press.

Lerner, Gerda. 1986. *The Creation of Patriarchy*, New York, Oxford University Press.

Lim, L. 1990. 'Women's Work in Export Factors: The Politics of a Cause,' in Tinku, I. (ed.) *Persistent Inequalities: Women and World Development*. Oxford, Oxford University Press.

Mather, C. 1985. 'Rather than Make Trouble, Its Better to Leave' in H. Afshar (ed.) *Women, Work and Ideology in the Third World.* London, Macmillan.

Mies, Maria. 1989. *Women the Last Colony*. London, Zed books.

Punjab State Human Development Report 2001.

Ranadive Joy Deshmukh. 2000. 'The Adjustment Policy Programme in India and the Household" in CWDS, *Shifting. Sands: Womens Lives and Globalisation.* New Delhi, Stree.

Rostogi, Preet. 2000. 'Identifying Gender Background Districts using Selected Indications' *EPW*, November 25, Dec. 1.

Safa, H. 1990. 'Women and Industrialization in the Caribbean' in S. Parpart and J. Sticker (eds.) *Women, Employment and the Family in International Division of Labor*. Macmillan, International Political Economy Series.

Salaff, J. 1981. *Working Daughters of Hongkong: Filial Piety or Power in the Family*. New York, Cambridge University Press.

Sandhu, H.K. 1976. T'echnological Development versus Economic Contribution of Women in Rural Punjab' *Social Change*, Vol. 6, Nos. 3 & 4.

Sen, Gita. 1985. 'Women Agricutultural Labourers: Regional Variations in Incidents and Employment' in Devaki Jain and Nirmala Banerjee (eds.) *Tyranny of the Household: Investigative Essays on Women's Work*. New Delhi, Shakti Books.

Sen, Krishna and Stevens Maila (eds.). 1998. 'Gender and Power in Affluent Asia', London, Routledge.

Sethi, Raj Mohini. 1982. *Female Labour in Agriculture*. Panjab University, Chandigarh.

Shah, Nandita, et al. 1994. 'Structural Adjustment, Feminization of Labour Force and Organizational Strategies'. *EPW* 29, No. 18, WS 39 – WS 48.

Shiva, Vandana. 1988. *Staying Alive: Women, Ecology and Survival in India*. New Delhi: Kali for Woman.

Shrinivasan, Viji. 1992. *Women, Work Experiences: Lace, Silk, Fish and Milk,* New Delhi, Haranand.

Singh, K. P. 1986. 'Female Labour Force, Population Growth and Development: The case of Punjab' in S.L. Sharma (ed.) *Development: Socio-Cultural Dimensions*, Jaipur, Rawat Publications.

Sutherland, Sally, J.M. 1991. *Bridging Worlds: Studies on Women in South Asia,* London, Oxford University Press.

Tong, E. 1989. *Feminisms*, New Delhi, Routledge.

14

Electronic Media and Altered Familial Spaces: Within and Without

RAJESH GILL

One way to gauge the transformation in any society is by observing the changing institution of family over a period of time. Like all other social groups and institutions, family too cannot remain unaltered, static, preserving its age-old structure and functions. On the contrary, family all over the world, so also in India, has witnessed radical transformations, especially in the wake of modern industrial society. Lazarsfeld and Merton (1977) talk about the normalizing powers of the media. They talk of the patterning of the values and norms in the media as representative of elite interests. They also discuss how these values and norms work as a kind of symbolic fabric in supplying people with what would be called the 'discourses' for making their social experience meaningful. Certainly, television sanctions and enforces social norms; it confers status on people, places, policies and events, simply by giving them coverage, and it sometimes removes people from active forms of involvement in their own lives.

Zitlin (1978), on the other hand, focuses upon the institutional power of the mass media. This, according to him, includes the preference given by the media to particular ideologies, the shaping of public agendas, the mobilizations of support networks for the policies of political parties and the state, and so on. Dominant ideologies are the most fundamental of symbolic structures in the mass media because they represent most directly the interests and worldview of elite. Adorno (1957) argues that the historical emergence of mass culture carries consequences both numerous and profound. Not only does the ideology of elite become a social fact of everyday living for the vast majority of ordinary people, but so do the standardization of ideas and eventually, the commercialization of public discourse. In the end, the idea of a public sphere, of something separate and separable from commodity culture, is rendered obsolete. Adorno (1974) demonstrates how television's objective structure is tied to the logic of producing and distributing commodities.

Apart from the production of ideologies, another function of television that has found prominence in literature is the reshaping of the everyday life routine of the audience. Because turning to television becomes a habit, a ritual, it in turn shapes the contours of the broader context of people's lives. It is this broader context of a person's life that shapes in important ways the meaning of viewing itself.

With the construct of discourse, cultural studies analysts have attempted to understand how television orders and organizes people's social experience. While it is the desire for entertainment and pleasure, they say, that often draws people into the world of television, it is the discursive power of television that is most salient because it provides them with normative guidelines for thinking and acting in their everyday lives (Lembo, 2000).

Television and Family

In contemporary India, one no longer comes across the large joint family, where members share a common kitchen and finances, sinking all individuality. What one finds today, especially in urban India, is a family which is predominantly nuclear, with the conjugal unit in the centre stage, children getting all the attention and individuality riding very high. Family no longer preserves the important traditional function of entertainment, with the members having their own individualized notions of entertainment and priorities, thus creating enough space between themselves. Among the innumerable gadgets a family must have today, is television, irrespective of economic, occupational or social status, both in rural and urban areas. Such an indispensable position does it occupy today within the family that while one could do well without cooking gas and get the food from outside, one cannot imagine a day without television, although it is often termed as an 'idiot box'.

While television has become a necessity of life today for everyone, the other electronic medium that has become a status symbol for the upper and middle class families is the computer. Apart from the educational and professional needs that it serves, many households acquire a computer just to support a status symbol, displaying it in the drawing room, like any other cut glass or expensive decorative items. Parents feel extremely proud when their six-year old child sits on computer for hours together, without any concern for what was happening in the other corner of the house.

Films are the third most important medium that has exercised a constant influence on individuals of all age groups, gender and social status, and above all, the institution of family. Out of the above three electronic media, it is the television and films, which have affected the Indian family, irrespective of income, ethnicity, rural-urban residence and region. Such deep has been their impact that the images of modernity, masculinity, femininity, virtues and vices that are entertained by people are all being created by either films or television.

In this paper, I shall be focussing largely upon television and, to some extent, computer because these two share commonness in that they keep the user fixed in space, thus exercising definite impact upon how members in a family are situated physically in relation to one another. The important difference between the two, however, is that while television can be watched simultaneously by a number of individuals, one computer can be used by one person at a time.

Efforts have been made to theorize upon television viewing. Typically, individuals must come to television from some other aspect of their lives, and similarly, they must turn off the set and fit television back into their lives. This progression from turning to television, to interacting with it, to leaving it and fitting it back in one's life is the basic cultural pattern in which viewers make their experience with television meaningful. Different things may go through different people's minds and they may feel a variety of things as they go about the business of situating themselves with television or in choosing to do other things. Turning to television thus becomes a habit, a ritual, which shapes the contours of the broader context of people's lives.

A large number of studies have been conducted, both in India and elsewhere, to understand how television affects family. These studies lead mainly to two contrasting perspectives. According to the first perspective, television viewing results into an increased interaction among the family members, often leading to a continuous dialogue between them on the issues thrown by the television (Dorr, 1986; Lull, 1980; Brodie et al., 1983; Goodman, 1983). Empirical studies by these scholars indicate that even when television viewing is not on, it works as a stimulates social interaction among members of a family. The other set of studies, however, insists that television viewing reduces the interaction between the members of a family substantially, often creating social spaces among the members (Robinson, 1972; Szalai, 1972; Neumann, 1981; Comstock, 1978). These studies observed a reduced interaction within the families as a result of television viewing. The question is which of the two viewpoints is correct. While one projects television as a socializing agent within the family, the other treats it as an isolating one, which pulls the individuals away from one another.

In view of the above discussion, it is inappropriate to make any sweeping generalization so far as the effect of television viewing on family life is concerned. Television occupies different spaces in the lives of different people. Further, it may hold different meanings in different situations for the same individual. Also, whether the viewing is mindful or unmindful makes a lot of difference. Apart from these factors, sociological studies indicate that the effect of television viewing on family, both intra and inter, would also depend upon factors such as socio-economic status and living style. Referring to the intervening factors in television viewing, Lull (1988) observes that there is a two-way relationship between television and family. Further, factors such as cultural norms, social and familial values etc., have been found to influence the television viewing patterns (Cantor and Cantor, 1986). The choice of programme too is found to vary with age and gender of the viewers. While more and more men watch programmes related to sports, news, action and detectives, more women prefer to view soap operas, music and comedy shows

(Morley, 1988). The music channel MTV is found in a study to be most popular among the youngsters (Dyal, 1992).

It is argued in this paper that the impact of electronic media on family cannot be generalized in such simplistic terms. For instance, television does both – increases as well as reduces social interaction between members of a family. How? The intervening factors are to be examined for this. One such factor, which puts direct impact, is the number of television sets a family has. Empirical studies show that in lower-middle and middle class families, where there is only one television set, the whole family views it together, although any conversation during the programmes is not tolerated. But, atleast physically, the members sit together, watching their favourite programmes, often resulting into social interaction consequent upon this viewing. But can this be taken as a socializing process, remains a question, mainly because studies also point out that one television leads to the major problem of 'control over remote control'. This was not a major problem as long as viewers had little choice. But, the tremendous alternatives in TV channels available to the viewers have often been found to result into serious conflicts within the family – between the siblings, between husband and wife, between grandparents and grandchildren and so on. A number of studies reveal that the parents in some cases were desperately fed up over such frictions television induced in their families, which had become a daily feature and they at times felt like throwing away this monster out of their house, since it had snatched away their peace of mind.

Interestingly, the families, which own more than one television set, are not without problems too. In such cases, mainly in the upper income group, television sets are generally situated in the bedrooms of different family members. Studies show that members go straight to their rooms, switch on the TV set and stick to them, often taking their dinner to their rooms. The tradition of taking food together, discussing the day-long happenings with the family members etc., all takes a back seat in all such cases. In one such study, the researcher came across a number of housewives who during the interview started crying, and narrated how they kept busy throughout the day in domestic chores, engrossed with various problems relating to children, adults in the family. They anxiously waited for their husbands in the evening, and when they came, the first thing they did on entering the house was switching on the television set even before keeping their brief case down. With eyes on television and sipping the tea, the wife was not supposed to disturb while the husband was listening to news or watching 'Bay Watch'. Similarly, many husbands complained that on reaching home tired, they had to wait for a cup of tea till the favourite serial their wives were watching came to an end. The timings of dinner were often moulded so as to an undisturbed viewing of the favourite programmes on television. In a very interesting study, Lembo (2000) examined three men, all married, who turned to television after work at all times. By turning to television every night after work, these men allowed the mainstream world of television imagery to enter their homes. Because they did not do other things during this time, they did not ordinarily have the opportunity to become engaged with other sources of information, with other ideas, or in experiences other than those that were provided by television. They were thus unable to engage their minds or stimulate their imaginations in ways that extended beyond the horizons of television's image worlds. Consequently, television came to have a certain power in their lives. It is the power to set the meaningful parameters of their social world. Television could set the agenda at this time, every night, because other things could not and did not (Lembo, 2000: 127-28). These three men turned to television after work precisely so that they could enter into the world of television imagery uncritically, with a willingness to accept what that world had to offer them. Remember, they wanted to be mindfully and emotionally involved in such a way that they could believe in what they saw and heard. As a result, for these people in this situation, it was television that had the power to shape a good deal of what they took to be 'real'. But studies also show that television viewing may not always be so 'mindful'. People also view television simultaneously, while doing other things like talking, studying, cooking, and so on. In such situations, then, the power of television to influence the ideology, attitudes, etc., would not be so strong.

Apart from the impact television exercises upon the intra-familial ties, it also has a tremendous effect on the inter-family interactions. The situating of television set in the sitting room often stands as a villain between the hosts and the guests, especially when the host refuses to move their eyes off the screen. While watching their favourite programme, without blinking their eyes, without looking at the guests, they enquire about their well-being etc. Very often, children refuse to come and join the guests because they at no cost can afford to miss a specific programme. Thus, what time the dinner will be served, which days of the week guests would be invited and whether children would join the guests or not, largely depends upon the idiot box.

The electronic media has affected family very intensely in still another way. In the traditional Indian system, the individual acquired the images, typifications in phenomenological terminology; from the elders in the family, religion, school, neighbourhood etc. The contemporary family is highly individualized, where members, especially the young, acquire various images of social roles from either films or television. How one can look modern, how to garner a masculine/feminine look, what one must eat, who is an ideal daughter-in-law, how should a professional woman look like, who is an ideal wife/husband etc. are all dictated by electronic media. While, on the one hand, it results into a kind of homogenization, on the other these images possess deep ideological underpinnings, which often clash with the ideology of a modern liberal civil society. Of course, these media present diverse images – of strong altruistic instincts as well as ego centrism; socializing as well valuing privacy; empowered woman as well as ignorant baby doll; and yet the viewers pick up some images more often than others, because they are celebrated in media, because they are fashionable; and because they buy status. In this game, then, family stands boldly, trying to hold itself back, trying to preserve its age old sanctity, and trying to neutralize the images which challenge its very integrity as an institution, without which no society can sustain itself.

References

Adorno, Theodor 1974. "The Stars Down to Earth". *Telos* 19. 1957. "How To Look At Television", in *Mass Culture: The Popular Arts in America,* edited by B. Rosenberg and D. White. New York, The Free Press.

Brodie, G.H. and Stoneman, Z. 1983. 'The Influence of Television Viewing on Family: A Contextual Framework', *Sociological Abstracts*. Vol. 32, No. 1, April 1984.

Brunsdon, Charlotte. 1991. "Text and Audience." In *Remote Control: Television, Audiences and Cultural Power* edited by Ellen Seiter, Hans Borchers, Gabriele Kreutner and Eva-Maria Warth. New York, Routledge.

Butler, Judity. 1995. *Bodies That Matter.* New York, Routledge.

Cantor, M.G. and Cantor, J.M. 1986. 'American Television in the International Market Place', *Communication Research*, Vol. 13, No. 2, April.

Comstock, George. 1980. *Television in America.* Beverly Hills, Sage Publications.

Dorr, A. 1986. *Television and Children: A Special Medium for a Special Audience.* Beverly Hills, Sage Publications.

Dyal, R. 1992. 'Public Response to Cable Television', *Mainstream,* Vol. XXX, No. 2, March, pp. 29-30.

Goodman, I.F. 1983. 'Television's Role in Family Interaction', *Journal of Family Issues,* Vol. 4, pp. 405-425.

Lembo, Ron 2000. *Thinking Through Television*. Cambridge, Cambridge University Press.

Lull, James. 1988. *World Families Watch Television.* Beverly Hills, Sage Publications.

— 1980. 'Family Communication Patterns and Social Uses of Television', *Communication Research,* Vol. 7, No. 3, July.

Morley, David. 1988. 'Domestic Relations: The Framework of Family Viewing in Great Britain', in Lull, James (ed.), *World Families Watch Television.* Beverly Hills, Sage Publications.

Noelle, Neumann, E. 1981. 'Mass Media and Social Change in Developing Societies', in Katz, E. and Szecsko, T. (eds.), *Mass Media and Social Change.* London, Sage Publications.

Robinson, J.P. 1981. 'Television and Leisure Time: A New Scenario', *Journal of Communication,* 3 (1), pp. 120-130.

Szalai, Alexander. 1972. *Daily Activities of Urban and Sub Urban Populations in Twelve Countries*. The Hague, Mouton.

IV

Corruption: A Challenge to Indian Society

15

Flourishing Market in a Corrupt State and Society

A.S. GILL

While corruption, on the one hand, is a hurdle in the development and sustenance of a market – domestic or international, it also lubricates its smooth functioning, on the other. It is a double-edged sword. Corruption does not recognize state boundaries, it is very much secular in nature and abounds, irrespective of caste, creed, religion, sex and even age. World market is a foreign market only in terms of trade statistics as observed aptly by Peter Drucker (1992). Honesty is not an advantage, let alone a prerequisite to market success. One additional skill, in addition to manufacturing and marketing, for being a successful exporter in the world market, is the ability to manage and thus avoid the various barriers, both domestic and foreign. It is knowledge, rather than national boundaries, which defines today's markets.

The term 'corruption' in this paper has been used in its wider sense, including both moral and physical aspects. It also implies favours, which though may not be of any personal gain to the one who indulges into it, but are against the rules and regulations in force. It also encompasses nepotism, bribes in kind and cash, misuse of authority and government machinery for one's own or family's use, e.g., misuse of vehicles, telephones, accommodation, etc., by bureaucrats or their political masters. It also includes all sorts of mal practices, allurements, pressures etc. As regards the term 'state' it has been used loosely and synonymously with government, bureaucracy and political leadership.

What matters in the present scenario of global village market ultimately is productivity. And, this cannot be disassociated from the state, which happens to be the ultimate decision-maker. More centralized the state, greater the control over products, factors of production and productivity. For example, productivity is determined by several factors like infrastructure, financial markets and the cost of capital, and educational standards, motivation, dedication, skills of labour and state's labour policies etc. Even a country like China has labour laws which are conducive to productivity but at times harsh for labour. Top quality infrastructure cuts the cost of production and movement, facilitates rapid and reliable delivery, and so increases labour productivity. Strong financial markets lower down the cost of capital and transactions, and so increase productivity. Flexible and well-enforced laws covering labour, land and capital (including bankruptcy) aid the rapid redeployment of these factors of production whenever needed, and so increase productivity. Substantial deregulation helps harness entrepreneurial energy. Rapid and fair procedures where regulations are still needed, judicial mechanisms to resolve disputes fairly and quickly, an alert and responsive bureaucracy and polity, a strong civil society with democratic rights and low levels of corruption, all are aids to productivity.

No developing country, including India, can claim to possess all the attributes, which are conducive to markets. Yet having a majority of them is enough to create economic miracles, as one Asian country after another have proved. India, alas, does not have a majority of these attributes. Literacy is barely 60 per cent. Infrastructure is in a terrible mess. The financial sector has serious handicaps. A legal system exists and in some respects works well (as Enron will testify), but legal *enforcement* is poor because of incompetent police and enormous legal delays. Markets for land, labour and capital remain rigid and largely unreformed coupled, with bureaucratic sloth.

The basic factor behind all this is corruption. India has a unique political economy where every political party is also a labour party (every major one has an affiliated trade union). They need huge funds to win elections, then to remain in saddle and finally for future elections and security. The prevalent political system thus serves as a breeding ground for corruption. Concessions, reservations, economic doles even at the expense of the state, are made to win elections, remain in power and secure personal future, not to talk of the national interest.

So, there can be no speedy redeployment of land, labour and capital to meet the fast changing market conditions. In sum, economic reforms remain half-baked. Although half-baked reforms have released entrepreneurial energy and helped improve productivity and growth, yet manufacturing remains plagued by a series of problems, which politicians are reluctant to correct due to vested interests. On the whole, the multinationals do not regard India as a cost-effective production centre for the global market, and are interested mainly in its domestic, protected market. Hewlett Packard considered using India as an export base but ultimately decided that the infrastructure was neither adequate nor reliable enough. Politicians, i.e., the state, have neither the guts nor an inclination. This explains why after years of reforms only a few multinational companies see much promise in shifting factories from other countries to India. India can, indeed, occupy atleast a few small labour-intensive niches in the international markets.

Yet, there remains cause for hope. There are still honest people left (although the tribe is shrinking day by day) who matter in the affairs of the state. India's economy, just like the world's economy, is shifting steadily from industry to services (Aiyar, 1999).

It is in this backdrop that the present study was conducted on India's export industry.

Objectives and Methodology

With a view to analyze systematically the reasons both of domestic as well of foreign origin, behind the poor performance of our export industry in the international market, a study was undertaken with focus on role of corruption, i.e., "*lal phita shahi* or red tapism or Inspector Raj". Another objective of the study is to suggest policy recommendations for (a) exporters – manufacturer and merchant; and (b) policy framers.

An attempt has been made to study the larger international set-up, wherein developments – political and economic – in one nation have effect on another, though remotely connected, governed by various agreements like MFA, WTO, barriers (tariff and non-tariff) and growing globalization. Further, efforts have been made to critically examine the technological developments, quality management and value addition etc. and their adoption and absorption by Indian industry, with the view to evaluate export prospects, especially the items and services that are value-added. Study of exporters' consciousness of the fact as to why 'India label' does not enjoy an enviable reputation in the international markets and of measures suggested to improve the value of India label, has been attempted.

Opinions were ascertained through personal interviews with exporters – both manufacturer and merchant – and officials of government agencies dealing with export related activities. In addition, published literature has been examined thoroughly.

So far, only a one-sided viewpoint of the trade and its spokespersons at higher echelons of bureaucracy, Chambers of Commerce and FIEO etc. has been highlighted in print media and published literature. However, what has been ignored but is equally important, if not more, is the viewpoint of the officers working especially in field formations of the various governmental and semi-governmental agencies dealing with exports. It is one of the significant contributions of this study that an attempt has been made, at a modest level, to understand the viewpoints of both the sides, i.e., exporters and the officers, especially when the latter are considered to be obstructions in export promotion, with the view to suggest measures which could be of some help in a better mutual understanding of each other's perspective and effective implementation of policies, so that exports get their deserved priority. The recommendations suggested for (a) exporters – manufacturer and merchant; and (b) policy framers, i.e., policy recommendations, is another contribution of the study.

The locale of this study was Mumbai. Mumbai is the commercial capital of India, being a premier port city. Majority of exports from India is routed through Mumbai. Both primary and secondary data have been used in the study. However, the study has primarily made use of secondary data for the purposes of trend analysis, examination of tariff and non-tariff barriers in industrial and developing countries and for the evaluation of trade practices and policies, for the simple reason that secondary level data at the national level were available. However, respondents' observations on barriers and problems, both of domestic and foreign origin, various incentive schemes and extent of their usefulness as well as abuse, and prospects of export have been elicited through personal interviews, discussions and group discussions. This analysis has been made on the basis of primary data because (i) secondary data on these aspects is not available, and (ii) a study of the practical problems faced by persons dealing in exports (viz., exporters and officials) and their perceptions about the different facets of export process is a prerequisite for understanding the export prospects. Valuable information, e.g., statistical data on export of garments from 1992-93 to 1998-99, was gathered from EPC, Mumbai and New Delhi, DGCI&S, Kolkata, RBI etc.

The respondents included exporters, officials and CHAs (Customs House Agents). The exporters are further divided into two categories: (i) manufacturer exporters, and (ii) merchant exporters. The basis for including these two categories is that they have different needs and exclusive problems. Thus, the primary data have finally been collected from three categories of respondents:

(i) Exporters (merchant and manufacturer);
(ii) Officers of the various law enforcing agencies, like DGFT, Customs, Mumbai Port, Air Cargo Complex, CWC, Airport Authority, Railway, CONCOR etc., involved in the processing of export; and
(iii) CHAs (Custom House Agents).

So far as the exporters are concerned, the sample was selected with the help of multi-stage stratified random sampling. The method of stratified random sampling was used in order to procure a representative sample of both merchant and manufacturer exporters. The universe consisted of the members of Apparel Export Promotion Council (membership of AEPC is mandatory for all apparel exporters). During 1998, AEPC had a membership of 30,383, consisting of 26,882 merchant exporters and 3,501 manufacturer exporters. Next, exporters dealing in knitwear were identified out of these two separately. Further, exporters dealing in cotton knitwear located in Mumbai were identified and this comprised the sampling frame (238 merchant and 126 manufacturer exporters). The lists of cotton knitwear exporters (merchant and manufacturer) were compiled on the basis of quotas of cotton knitted garments assigned by AEPC. Two samples consisting of 60 manufacturer and merchant exporters each were randomly drawn by the lottery method from the two lists of exporters, respectively. Personal interviews with the exporters of cotton knitwear were also conducted in order to gauge the problems they faced in their day-to-day routine work in their respective fields, apart from their perspective of the problems faced by the officials. Some manufacturer exporters had multi-location offices as well as multi-point export locations. Contacts with these exporters were made at Mumbai, at their registered offices, with prior appointments. Interviews and discussions were conducted with responsible persons as well as with the lower level staff of the exporters.

As regards the officials in various law-enforcing agencies, they make a heterogeneous group comprising diverse types, background etc. The only common thread among them is that they are dealing with exports at one stage or the other. At the time of pretesting of interview schedule, it was realized that interviews with the officials of Railways, CONCOR, CWC and ICD/CFSs were very necessary in order to gauge the proper perspective of problems faced by the exporters and the reasons behind the relative failure/unpopularity of ICD/CFSs against the popularity of Mumbai/JNPT.

The officers, fifty in number, were selected and interviewed, depending upon their availability and convenience in order to gauge the problems they faced in their day-to-day work in their respective fields and their perspective of the problems of exporters as well.

A list of Custom House Agents (CHAs) was procured from Bombay Customs House. The list contained names and addresses of 1,015 agents. This constituted the universe. Subsequently, a list all the CHAs dealing with apparel exports was obtained with the help of Customs Computer System, constituting the sampling frame and this contained 105 CHAs. Finally, a sample of 30 CHAs, handling apparel exports, was randomly selected using the lottery method. These CHAs were, thereafter, interviewed personally. The CHAs have all sorts of experiences as they have to face both the exporters as well as enforcement officials. Interviews with CHAs were the most revealing and interesting, especially with reference to actual nature of the goods, attitude of the exporters and officers as regards the liberalization of policies and practices etc.

Primary data from exporters, CHAs and officials of various law-enforcing and exports related agencies have also been obtained through the use of an interview schedule, formulated specifically for these categories of respondents.

The survey of literature was conducted, prolonged and extensive informal discussions were held with exporters and representatives of law-enforcing agencies with the specific purpose of formulating the interview schedule. After this exercise, a tentative interview schedule was prepared for the collection of primary data from exporters and officers. Two sets of interview schedule were prepared and pre-tested on a small group of respondents and these were finalized after necessary modifications. However, another interview schedule was prepared for CHAs afterwards.

Findings and Discussion

There is a shift, internationally, towards outsourcing from underdeveloped and developing countries with main objective of cost cutting. India too has boarded the bandwagon though somewhat late. That India has shown a positive trend in exports of goods and services in recent years, is evident from strength of rupee vis-à-vis US dollar and other European currencies, erection of tariff and non-tariff barriers, threat of anti-dumping duties, especially the developed nations who for so many decades have been espousing the cause of free international trade. Analysis of secondary data reveals that future of exports from India is bright.

The problems and barriers could be looked at from different perspectives, e.g., as an exporter – merchant and manufacturer, as an officer dealing with exports and finally as a researcher with an objective attitude. (Although the word 'problem' includes the barriers, yet, for the sake of emphasis laid on the term 'barriers' in international trade and to give it due attention from an analytical point of view, it has been dealt with separately). An endeavour has been made to enlist the problems and barriers on the basis of data elicited from respondents, and then critically evaluate the same with the purpose of recommending the possible solutions. The present paper discusses the various barriers while making suggestions and recommendations.

The problems and barriers are fountainheads of corruption. More the problems better, it is for breeding of corruption. In fact, these problems act as entry barriers and hence discourage new entries. These barriers are blessing in disguise for those already in this business. And that is why exporters hardly complain of corruption as a problem. Inconvenience because of corruption is not much of problem.

The reasons for India's late response to emerging trends in international market and its inability to take the full advantage of its strengths are not far to look. These include:

— lack of sophisticated technology,
— generally poor quality of goods,
— inadequate and costly transportation facilities from factory to warehouse and then to port of loading,
— unorganized industry,
— stiff competition from other Asian countries,
— trade barriers,
— a general recession on the whole and the consequent lack of resources, and
— lack of whole hearted political will and initiatives. Wherever and whenever feeble initiatives are taken these do not deliver most of the times, incentives to right people at right time,

In fact, all the above said weaknesses or barriers are manifestations of one basic factor, i.e., corruption, whatsoever we may call it – red tapism, speed money, commission, party fund, nepotism and/or protocol, etc. There is no dearth of barriers erected by the importing countries because of their own domestic socio-political and economic compulsions. These problems exist over and above the problems faced by the exporters because of Indian policies, bureaucratic set-up, culture and lack of basic amenities subsequently culminating into a weak image of Indian products abroad.

The problems, which are the creation of India's own socio-politico-economic and bureaucratic set-up, can also be examined from two perspectives. First, from the perspective of exporters and secondly, that of officers dealing with the trade. Both the viewpoints have some elements of truth. Efforts have been made to put forward the viewpoints of both, with some moderation here and there, without losing any content. The focus was to capture unbiased ground realities, mitigate the irritants and suggest remedial measures towards improvement of export prospects. The viewpoints of exporters as well as officials are assessed on the basis of personal face-to-face interaction with them. However, over and above the problems described by these two types of respondents, additional problems have been gauged from various publications scrutinized by the researcher and out of personal observations borne out of day-to-day experience while coordinating with various departments, apart from exporters and importers.

The problems as expressed by the exporters and the representatives of law-enforcing agencies are given in Table 1.

Table 1

Problems Enlisted by Respondents

Respondents	*Problems*
Merchant Exporters	Red tapism; shortage of funds, working capital, pre- and post-shipment finance etc.; excessive paper work; multiplicity of inspection agencies; lack of assistance in international marketing; poor image of 'Made in India' label; absolute dependence on foreign markets and lack of sales avenues in DTA to fall back during lean periods in exports; tariff, non-tariff and administrative barriers; quota system and the ad hocism in its administration; phasing out of MFA; competition from new emerging East Asian, South Asian tigers and preferential treatment meted out to in-group/bloc members by US and EU.
Manufacturer Exporters	Lack of infrastructure; red tapism; non-availability of capital goods and obsolete technology; shortage of funds, working capital, pre- and post-shipment finance etc.; multiplicity of controlling agencies; excessive paper work; low productivity of labour and archaic labour laws; lack of assistance in international marketing; poor image of 'Made in India' label; and trade Barriers – tariff, non-tariff and administrative; quota system and the ad hocism in its distribution/administration; phasing out of MFA; shortage of embellishments; competition from new emerging East Asian, South Asian tigers and preferential treatment meted out to in-group/bloc members by US and EU; ban on Azo dyes; handicaps being a small-scale industry; increasingly a capital-intensive industry; absolute dependence on foreign markets and lack of sales avenues in DTA to fall back during lean periods in exports; erratic supply of good quality yarns of medium and long staple cotton; and shortage of machinery spares and technical hands for maintenance.
Representatives of Government Agencies	One-sided liberalization; lack of confidence in and among officers; officers avoid decision-making; corruption; lack of working environment and basic amenities; and lack of knowledge among exporters.

During the interviews and discussions with the respondents, it was discovered that though they were able to specify and rank the problems and barriers in the order of their significance, they lacked the ability to provide an analytical explanation of the problem. Therefore, having procured the list of problems and barriers from the respondents, the researcher scanned through the relevant documents and literature in order to examine in detail each of the problems. The analysis is presented, in brief, in following discussions.

Table 2

Problems in Terms of Origin (Foreign and Domestic)

Origin	*Problems*
Foreign	Trade barriers; competition from other developing countries – countries, especially those enjoying the 'Most Favoured Nation' (MFN) status and/or not covered by quota restrictions; abuse of position and hold over world organizations like WTO, World Bank, IMF etc., by EU and US.
Domestic	Lack of funds, bureaucratic set-up including customs and port problems, and inflexible labour laws.

PROBLEMS OF FOREIGN ORIGIN, i.e., creation of importing countries and other competitors to export, were identified by respondents and these have been placed into a hierarchy on the basis of their responses:

(a) *Trade Barriers*: (i) tariff; and (ii) non-tariff.

(b) *Competition from other developing countries:* Countries, especially those enjoying the 'Most Favoured Nation' (MFN) status and/or not covered by quota restrictions give Indian apparel exporters a tough time.

(c) *Big brothers' attitude of US and EU*: EU and US abuse their position and hold over world organizations like WTO, World Bank, IMF etc. in all possible manners.

Problems of Domestic Origin: Fountainheads of Corruption

It is meaningful to delineate these problems, since these are amenable to corrective measures at the level of national policy. The major problems of domestic origin enlisted by the respondents are the following:

Red Tapism

While big policy initiatives may set the trend, it is the minor irritants, which need to be looked at in order to push exports, as pointed out by the exporters. For example:

— Delay in import of labels and tags as exporters have to first prove their 'bonafide';
— Shipping bills not cleared without Modvat certificate;
— Drawback clearance normally delayed;
— Octroi demanded in some states, though the law says no octroi on export goods;
— Commerce Minister promised one-time revalidation for expired advance licences where exports have been undertaken. But, no notification so far (Viswanath, 1999c); and
— Clearances of licences, setting and publication of input-output norms, fixation of drawback rates and DEPB rates are slow and tedious, especially the application for DEEC.

Serious doubts have been expressed regarding the implementation stage of many policy measures, because of bureaucratic red tapism, procedural bottlenecks, e.g., Commerce Ministry is empowered to frame policy but implementation lies with the Ministry of Finance (Customs & Central Excise Department) and the outlook of the latter is biased towards revenue collection.

Further, there are too many agencies involved in monitoring exports and the problem is compounded by lack of coordination and cooperation among these agencies. Moreover, various agencies are located at different places causing delays and losses, belying hopes on the part of exporters for prompt deliveries of quality goods in a highly competitive international market.

Viswanath (1999c), in an article entitled 'Small exporters at their wits end to get out of red tapism', posed the question, "What ails India's exports?" The instant reply is: "Procedural irritants and some broken promises". Panigrahi (1999b), while examining the role of procedural bottlenecks as a barrier in export promotion efforts, has arrived at a conclusion that procedural maze, overdocumentation and multiplicity of exportincentive schemes are a big hurdles to export drive to be reckoned with. Coming heavily on government claims of simplification of procedures, he finds the claims, only an eyewash. It is a widely acknowledged truth that procedural wrangles have had an altogether negative impact so far on industrial growth and exports, having dampened economic progress. Lack of clarity, simplicity and transparency is creating all sorts of confusions. Contradictory provisions and notifications, coupled with frequent changes, flip-flop policies and inconsistent rules, are multiplying uncertainties, throwing industry plans out of gear. To make the matters worse, the corrupt culture and bureaucracy are adding woes to the industry.

However, whenever there is a movement of goods from the factory to the port, the octroi posts stop the vehicles. To avoid delays in delivery schedules, the small exporters are forced to pay up.

On the insurance front, exporters said that the insurance company states that covers would be given only to products which are under deck. They point out that they have no say on where the product would be kept and, therefore, there was always a probability that in case of a damage, the insurance company may not pay up stating that the product was kept on the deck and not under the deck.

Transportation – Corruption-Ridden!

Local transport unions, especially in areas declared as 'backward' for trade and industry, compel the exporters to pay exorbitantly high freight and loading/unloading charges. Infrastructure is very poor at most of the ICDs/CFSs, empty racks are not available, train frequencies are very less, and moreover, railway schedules for cargo/goods trains are not confirmed and hence the uncertainty. Goods trains carrying goods for export are not on the priority list of Railways. It takes more time to carry goods to a port than from the port to a foreign destination. Consignments get delayed and hence orders are cancelled. The credibility of exporter remains at stake for no fault of his. This has an unintended consequence of unpopularity of ICDs and CFSs. Transport of goods from Mumbai and its surrounding areas to JNPT, otherwise an ultra-modern port, is a hell of an expedition because of locals of the area and 'goonda' elements amongst them. There are routine cases of extortion and violence, en route as well as at the port. Exporters claim that there exists a criminal nexus between agents and railway authorities and nothing moves without palm greasing.

ICD/CFS Sans Facilities

Inland Container Depots (ICDs) and Container Freight Stations (CFSs) have poor infrastructure and godown facilities. Even containers, which are the basic item for packing and transportation, are not available. ICDs/CFSs lack handling equipment too. If these are somehow available, they are not operational either for lack of trained manpower or for being out of order. Problem is further compounded because of too many strikes and 'work to rule'. Problem is limited not only to "cart in" (the term "cart in" is used to imply that goods meant for export have been brought inside the port/ICD/CFS) and stuffing inside the container but also in taking the goods "back to town" from the port/ICD/CFS. These problems are equally valid for ports too.

Shipping Ports – Short Cuts Available!

Cornell Group, on behalf of Government of India, had examined the issue of poor port facilities and thus a hurdle in export promotion (Whines & Handgovers and Gogoi, 1999). The Group has suggested three-pronged reforms – structural, administrative and operational – to rein in the slide in performance of the ports.

In the first place, the boards of the major ports need to be changed by bringing in more commercial experience and ideas and most importantly, with no conflict of interests. Short of calling the members incompetent, the Group has stated that there is an inconsistency in management decisions primarily because the members lack commercial decision-making background. And, then, there is political interference. This repositioning will involve getting rid of institutional rigidities, policy distortions, current maze of labour regulations and product reservations in the name of promoting small-scale industry (SSI).

Time taken for movement of containers from dry port, i.e., ICD/CFS to the ship is high and hence delays in shipments. Quite often, the materials are not dispatched in the ship for which the bill of lading has been issued. There are frequent computer breakdowns at Kandla and Mumbai ports besides the slow pace of work. At Mumbai port, labour gang of minimum persons has to be booked in advance but they are very slow. If one wants faster work of loading-unloading, stuffing etc., one can bring outside labour but subject to minimum gang charges, whereas at JN Port labour unions do not allow outside labour at all and hence one has to pay through one's nose for the timely stuffing of the containers. Respondents said that invariably for bigger consignments, they engaged their own labour on payment of minimum gang charges and still it was more economical than employing official gang labour. There are frequent thefts, especially of expensive goods, which are most of the time noticed and reported at destination, causing not only embarrassment but also economical loss as the buyer may demand replacements.

Pilferage/Theft

Exporters in our study reported cases of loss of samples as well as of the goods ready for export, duly packed but pending stuffing in containers and shipping on board. Goods of common use are very susceptible to pilferage. Exporters also expressed that CHAs and officers of customs/port/ICD/airport etc. carry the samples or distribute them to oblige the people at their cost.

There are, no doubt, well-organized gangs operating within and outside the port (including air cargo and dry ports) areas, indulging in thefts of imported as well as under-export goods. Sometimes importers themselves get their goods stolen through these gangs to avoid customs duty (because there is no duty on goods lost or/and destroyed forever), evade sales tax and claim insurance (which is generally 110 per cent and may run up to 300 per cent depending upon the nature of the goods). Further, such goods may have an added advantage of non-accountal for manufacturing purposes and ultimate evasion of state/central excise duty and income tax etc. However, thefts of goods under export are few and petty, a handiwork of small-timers.

Problem of Half-Baked Measures and Selective Partial Implementation by Customs and DGFT

Exporters in general expressed during interviews and discussions – both formal as well as informal – that measures taken by the government and its agencies were inadequate and ineffective. However, officials claim that exporters most of the time lack knowledge regarding the facilities provided by the government and hence these remained unavailed.

Procedures for expeditious assessment and clearance of imported goods, e.g., self-certification of export consignments, removal of export goods from the factories on the basis of self-certification and self-sealing of export consignments, rationaliszation of duty structure, duty payment on monthly basis for SSI units, relaxation of maintaining statutory records of excise by companies paying over Rs. 5 crores duty in one year, self-clearance procedure for 100 per cent EOUs, relaxation in strolling duty paid goods, introduction of electronic data interchange (EDI) in major ports, etc., are some of the recently introduced measures intended to simplify the procedures. But, for a bewildering array of reasons, the net result of all these efforts has failed to bring in any tangible change in the system and practices prevailing in the Revenue Department.

For example, the facility of removal of export goods from the factories on the basis of self-certification and self-sealing of export consignments has only a limited usefulness. The real problem under the new dispensation consists of the surprise inspection and checks by the Customs and Central Excise officials. The industry fears that in the name of checks there will be more harassment and delays. Because of these practical difficulties, the scheme has not enthused the exporters. Those, who opted the route out of ignorance, are now repenting having had a bitter experience. The views of exporters and law-enforcing agencies were obtained on the steps taken by the government to simplify procedures and hence make exports less costly. Though exporters have welcomed the initiatives taken but officials have some reservation. Their main objection was that these cause loss to the exchequer in absence of effective controls.

Table 3

Respondents' Reactions to Simplification of Procedures

Reactions	*Exporters*	*Officers*
Positive Development	100%	36%
Effective	48%	20%
Very Effective	62%	06%

Effective means that it has cut export cost and time.
Positive Development implies that it is a step towards liberalisation and helps to boost exports.

Administration of Quota-Breeding Corruption

Exporters basically levelled two charges against the policy of distribution of quota: (i) frequent and uncalled for changes in quota distribution policy, and (ii) malpractices in distribution. And, then, there is the problem of late release of quota causing economic hardship to exporters. Exporters claimed that this is done intentionally for the benefit of quota traders who corner the quotas in bulk and sell them on premium.

Those who have quota are not exporting and those who want to export are not getting quota. Quota holders and quota brokers reap huge profits at the cost of exporters by charging premium. Inordinate delays in release of quota force them to approach brokers to fulfil the commitments in time. Further, the government proposal to sell quota on NSE did not catch the fancy of exporters. One reason for this is that the premium now being paid is unaccounted for. Moreover, official sale shall attract other taxes like sales tax and income tax etc.

Quota policies come under heavy firing from all types of entitled exporters because of quota restrictions and ever-changing policies of allotment of quota. Criteria for allocation are always changing for first come first serve, new units, past performance, etc., to suit a few big and politically active. Quotas should be streamlined and made transparent. Even the releases of annual ceilings for exports are inconsistent and ignored at international level for lack of initiative or motivation. Exporters during interviews did claim that FCFS quotas were, on the one hand, being granted to some on dummy Letter of Credit while being denied to other legitimate exporters on petty monetary and typography errors; and that ETS charges being levied on quota transfers were not justified. Recently, All India Garment Exporters Common Cause Guild, while appealing to the Prime Minister, has alleged that Rs. 4 lakhs are being collected per day as ETS charges even covering mutual quota transfers among exporters (AIGECC Guild, 2000).

Lack of Dissemination of Knowledge Among Exporters

There is an adage "knowledge is power" and there is nothing more true than this in the present global scenario of information technology. Knowledge about latest fashions, strengths and strategies of competitors is the buzzword of international marketing. However, apparel exporters claimed that neither AEPC nor other associations and Chambers of Commerce were disseminating any useful information to them though they were being heavily charged for the same.

Excess of Documentation and Under Staffed Ports

All the authorities linked with export have their own set of documents for giving no objection or clearance for exports, claim the exporters and they had often raised this issue through their associations and Chamber of Commerce. For example, there are documents for RBI, DGFT, EPCs, Port/ICD/CFS and customs authorities etc. The paper work is not only time-consuming, leading to wastage of money, but it also hinders the movements of the export goods and their timely delivery. Safe and sound timely delivery is crucial in the buyer's market, especially when good quality products are available in competitive market. However, this problem is being taken care of with the inception of EDI and online assessment/clearance by customs authorities at most of the ports/ICDs and DGFT.

Another grudge of the exporters is that Customs Houses/ports etc. are understaffed and lack appraisers who are well-versed with export formalities and items. The later problem relates to the post-export irritants, e.g., delays in disbursement of drawback, export-related no objection certificates, acceptance of proofs of export, issuance of DEPB, DEEC etc. The department, in its turn, has issued Citizen's Charter, enumerating the efforts of the department as well as what public at large can expect from it.

Problem of Being a Small-Scale Industry

Industry in India is classified into three categories on the basis of investment in capital goods, viz., large, medium and small-scale. The growth of SSI sector is getting stunned and big players' entry is virtually banned. Exporters, both merchant and manufacturer, expressed the opinion that the restrictions on capital investment, especially for export-oriented units, should be removed.

Most of the exporters were found to be concerned only with the items of export they were manufacturing or dealing with. They were also found to be lacking in an initiative even to know about other items. Further, the source of their knowledge about barriers is the buyer, who guides them regarding their requirements. In fact, their whole attention is on export, i.e., either what is in vogue or whatever they are manufacturing. Hence, they lack in developing the products where barriers – tariff and non-tariff – are the minimum. It is seen that the awareness is more among the merchant exporters vis-à-vis manufacture exporters (Table 4). The observations revealed that the difference is explainable by the fact that merchant exporters were more marketing-oriented and that too outside India. Manufacturer exporters, in contrast, were looking after both manufacturing as well as marketing on their own. Moreover ,they were catering to markets within and outside India. Hence, they were unable to concentrate fully and equally on both.

Table 4

Awareness Among Exporters About Barriers

Barrier	*Market*	*Awareness (%)*	
		Merchant	*Manufacturer*
Quota•	USA, EU, Canada	100%	100%
Anti-Dumping Duty	EU	60%	45%
	USA, Canada	75%	52%
Health Standard (ban on dyes, flammability etc.)	EU	100%	100%
	USA	75%	55%
Tariff Rates	EU	52%	35%
	USA, Canada	60%	45%
Customs Procedures	EU, USA, Canada	68%	45%
Requirements of Labelling and Packaging	EU, USA, Canada	70%	45%

Ranking of Problems by Exporters

Respondents were asked to rank the problems confronted by them, according to their significance (in descending order). After obtaining this ranking from all the respondents, the median score for each problem was calculated and finally these problems have been ranked according to the median score (Tables 5 and 6). An important observation is that both the types of exporters – manufacturer as well as merchant – rank lack of finances, especially the working capital, as number one problem. Among the problems faced by manufacturer exporters, those on the domestic front, such as shortage of working capital, administration of quota for export of apparels, retrograde labour laws, etc., are on the top, whereas the post-manufacturing problems, like trade barriers to Indian garment in the foreign market, poor image of Indian products, etc., have been relegated to the rear end.

Table 5

Ranking of Problems Perceived by Manufacturer Exporters

Problem	*Median Rank*
Shortage of funds, working capital etc.	1
Quota administration	2
Archaic labour laws	3
Inadequate Infrastructure	4
Non-availability of capital goods and obsolete technology	5
Multiplicity of controlling agencies	6
Excessive paper work and customs procedures	7
Lack of assistance in international marketing	8
Poor brand image of 'Made in India' label	9
Red tapism	10
Trade barriers in importing countries	11

Whereas merchant exporters have lesser problems confronting them as compared to manufacturer exporters, the ranking of problems by them is invariably consistent with that by the manufacturer exporters (rank order correlation=0.924). Merchant exporters, just like the manufacturer exporters, ranked the problems faced on the domestic front on the higher end vis-à-vis problems of marketing confronted abroad.

Table 6

Ranking of Problems Perceived by Merchant Exporters

Problem	*Median Rank*
Shortage of funds, working capital etc.	1
Administration of quota	2
Multiplicity of controlling agencies	3
Excessive paper work and customs procedures	4
Inadequate infrastructure	5
Lack of assistance in international marketing	6
Poor brand image of 'Made in India' label	7
Red tapism	8
Trade barriers in importing countries	9

Ranking of Agencies as Hindrance to Export Promotion

Apart from the problems faced by the exporters as discussed earlier, they also expressed concern about certain government agencies as problems in themselves. Respondents, both merchant and manufacturer exporters, were asked to enlist these agencies and rank them according to their significance as problems in themselves (in descending order). After obtaining this ranking from all the 60 respondents of each type, the median score for each agency was calculated and finally these agencies have been ranked according to the median score (Tables 7 and 8).

Table 7

Ranking of Agencies by Manufacturer Exporters as Hindrance to Exports

Manufacturer Exporters	*Median Rank*
State agencies (like State Electricity Board, Octroi, Sales Tax Department etc.)	1
Central Excise	2
AEPC	3
Customs	4
DGFT	5
CHAs and touts	6
Port authorities	7
Banks	8
Shipping agencies	9
CONCOR/Railways	9

Table 8

Ranking of Agencies by Merchant Exporters as Hindrance to Exports

Merchant Exporters	*Median Rank*
AEPC	1
Customs	2
DGFT	3
Port authorities	4
Banks	5
Shipping agencies	6
CONCOR/Railways	6

Agencies as obstacles co-efficient of correlation 0.995.

Views of the individual exporters regarding negative role of agencies as problem creators have recently been further endorsed by All India Garment Exporters Common Cause Guild in an appeal-cum-advertisement (2000) as under:

— AEPC spends crores of rupees annually on export promotion/study tours benefiting only EC members or their coterie; ATD centres built with common exporters funds have been gifted to the selected few for a fee of Re. 1; FCFS quotas are granted on a dummy Letter of Credit to a selected few and are denied to others on petty monetary and typography errors; exorbitant EMD are slapped on exporters; selected exporters associations with microscopic memberships walk away with profits from international fairs at the expense of a common, unrepresented exporter.

— AEPC commits errors and exporters suffer; and there is no accountability for exporters' grievances.

— Customs hold shipments for valuation; audit system is circumvented to suit vested interests.

— DGFT talks of compulsory Barcode without talking of methods to make exporters competitive.

— Inspector Raj of Labour, PF, ESI and Pollution Departments is engaged in large-scale extortion of money.

Officers' Viewpoint regarding Problems Confronting Exports

An attempt was made to seek the views of the officers on the trade allegations that the various law-enforcing agencies, instead of being facilitators, are in fact obstacles in the way of international trade. In other words, the trade believes that exports would be better off in absence of these law-enforcing officials. Reacting to this, however, the officers draw a different picture of the trade, government policies in particular. Officers did feel that although there were genuine problems, yet these problems were the creation of lopsided policies, lack of political will, lack of or delay in decision-making, corruption and exporters' own shortsighted gains etc. The representatives of government public sector and private agencies involved in export-related procedures were asked to give their opinion as to whether problems expressed by exporters were genuine or not. Responses are presented in Table 9 below:

Table 9

Officers' Perception about Exporters' Problems

Problems	*Genuine*	*Not Genuine*	
Foreign origin			
Quota restrictions	80%	—	20% not aware
Anti-dumping duties (tariff)	70%	30%	
Various health (ban on dyes), product and packaging standard etc.	84%	6%	10% not aware
Lobbying (for domestic products and against said to be subsidized imports)	90%	6%	4% not aware
Customs entry procedures etc.	36%	36%	28% not aware
Domestic origin			
Shortage of funds (working capital, and for upgradation of technology etc.)	70%	10%	20% not aware
Quota administration	70%	30%	
Archaic labour laws	100%	—	
Inadequate infrastructure	80%	10%	10% not aware
Obsolete technology	90%	10%	
Multiplicity of controlling agencies	100%	—	
Excessive paper work and customs procedures	66%	34%	
Lack of assistance in international marketing	65%	35%	
Poor brand image of 'Made in India' label	90%	10%	
Red tapism	76%	24%	

Various problems and the reasons behind the genuine problems of the exporters, as indicated by the various officials, are discussed as below.

Officers Pushed Against the Wall

Officers, when interviewed, complained that although the policies were pro-trade, yet at the same time these were harsh towards officers. Seniors act under the influence of pressures and most of the time oral instructions are given. The common excuse to keep one in check is the statement: "lots of complaints are coming against you". If anything goes wrong, junior officers are made the scapegoat. As a result, if one is doing a job, one is either conniving with the trade or is harassing the trade.

Liberalization rules and regulations, framed with the best of intentions to curb some evil, sometimes lead to totally contradictory results. Such laws and rules are like 'scarecrow' as rightly pointed out by none other than N. Vittal (1999a), Former Chief Vigilance Commissioner (CVC). The scarecrow is initially put to protect the crops and to scare away the birds. However, soon the birds start sitting and building nests over it, perhaps realizing that it was only a dummy. The scarecrow effect is obvious if we attempt a close scrutiny of many of our rules and regulations. In fact, the greater the idealism and altruism behind the law or rule, greater would be the scarecrow effect.

Many a time, people bemoan the fact that our system is not effective. Vittal (1999a) has suggested that a good exercise to improve governance and its effectiveness, implying an effective implementation of policies, is to apply the scarecrow index to every policy measure, rule or regulation and see whether it is positive or negative. All those with a negative scarecrow index should be scrapped. If we are not specific, we will be like the lady who went to Bob Hope with the best intention and said she wanted to do something clean and big. Bob Hope replied, "Go and wash an elephant"(ibid.).

Demoralizing Effect on Officers

One common grudge among officers against the seniors is that the latter entertain the traders even when they are known to be habitual offenders, are offered tea while the subordinate officers are made to wait outside the room. Open door policy is applicable only for trade, who can meet the boss any time while the subordinate has to seek prior appointment or atleast send a slip stating the purpose of visit. General opinion of the officers about themselves and trade at large as in the eyes of their higher ups can be summed up as under:

> While trade is not guilty unless proved otherwise, subordinate staff is guilty unless one proves oneself innocent.

What is required therefore is a need to instil confidence among officers. They also need to be treated with the same regard as the trade, if not more.

Officers Avoid Decision-Making

Files keep on moving here and there, up and down with no result except that the file is not pending on any table, especially the case files involving revenue. Reason – officers are wary of committing a mistake and later face the flurry of explanations. Alternatively whenever in doubt decide in favour of the revenue. Recently, Cogentrix, and earlier Tata, cancelled their projects of power and airport as well as airline respectively in India out of frustration and fatigue.

The US-based Cornell Group, in its interim report to the Government of India, on the possibilities of commercialization and corporatization of the Indian port system, has critically examined the problems and prospects of major Indian ports (Gogoi, 1999). In its report, the Group, short of calling the members incompetent, has stated that there is an inconsistency in management decisions primarily because the members lack commercial decision-making background. And, then, there is political interference.

Corruption: The Ultimate Virus

Respondents, both exporters as well as law-enforcing officials, were of common opinion that corruption is very much a fact of life while doing business in India. Interestingly, 'corruption' has neither been listed by merchant exporters nor by manufacturer exporters as an obstruction to export promotion. Respondents were of the view that it is very difficult for an honest exporter and an officer to work and survive in the system. Corrupt only were thriving. It is pervasive among almost all the echelons of bureaucracy, politics, public and private sector manufacturing, trading, importing and exporting concerns. Corruption is the most secular and all-embracing phenomenon without any caste, creed and class discrimination. In the words of Vittal (1999b), there are five elements, viz., the corrupt politician, the corrupt bureaucrat, the corrupt businessman, the corrupt NGO and the criminal, who are the major players in the corruption scene. It may be known by any name, e.g., protocol, *hafta*, speed, *chaya-pani*, etc. It is nothing but a naked, indirect and explicit corruption. For example, 'protocol' may include anything under the sun, but in kind. As reported by the respondents, protocol requires cash that comes directly or indirectly from the trade most of the times, though sometimes an officer has to spend from his own pocket too. These officers enjoy postings of their choice with the blessings of seniors and their wives. Officers who do not care for protocols, on the other hand, are termed either as 'arrogant' or 'useless' and hence are dumped. Most of the officers in the process fall in line, sooner or later. Cash payments are quite common for prize postings. Most of the time, officers with outstanding annual confidential reports are the biggest sycophants (referred to as 'chamchas') as revealed by the officials during interviews.

India is perceived to be the 19th most corrupt country in the world by a German NGO, 'Transparency International', which grades countries on the basis of what is called the 'Corruption Perception Index'. According to the 1998 report, out of the 85 countries graded in the order of honesty, India ranks 66th. This means that 65 countries are less corrupt than India while 18 countries exceed (Vittal, 1999c).

In a news item "Corrupt Nations", published in *Financial Express*, Mumbai, on October 29, 1999, India has been viewed as the 27th most corrupt country in the world. However, this is the opinion of the First World, according the Berlin-based Transparency International (TI), which tapped, among others, the World Bank, the World Economic Forum and the Economist Intelligence Unit. TI has ranked 99 countries (curiously, the oil-rich countries of West Asia have been kept out of purview) on its scale of corruption, the cleanest scoring 10 (Belgium) and the most corrupt collecting 1.5 (Cameroon) out of 10. India scored 2.7 and Pakistan 2.2. It is fashionable abroad, among NGOs and multilateral institutions, to berate corruption in developing countries. But, even a free economy leader like United States of America, is 16 rungs below Belgium on the cleanliness scale: the US scores 7.5. TI very cleverly says that a score of less than 5.5 points to a problem for the concerned nation. Why does the 2.5 deficiency of the US or the 3.4 shortfall of France pass muster?

Economic liberalization, it is said, does away with corruption, but Brazil scored only 4.1 and Mexico (post-NAFTA) 3.4, at par with China. Both the Latin American nations play hosts to multinationals. And China, despite its trouble-spelling low score, attracts sustained mega foreign direct investment. Perhaps, there is a connection between foreign investment and corruption in developing countries (ibid.).

The current debate in the Indian business community about ethics is based on the growing realization that ultimately, the adage "honesty is the best policy" can be a practical guide. Vittal (1999c) suggests an exercise, similar to Transparency International, of preparing a Corruption Perception Index, listing government departments, public enterprises and public sector banks, in the order of increasing corruption? Vittal is of the view that such an exercise would shame those who are badly off and perceived to be very corrupt. However, it may result in creation of another scarecrow, as in case of latent heat and energy, most corrupt departments may not be perceived corrupt. There is a very pertinent and old adage having some truth in it: "*bad se badnam bura*".

Causes and Way Out

Growing materialism and mismatch between income and cost of acquiring the necessities is the main cause of corruption according to most of the respondents from the category of representatives of government agencies. Most of the officials were of the view that if minimum necessities like telephone and electricity bills, education expenses of the children, maintenance of conveyance commensurate with times and economic security after retirement were taken care of, then 70-80 per cent of the government employees would not indulge in such nefarious activities. They were also of the view that given a decent and respectable salary, extra money collected through corruption was not worth the risk involved. In other words, if one is economically satisfied, he/she may not venture into economic corruption.

However, the views of the general people are different. They argue that feeling economically satisfied and having no desire for more and more is the end of the development and growth. Dissatisfaction with the present is the very essence of progress. Secondly, they find the risk involved in corruption vis-à-vis benefits as very low, unlike the officers.

In a nutshell, if a public servant feels satisfied with his emoluments, there may be lesser inducement to corruption, whereas if a businessman (manufacturer, importer, exporter or trader) feels satisfied, there may be less of growth. For progress/growth, outsmarting one's competitors in the world of "survival of the fittest", a businessman may tend to indulge in corruption given the low risk. Another fallout of this thinking is that supply side of corruption is the precursor.

A retired judge of Supreme Court of India opined that (1) there are 10 per cent extremely honest persons, (2) 10 per cent most corrupt, and (3) remaining 80 per cent in a fluid state. The trend in public life is that whosoever between the categories mentioned at (1) and (2) rules the remaining category of 80 per cent, i.e., (3), becomes a part of it. In other words, if honest people are at the helm of affairs, 90 per cent people will be honest and if the corrupt is ruling the show, 90 per cent will be engaged in corruption. Hence, in his opinion, efforts should be made to make honest persons sit in the hot chair.

Respondents, however, irrespective of the category, were still of the view that honest exporters and officers, though a rare commodity, commanded respect and are held in high public esteem.

Vittal has critically examined the role of corruption in Indian society and its impact as a hurdle to business including the international trade. The corruption involves two sides: (i) donor/giver, i.e., supply side and (ii) recipients, i.e., demand side. Vittal, in an article, entitled "The Supply Side of Corruption" (1999c), has elaborated on the donor. Recipient side, i.e., the public servants or politicians, has already been attracting the attention of the media. He has emphasized that as far as the supply side of corruption is concerned, there has been a thundering silence. Corruption, in the words of Vittal, is like two hands clapping. He has raised a very pertinent question, "Why is it that the supply side of corruption flourishes and not commented upon?" and he himself has answered: "This is because viewed from the supply side, corruption offers a good price. In monetary terms, it is a small price to pay for a bigger benefit". He has pointed out that at international level, today, there is a legal framework and a consequence emerging that giving bribes must be checked. In the 1980s, the United States government came up with the Foreign Corrupt Practices Act to ban the payment of bribes by the US companies in foreign countries. In 1996, 34 OECD countries signed the anti-bribery convention. The World Bank estimates that FDI goes down by 20 per cent if a country is corrupt and 35 per cent if it is perceived to be very corrupt. At the time of disbursal of the loans, the World Bank is now looking into issues of corporate governance and is controlling corruption also.

The permit-licence raj had led to the development of a vicious cycle of corruption which involves the corrupt politician (*neta*), the corrupt bureaucrat (*babu*), the corrupt businessman (*lala*), the corrupt NGO (*jhola*) and the criminal (*dada*). To get out of this cycle, organizations like the CVC and the courts may be able to bring some people to book but this has a limited impact. What we need is a movement in the country from the supply side of corruption. If the Indian industries and business people decide that they would not bribe the public servants, we would have taken a major step in fighting corruption (Vittal, 1999c).

Unless the deep-rooted culture of corruption and bureaucracy also changes, no good intentions can be implemented. Earlier, many good schemes simply flopped because of the work attitude of the staff. The recent example is Electronic Data Interchange (EDI) system, which is intended for faster clearance, but has failed to deliver the expected results simply because there is no truly willing acceptance by the departmental staff. They feel that all these procedural simplifications may drain their easy money earning (Panigrahi, 1999b).

Rajeev Gupta, in an illuminating article, "Export Promotion Scheme Favours Unscrupulous Exporters: Investigative Revelations" (1999), after examining most of the incentive schemes in vogue, is of the opinion that the export promotions schemes favour unscrupulous exporters. This is also the opinion of the Public Accounts Committee (PAC). If one takes into account the cumulative effect of export promotion schemes such as duty exemption, duty drawback, etc., then, the cost of export promotion is ridiculously high. As a matter of fact, since these are administered separately by different agencies/ministries, the cumulative effect will not be known even. The subsidization is the main cause for corruption in this area. The schemes, plenty in number, with permutations and combinations, and with various loopholes, are made available so that exploitation continues unabated and the interest of all concerned is best served. The Ministry of Finance had estimated misutilization of Value-Based Advance Licensing Scheme (VABAL) to the extent of Rs. 10,000 crores, which is not a small amount in any case. There are hundreds of cases pending in the Customs Houses to be finalized on account of overvaluation problems, related to VABAL, leave aside the recoveries.

Gupta, in a scathing note, concluded:

> Policy makers proved morons through VABAL lacunae and misuse, they proved they are imbecile through passbook and now through DEPB they are proving idiots and claiming revalidation of this status by continuing the DEPB for the reason of no alternatives. Though it is a prerogative of the bureaucracy to formulate the policy but it is more to be seen as responsibility and not an unbridled authority to permit looking of the nation in concert (Gupta, 1999).

The Comptroller and Auditor General of India (CAG), as per press reports published in the *Business Line*, New Delhi, on 1 November 1999 reprinted in *ELT,* Vol.114 (1999) A44-A46, entitled "CAG Flays Misuse of VABAL Scheme – Pulls up Customs, DGFT for Rs.3,532-cr Revenue Loss", took the customs authorities and the Directorate General of Foreign Trade (DGFT) to task for allowing the VABAL to be misused entailing a revenue effect of Rs. 3,532 crores.

The CAG, in its report on 'Indirect Taxes-Customs' for the fiscal year ended March 31, 1999, tabled in parliament, conceded that customs duty of Rs.11,798 crores was foregone during 1997-98, on account of export promotion schemes including duty drawback, while under-assessment of tax and loss of revenue amounted to Rs.5,093 crores for the period under review.

The report also indicted the government for its failure to draft a suitable mechanism to identify cases of default and effect recoveries till date, though an enabling provision in the Customs Act had been made in

1991. A sum of Rs.14,346 crores has been paid as drawback from April 1991 till March 1998. The CAG also detected non-levy/loss of customs revenue arising from operation of certain duty exemption schemes such as the VABAL, EPCG, EOU and EPZ, amounting to Rs.227.67 crores.

In fact, various investigation agencies and even some trade analysts term the exemption schemes as a breeding ground for corruption. CAG and Customs point out to various cases of under/overvaluation of imports and overvaluation of exports in order to substantiate their viewpoint. The list of cases investigated is replete with umpteen number of cases of overinvoicing, misdeclaration and fraud, e.g., export of ball pen at the rate of Rs.100-200, plastic bucket at the rate of Rs.700-1,000; export of rags in garb of costly garments; export of *masoor dal* as against declared description of polyester yarn/fabric; export on papers only, without actual shipments etc. In a nutshell, there are cases of misdeclaration of valuation, description, quantity and weight and even total frauds.

Further, the respondents, both from trade as well as official agencies, were critical of these incentives (Table 10), whereas the exporters claimed that incentives were insufficient and discriminatory. Insufficient for the reasons that total export costs are more as compared to remuneration received, exports are not viable, competing countries were doing more than the Indian government, etc. Discriminatory, because the big and established units were being favoured by government agencies in the allotment of garment quota, disbursement of loans, facilities like green channel, cargo clearance, self-certification and self-sealing of export cargo, besides providing facilities like repeat licences, status, e.g., star trading house/trade house, etc., and the accompanying benefits. However, representatives of government agencies are of the view that these schemes are abused and officers are subsequently made the scapegoat both for following the rules scrupulously if exports are delayed in the process, as well as for not doing the same if the exporter is found to be availing the benefits fraudulently. These incentives are not in consonance with the spirit of the WTO. However, they do agree with the exporters that government policies are discriminatory as far as the distribution of incentives is concerned.

Table 10

Respondents' Reactions to Incentives

Reaction	Exporters	Officers
Desirable	100%	—
Not desirable	—	80%
Insufficient	95%	—
Discriminatory	70%	64%

Both the trade as well as officers agree that there is corruption-cum-politico-bureaucratic pressure, especially in ICDs/CFSs and Air Cargoes, where staff and the trade are not well-versed in rules and regulations, nature of the products and consequent importance of various restrictions/prohibitions, economic and other benefits to the importers and exporters, etc.

The respondents were further asked to respond to some specific aspects of incentive schemes, especially the extent of their abuse and corruption involved therein. The responses are tabulated in Table 11.

Table 11

Respondents' Views on Some Aspects of Incentives

Statements	Exporters		Officers	
Are incentive schemes abused?	Yes	90%	Yes	100%
What is the extent of abuse?	—	5%	—	30%
Which is the most abused schemes (w.r.t apparel exports)	DBK	DEEC	DBK	DEEC
Are exporters a party to corrupt practices?	Yes	65%	Yes	95%
Is corruption injurious to exports?	Yes	12%	Yes	15%
Does corruption cause loss to government?	Yes	60%	Yes	35%

Lack of Work Environment and Basic Amenities

Working conditions are pathetic. Most of the times, there are no chairs for visitors. Some officers kept their chairs having names of the branch/section inscribed on these, tied to the tables to avoid misplacement. Officers are not provided with basic tools for their work. Customs officers complained that books like Tariffs, Import-Export Policy, Manuals and Allied Acts are hardly supplied to them, especially when they are supposed to consult them and implement the instructions contained therein. The officers have to depend either upon the trade or their own pockets for the books to which they are otherwise entitled.

Incongruity in Theory and Practice

"There was no lack of commitment at the higher level in government towards exports, but the problem arises at the operational level", claim most of the exporters. Law-enforcement officers of middle and lower ranks are of the view that officers at higher echelons of bureaucracy are more of diplomats, preaching something while doing something different. One respondent went to the extent of saying that barring a few glaring exceptions, seniors follow Machiavelle's "The Prince" in letter and spirit and that is why they always remain near the hot seat of power.

Lack of Knowledge: A Source of Speed Money

They lack knowledge of both laws and procedures. Result is avoidable delays as well as corruption or speed money as it is called. Sometimes, the delay may be because of one agency but another may be blamed for it. For example, valid visa is required under MFA. It is allotted by AEPC, but its implementation is enforced by Customs and hence Customs is blamed for delay even if visa is not valid. All agencies working at the airport or seaport are mistaken as Customs only.

There is another significant corollary to the problem of lack of knowledge among exporters. It is observed during interviews with exporters, CHAs and representatives of law-enforcing agencies that sometimes CHAs or their employees take pecuniary advantage of a lack of knowledge among the exporters. They also take an advantage of greed among officers.

"Made in India" Tag

Swiss watches, German automobiles, Japanese electronics, French perfumes, Danish cheese, Italian designer, apparel and shoe, *Indian what...?* That's the big question. What category can India own that can add value to "Made in India" brands in the international market? India's rating in terms of image abroad, as brought out in the World Competitiveness Report, is 45th among 48 countries (FICCI, 1996). In order to achieve a quantum leap in exports, the question of how far a "Made in India" label can add value to a brand name is moot. In fact, only recently, the efforts to promote 'India' label have been initiated seriously by Ministry of Commerce and Trade, the result being the creation of the India Brand Equity Fund (IBEF). However, still much action in concerted way is desirable.

Problems Identified by Researcher

Export: A Service to Nation!

Exporters, wherever and whenever given a chance, whether in a meeting with the Finance or Commerce Minister or Ministers of State or meeting with representatives of government agencies or their own Chambers of Commerce, industry and associations, usually harp on one point that by exporting they were doing the country a favour since they were bringing foreign exchange into India. They blame the government and its agencies for all the failures, clamouring for more and more concessions. A big question therefore arises: Is exporting a service to nation, especially when government is throwing economic benefits to exporting trade? Answer to the question lies in another introspectionary question posed to one's own conscience: Will one export at par, i.e., at cost to cost, not to talk of export below cost, in absence of any subsidies/incentives – direct and indirect? If the reply is affirmative, then exporting is definitely a service to the nation.

It was revealed during fieldwork that the merchant exporters, and their CHAs in particular, spent a substantial time and efforts on as to how to milch the incentive schemes to the maximum extent. That the immediate short-term advantages constitute the top priority for the exporters and CHAs, and that "the money has no colour, it is neither black nor white, money is money and it has same buying power" revealed the discussions.

Inertia of East!

"Export or perish", "export is a national priority" and euphemisms like these are mainly for textbook consumption or at the most for bureaucracy. Service to nation, national interest, humanity, export promotion, etc., are all jargons having little relevance in business except for lip service. In general, if one looks at economic history of the world, for a businessman all over the world, profit and maximization of wealth is the first priority. Even, in word 'businessman', the word 'business' comes first and 'man' comes later. Indian exporters are no exception. They, too, are driven by the motive of profit/wealth maximization.

Exporting is not the priority of Indian businessmen till the time they continue is getting enough returns. They often lack self-motivation. One of the factors, restraining Indian entrepreneurs from going into exports whole-heartedly, is the theory of 'Karma', though with the passage of time, it is getting weaker. Dissatisfaction with the present is the key to worldly progress, according to the western capitalism, but they feel happy and satisfied with their lot, lacking a spirit of adventure and the killer instinct. Their attitude to developments in the field of exports, both within India and abroad, is of a defensive and reactive kind and not pro-active.

In fact, this behavioural pattern of Indian exporters is not limited only to exports, it is also affecting our sports and foreign policy. A corollary of this is that Indian strategic export marketing lacks identification of markets, product development and adaptation, market research and development.

Inferences

Following inferences can be drawn from this study:

— The exports from India have been a result mainly of the push factors like the lack of domestic market and direct and indirect incentives in the form of duty drawback, subsidies, tax saving, etc.

— Short-term perspective, viz., most of the exporters are concerned only with immediate gains, i.e., how to sell what they are producing.

— Their sixth sense, i.e., how to avoid domestic taxes and take advantage of various incentive schemes, often, is employed by them very effectively and efficiently. Their philosophy can be described in a nutshell in the form of proverbs such as "make hay while the sun shines" and "a bird in hand is better than two in the bush".

— The myth of service to the nation, i.e., the exporters are bothered about the nation and that they earn foreign exchange for the sake of country, stands exploded. On the contrary, they export because it is more profitable to them and they shall not do so if all their products are consumed in the domestic market.

The analysis of primary data leads to the conclusion that both the exporters as well as the officers, especially those involved in direct public dealings, have consensus on the following issues:

- There is corruption in all spheres of public life – political, government and private.
- Corruption is so rampant and exporters have become so used and insensitive to its existence that they no longer treat it as a problem. Rather amazingly, the officers feel that there is no reward for integrity and honesty.
- The higher one goes, more is the magnitude of corruption. There is an old saying: "*sowh sunar di ek lohar di*"(one stroke of blacksmith is equal to hundred strokes of goldsmith).
- Government policies are to share the blame for the inconsistencies, erratic behaviour of officers and an undue interference and concomitant corruption.
- Indian exporters have a bad name in international market because of their own deeds, acts of omission and commission, sub-standard quality of goods, lack of credibility etc.
- Incentives were insufficient and discriminatory. These are the breeding grounds for corruption.
- Full stop to ad hocism and adoption of long-term consistent government policies.

Even, the government admits that its policies have to share the blame for the failure to achieve targets and growth envisaged by itself.

The classification of problems, according to domestic or foreign origin, helps one in understanding the grey areas where remedial measures can be taken at the national level. Indian exporters have become accustomed to red tapism and a cumbersome system of paper work and they are more concerned about finances, administration of quota and archaic labour laws. Rather than all the time crying over the problems emanating from other countries, it is better if we set the things right at our own home first.

Another conclusion drawn from the study is that a perceptible difference exists between the exporters and the officers with respect to the identification of problems in exports. Both the views have to be weighed before taking any major policy decision on exports. It also underlines the need to improve communication between the two major players in the game of exports. Thus, for immediate best results, atleast the administration of quota and labour laws can be suitably amended with ease provided there is a political will.

Presently, while there are watchdog and grievances committees for the trade but no committees for the officers where they could explain their problems. There should be a similar body of staff too. Further, in such meetings of the field staff, there is a dire need for an 'ice-breaker' so that officers could express their views without any reservations. It must also be made obvious that action had been and would be taken on their grievances to build confidence in them.

There is also an urgent need for a forum where representatives of enforcement agencies, actually facing the realities in the field, and representatives of the exporting community should sit together to sort out the problems. In the present scenario, policy makers, while sitting in ivory towers, interact with the trade calling explanations of the field officers. While they may be visiting fields to interact with the officers, interaction is only one way, i.e., top to bottom. Secondly, a subordinate can hardly open up before the visitors in presence of seniors. Motto followed during such meetings is "boss is always right". It is the feeling of the researcher that ice can be broken during informal dinners where officers of the same rank are present.

Lastly, most of the officers were either not bothered about export promotion or they were passing time and paying a lip service only. Reasons for the apathy seemed to be insensitivity to the nation, lack of motivation and most important, an acute desire for 'prize' postings only and for that matter interference from the higher levels. Situation is, in fact, grave, needing immediate attention. Alas! People hardly have the dedication and time. Definitely, the distracters are more.

Recommendations

Just as it takes two to clap, efforts are required both at the levels of government as well as the trade, in order to give the much-needed impetus to exports. Also, both need to introspect into their respective domains. First and foremost suggestion, both for government and trade, is to perform SWOT analysis. Next, a corollary to above suggestion is to adopt pro-active approach, instead of catering to the demands and simultaneously take corrective measures to convert weaknesses in strength. And, this exercise should go on perpetually irrespective of the fact as to whether the exports are doing well in foreign markets or not. This can be done by collective efforts at the level of associations of manufacturers and exporters. There should be a permanent, transparent and aggressive body of exporters with a positive attitude, instead of fault-finding, preferably a non-government organization (NGO), in addition to the Export Promotion Councils, to push exports, for lobbying, advising and also fighting, if need be, against the anti-dumping and other barriers abroad.

Recommendations can be, for the sake of convenience put into following two broad domain categories:

- *Manufacturing and export domain:* Raw materials; Manufacturing and ancillary fields like packaging; marketing; moral obligation to government and the nation; and
- *Government domain:* Infrastructure; trade policies, including steps and incentives to boost exports, especially the cotton knitwear; change in mental make up of public servants, simplification of procedures and transparency; and labour laws.

Suggestions for Exporters

Remember an old saying, "God helps those who help themselves". The moral is very simple and unambiguous: let the exporters help themselves, letting the government in turn help them and the country, in the process in boosting exports.

Go Green: All efforts should be made not to violate international ecological standards.

Increase the Value Addition: Value can be added to products in two ways: (a) by improving the appearance of the product and its packaging i.e. cosmetic effect, and (b) by making peculiar and attractive designs, ethnic designs depending upon the nature of the export product. Or, by catering to niche markets or by building brand image. Packaging is the most neglected aspect of an export item.

Quick Delivery, strictly according to schedule. It takes almost 40 to 60 days for the garments to reach a retail outlet in Europe from India in contrast to 25-30 days from Hongkong and Singapore. Indian exporters have been alleged to making 'false' promises regarding delivery of goods, leading to a lack of credibility and a negative image (Koshy, 1995).

Modernize the Industry: A general tendency, observed among the manufacturer exporters during interviews, is that till the time their products are selling, they remain satisfied with the age-old machinery and old worn-out designs. They lack the urge to modernize, improve and improvize. Yes, trade policies need to be amended too in this regard but there should also be a willingness on the part of manufacturers.

Diversify Product Base: Indian exports are dominated by raw materials and low value-addition item. Of course, we now excel in export of software services. But, there should be always continuous search for new, high value-added goods and services.

Strengthen Marketing: Marketing tie ups in a short run may assist us in gaining access to foreign markets though not necessarily be of much help in establishing our brand names and "Made in India" label. The distribution channels of leading brand names can also be utilized. Strategy is very simple: come what may, be honest and supply quality goods at competitive prices on scheduled time. However, it takes time to establish an image. Secondly, create demand for our products. Our marketing being quite weak, we have become followers and produce only what buyers tell us to manufacture. Hence, we remain at their mercy, kowtowing to their price lines.

Develop a Positive Attitude, Making the Best of What is Available: Let every exporter do an introspection of what one is doing for oneself and the nation vis-à-vis government efforts for export promotion. No doubt, there is both a need and scope for further improvement in government's action. Yet, the fact remains that for a successful working of any scheme, including that of export promotion, some essential ingredients are a must, e.g., understanding of *raison d'être* of the scheme, mutual trust between government and its agencies on one side and the trade on the other and fulfilment of the faith put in by the government in exporters. Let there be no betrayal of the confidence and genuine expectation of the government, lest all incentive schemes including the genuine ones are dubbed as tax avoidance schemes and a source of corruption.

Suggestions for the Government

Government is the fountain of authority and representative of the people at the international forums. For any sort of woes that exporters confront within and without India, they look towards this authority for the solution of their problems and for guidance. Even, in the capitalist economies, a minimum level of government interference to protect domestic industry against invaders, and more so to protect national interests at the international level, is desirable and most often sought after. Accordingly, the suggestions having policy implications call for action at two levels, viz.,

— national level – industrial and economic policies, incentive schemes, and

— international level – trade policies.

However, the boundaries between the domestic and international domains are hazy and overlapping, especially with an increasing globalization and opening up of the national boundaries for commerce where domestic policies of one country become a concern for another because of their impact on international business.

Provide Export Credit at Concessional Rates

Making the availability of working capital to purchase raw material in advance extremely critical. Banks give advances first to those they find creditworthy, the yardstick for that being a consistently good performance shown by the unit last year or for whom somebody can stand surety. Secondly, the interest rates on such finances though reduced, are still considered to be on the higher side as compared to the international level. Export credit should be at a rate closer to the LIBOR rate so that competitiveness of the country's export increases.

Improve the Infrastructural Facilities

Infrastructural facilities like ports, power, roads and railways must be upgraded on priority. There is an urgent need to develop express ways and railways arterial linkages with major and minor ports having special handling facilities and more container hubs. One option is to privatize these facilities on build and operate basis that the government is already going ahead with.

Reduce the Cost of Production and Exports

The cost of production for exports has to be brought down to the global level. Setting up export zones can do this. Government has taken some steps in this direction. Another option is of setting up of global size factories or by upgrading existing facilities. Yet, another step may be to remove SSI restrictions so far exports are concerned. This will help manufacturers and exporters to become globally competitive. Another step in this direction on which the government has already taken an initiative is the simplification of export procedures and believing the exporters and the officers alike, atleast once and then adopting zero tolerance to the abuse of incentives as well as corruption. The employer should be given freedom to retrench 2 per cent of the workforce per annum, may be with the provision of giving employment to double the number of workers.

Governments both at Centre and in states should establish research institutes and encourage R&D in private sector, dedicated exclusively to the development of eco-friendly non-carcinogenic high value-added products and services. Interface between research and application of products and services is utmost necessary. More trade fairs and exhibitions for the foreign buyers should be organized.

Plans for the Future

Create a specialized cell consisting of professional negotiators: There is an urgent need that India should prepare and plan for future talks and other international negotiations as a caution against getting caught unaware of the decisions already taken by various world forums. Negotiation briefs should be based on well-researched substantive facts and negotiators should be well-versed. There should be a proper coordination between exporters and government representatives, whose point of view must be grasped before going in for negotiations. Most of the time, Indian representatives, who are invariably bureaucrats with heavy clouts and are least concerned with negotiations, are found to be indecisive and lacking in knowledge, resulting into defensiveness on the part of India. Indian embassies abroad should acquire a more commercial orientation. Right now, the image of Indian embassies abroad is that of the protocol offices catering to the needs of visiting politicians and bureaucrats, staffed by either hi-fi or disgruntled appointees and occupying the offices either as a reward or a punishment.

Tap new markets: We should not only consolidate our share in the existing export markets but also tap new markets. For example, economies of Eastern Europe are in transition rendering our entry easy in these markets. Our major competitors in these markets are other developing countries. In identified new markets, therefore, India must set up professionally-run trade promotion offices, may be with the assistance of exporters.

Keep abreast of the commercial developments both national and international: The government needs to be consistently vigilant of international commercial, economic and political developments, for the reason that in the prevailing world scenario, the dividing lines among commercial, economical, political and military spheres are thin and impervious. Further, the government should, keeping in view changing scenario, modify its export thrust and related strategies well in time and also appraise the manufacturers and exporters at large.

Revitalize 'Made in India' Label with Zeal

'India Brand Equity Fund', though a right step in right direction, has remained at low ebb for want of commitment. Operationalization of the fund with zeal at full throttle is the key to image building of "Made in India" label, as India's image abroad is very poor. The government should further create a fund for market development and for fighting anti-dumping cases abroad headed by apolitical professionals. No doubt, efforts are also required at the level of exporters but then government backing not only motivates the exporters but also strengthens their initiatives in this direction.

Enthuse Commitment

The strongest political will, deepest political commitment and earnest administrative and systematic support are *sine qua non* for quick export growth. Government's role has to be that of a problem-solver and a trade-facilitator.

State governments too have an equally responsible role to play. So far, state governments have not been paying adequate attention to promoting exports as compared to attracting foreign investment. One reason for this could be that states do not seem to have any tangible stake in export promotion. Hence, a share in the foreign exchange could be given to respective states to encourage their participation in export promotion. There is an urgent need to evolve an export policy at state level to remove inter-state barriers and levies like octroi on export items. These can go a long way in providing infrastructural support and removing bottlenecks.

Both, Union and State governments should therefore take immediate steps to inculcate an export culture at all levels of the administration in State and Central Govt. Need is to take steps to motivate the officers especially in the field formations to encourage exports. The Government, in its earnest did introduce schemes like reward to officers and informers; appreciation certificates and awards to best performing officers. However, the implementation of such schemes in practice acts as a demotivating factor, both in the short as well as long run. Officers who are non-performers, by choice or otherwise in performance of official duties, but are very efficient in public relations, sycophancy and "Protocol" duties, enjoy cushy & remunerative postings as well as rewards *("Protocol" in its present incarnation in the context of Indian bureaucracy has assumed the status of institutionalised corruption)*.

The system needs revitalisation. The *first* and foremost task should be to evolve a system of two-way communication in the bureaucratic set up. *Secondly*, the system should be made transparent, especially with reference to transfer & posting policies and reward schemes, to revive the faith in the system. Utmost care should be taken to ensure that the heads of various departments are persons of high integrity, intelligence and conscience. *Finally*, the system of "Protocol" must be demolished, paving the way for a healthy and sustainable bureaucracy, a prerequisite for an effective implementation of otherwise meticulously framed policies.

In a nutshell the approach of the government as well as that of exporters should be proactive instead of reactive.

- While problems of the domestic origin *can be tackled* at the levels of government and exporters, individually and together, the problems of foreign origin are more *difficult to resolve* because of their exogenous origin and inexplicit nature. Best that can be done is to study these, avoid the known barriers and counter them in the world forums if possible. The role of the Government has been very responsive and laudable especially with reference to grievances of the exporters.
- Government policies, rules and regulations in themselves do hamper the genuine export trade for want of practical solutions:

— Government has double standards of liberalization – one for the trade and another for field formations.

— Communication within the government machinery is one way and there is in fact a deliberate discouragement to the flow of information in the opposite direction.

— Supply of books is both negligible as well as late and clarifications to field formations are often belated as a rule.

— There is corruption and encouragement to sycophancy at high places where it matters.

— Bureaucratic set-up needs revitalization for its sustenance and an effective implementation of dexterously framed policies.

- Corruption is there, working as a double-edged sword. It is both a hurdle and a facilitator. It hits genuine exporters, at the same time facilitating not so genuine exporters. It assists unscrupulous exporters in availing of various incentives without which they would have never exported. An amazing revelation which came out during the course of interaction with exporters and CHAs was that they are least concerned about corruption which they find quite handy to manipulate for their own gains. But, they were particularly wary of dishonest officers who sometimes do not clear an improper piece of work even after having been offered and actually provided with bribes. They are even more skeptical of officers of integrity who would not perform any wrongful activity knowingly. An officer who would do any work, right or wrong, for a paltry sum is called 'Raja'. On the other side, the representatives of law-enforcing agencies asked, "what is the premium on honesty?" Bureaucrats only, in fact, have raised the issue of corruption in public life and particularly in bureaucracy. Researcher feels that in any case of corruption and bribery, there are two sides – a giver and an acceptor – and if either side takes a vow not to be a party to it, atleast 50 per cent the problem shall be 'reduced'.

While India has all the ingredients and potential to face the challenge, the need on the part of government and exporters is for the shedding of complacency on the one hand and adoption of dedication and perseverance, coupled with dexterity, on the other, placing all the ingredients at right place, at right time and strengthening of the commercial intelligence.

References

AEPC, 1995, *Hand Book of Export Statistics*, 1992-93, 1993-94 and 1994-95, New Delhi, AEPC.

— 1996, *Hand Book of Export Statistics*, 1993-94, 1994-95 and 1995-96, New Delhi, AEPC.

— 1997, *Hand Book of Export Statistics*, 1994-95, 1995-96 and 1996-97, New Delhi, AEPC.

— 1998, *Hand Book of Export Statistics*, 1995-96, 1996-97 and 1997-98, New Delhi, AEPC.

— 1999, *Hand Book of Export Statistics*, 1996-97,1997-98 and 1998-99, New Delhi, AEPC.

Aiyar, Swaminathan and S. Anklesaria. 1999. 'India Fails as a Manufacturer-Exporter', *The Economic Times*, June 9th.

All India Garment Exporters Common Cause Guild (AIGECC Guild), 2000, 'Sawal 6 Billion Dollars Ka', *The Economic Times*, October 20th.

Bhatacharyya, B. and A.K Sengupta. 1996. *Exporters Handbook: Strategic Information and intelligence*, IIFT.

'CAG Flays Misuse Of VABAL Scheme – Pulls Up Customs', DGFT For Rs. 3,532-cr Revenue Loss, 1999, *ELT* Vol.114(1999) A44-A46 (Source: *Business Line*, New Delhi, dated 1-11-99).

'Corrupt Nations', 1999, *Excise Law Times* ELT Vol. 114 (1999) A-42 & A-43) (Source: *Financial Express*, Mumbai, dated 29.10.99).

Customs and Central Excise, 1998, *Citizen's Charter*, New Delhi, Directorate of Publicity and Public Relations.

Drucker, Peter F. 1992. *Managing For The Future: The1990s and Beyond*, Oxford, Butterworth-Heinemann Limited.

'Exporter's Cramp?', 1996, *The Economic Times*, October 10th.

500 Corporate Giants to be Harnessed in Export Drive (MITI – type approach to evolve specific policy initiatives',1998, *The Economic Times*, April 9th.

Gogoi, Mukul Chandra. 1999. 'Port Whines and Hangovers', *The Economic Times*, October the 1st.

'Government agencies are creating hurdles for exporters', 1998, *The Indian Express* (BUSINESS Inc.), April 27th.

Gupta, Rajeev, 1999, 'Export Promotion Scheme Favours Unscrupulous Exporters-Investigative Revelations', *ELT*, Vol. 112 (1999), A134-A139.

Koshy, Darlie O., 1995: 'Export Marketing of Apparel to US, EU & Japan (Effective)', *Accelerating Exports in 1990s: Challenges and Vita Steps – A Brief Review* (Background Paper), FICCI.

Malhotra, B.L. 1999. 'Sundar Committee's "ATTI SUNDAR" Report', *Impex Times*, June 25th, Vol. XVI, No. 10, pp. 23-25.

Panigrahi, S.N., 1999b, 'Procedural Simplification: Only An Eyewash', *ELT, Vol. 113 (1999) Part-I October.*

Vittal, N., 1999a, 'When the law is a [failed] scarecrow', *The Economic Times,* August 5th.

— 1999b, 'Why is Indian Business Interested in Ethics?', *The Economic Times*, August 19th.

— 1999c, 'The Corruption Perception Index', 1999, *The Economic Times*, November 19th.

— 1999d, 'The Supply Side of Corruption', *The Economic Times*, December 9th.

— 2000, '2nd Generation Reforms: A New Approach', *The Economic Times*, January 6th.

16

Corruption in Governance: Is There a Way Out?

RAJESH GILL

India is the largest democracy on earth, celebrating its vows to ensure equality of opportunity and distributive justice to its people, irrespective of their caste, class, ethnicity or income. While the country has come a long way, paving its way with dignity out of the colonized past, abolishing many of the social evils by adopting world's most modern and secular constitution, it finds itself today among the most corrupt countries of the world. While corruption has proved to be the worst challenge to a growth-oriented economy, a competitive society and a secular polity, it has poses today the greatest threat to the systems of governance in the country, especially when efforts are on to decentralize and democratize the governance. In recent past, an enormous deal of concern has been shown for 'governance', mainly due to the problems of non-performance along with an erosion of people's faith in the systems of governance, especially in countries like India undergoing tremendous social and politico-economic turmoil. Alternatively, the concept of 'good governance' has been generally floated in various circles, both government and academic, as an ideal system ensuring transparency, accountability and people's active participation.

This paper brings out the interface between the institutions of power, bureaucracy characterizing the modern Indian society on the one hand, and corruption, on the other, besides identifying the processes through which this nexus has not only been accepted by the people at large, but has been institutionalized too. The main argument put forth is that the transformation of present system of governance into good governance is not an easy one, given the vested interests at stake. On the contrary, such a transformation goes against the interests of people who thrive upon the present system of governance. Is credibility of governance a simple issue to be tackled merely by a conceptual substitution of 'governance' by 'good governance'? This paper takes up this question and argues that transforming the system from governance to good governance is a job easier said than done. In this scenario, then, it is pertinent to pause and explore: is the problem incurable or is still a solution round the corner?

Most of the societies have been governed – initially through more traditional, personalized and informal modes, and now in the most formalized and modern modes of governance. This transformation has been conceptualized by Max Weber as a process of 'rationalization' or 'bureaucratization' which is marked by the organizational structures that are most rational, impersonal, formal and hierarchical. Weberian conceptualization comes quite handy, especially in understanding the varied manifestations of bureaucratized governance, which have emerged in the developing countries like India. That such a system of governance has no human face, little sensitivity or elasticity, was well recognized by Weber himself. What is most interesting for social scientists however is a sharp deviation of bureaucratic governance among developing countries, from the Weberian ideal type. Drawing its strength mainly from hierarchy, the system attaches a specific kind of power with each level of hierarchy, right from the lowest to the highest, making the bureaucratic and power structures synonymous. Right from the days of colonial rule, India has tasted such a bureaucratic system of governance at every level – national, regional and local; rural and urban; and so on.

Governance in India has mainly been bureaucratic in nature – something the nation has continued even after the exit of the colonizers and acquisition of the hard-earned self-rule/governance. The very term 'governance' divides citizens broadly into two categories – those who *govern* and others *governed*. Of course, these two are not always independent and exhaustive categories, but in specific contexts, yes, they are! For instance, a senior professor feels absolutely weak (just like any other poor illiterate citizen) while standing in a never ending queue, to get his licence renewed, or pay his electricity bills. Actually, the very fact that you are standing in a queue indicates your status in the system of governance. It is always the person on the other side of the window who holds primacy. Why? The simple answer is – he holds POWER! In simple terms, this would mean that those who are participants in the system of governance (at whatever level), are more powerful than those governed in a given context. Of course, the situation would change depending upon the situation. The same person who is on one side at one point of time, may be at the other end at another point of time. It is exactly this relativity and contextuality in the acquisition of power that often leads to an negotiated exchange of power between the wielders, i.e., you please me and I please you and the nexus goes on. Most of the relationships today are based upon this reciprocity of appeasement rather than any emotional or altruistic exchange between the individuals. It is the pragmatism of the relationship that decides how long the relationship is going to end and how strong it is going to be. Hence, 'power' happens to be the most pertinent ingredient of governance.

Governance is thus characterized by the structures of power attached with public office, irrespective of whether occupied by elected or appointed incumbents. Of late, our system has made it almost mandatory that this public office can be grossly misused by the incumbents for their own personal gains. This misuse of public office is conceptually defined, in broad sense, as 'corruption'. Actually, a person who possesses power as a result of his official position, but does not 'misuse' it, is considered to be incapable, inexperienced and weak, not deserving to be in that position. Hence, most of the times, almost every new entrant undergoing the process of professional socialization internalizes the different ways to misuse public office and make his presence felt in an otherwise impersonalized and insensitive system of governance. So much so that gradually it becomes rather impossible to distinguish between what is corruption and what is not; between who is corrupt and who is not. In fact, a corrupt individual being most cautious, methodical and far-sighted often escapes the problems confronted by an honest, committed and hard working individual, who in his innocently honest functioning, often antagonizes people around him – both in the office as well as outside.

Such a bureaucratized and centralized system of governance, suffering from a heightened level of corruption, has recently come under the focus of planners, academics and seminarians. They are now talking not merely of governance but 'good governance', which is people-friendly, participatory and sensitive to human needs. Policies at the national, regional and even grassroots levels have been modified, amendments enacted and implemented, with the objective of decentralizing the process of governance, making it people-friendly and participatory. Here, I see a sharp contradiction between the existential reality and the vision that is being projected by us collectively as academics, planners, policy makers and so on.

The existing system of governance, whether it is the police, panchayat, municipal corporation or any other body, is highly bureaucratic, hierarchical, with strong strings of power attached at every stage, often put to misuse by incumbents for their own personal gains. Making it transparent, participatory and people-friendly, therefore, threatens this power structure. Such a transparency, decentralized power structure and system of accountability, ultimately making way for the devolution of power to the grassroots, simply would rob the present incumbents off the powers they wield owing to their official positions. The most common, rather the only, reason why young men and women are striving hard to join the ranks of those 'governing', even after obtaining professional degrees, is POWER, and not an altruistic instinct to serve the country. Once this goal is achieved, one starts craving for the luxuries (perks) attached with it, e.g., an official car with a red light atop (which must blinker even if not required); a cook, a driver, a gardener, and so on. All this becomes feasible only because all these people receive their salary from the government exchequer while the fruits of their labour are enjoyed by people at home. This is POWER. As all this goes on, the power holders no longer remain in the habit of spending out of their own pockets even to meet their personal/domestic expenses. Hence, it becomes a double gain which has proved to be disastrous for the government exchequer. Unfortunately, when it comes down to economic recession and financial crisis, benefits to the poor are immediately withdrawn because they have no voice. The real culprits however manage to save their skin. The latest example of this is the pressure being put upon the CVC, India, to first seek permission from the concerned department before placing any charge of corruption against senior officers in bureaucracy. Various professional bodies have successfully managed to insulate themselves from the threats of anti-corruption drives of the state by putting pressure at appropriate places.

The most blatant example of nexus between governance, power and corruption is found in Indian Police Services today. Although these services have, for a long time, since the British rule, been known for this nexus, some metropolitan cities enjoyed an envious position of an extremely efficient police force. The case of Mumbai may be taken here. In a recent article, written by a former police commissioner, it is brought out how corruption was confined to the junior ranks in Mumbai's police till as late as twenty to thirty years ago, while their supervisory staff ensured justice for the common citizens (Ribeiro, 2003). By the end of the last decade of the century, however, a growing number of officers shifted their focus from serving the people to serving their own interests. The author further argues that corruption has thus ceased to be need-based and has become greed-based today, engulfing the whole police force right from top to bottom. With the result that nobody can point a finger at any body else. These views get further substantiated in the light of the recent involvement of top brass police officials in the infamous stamp scam case again in Mumbai. Actually, a stage has come where social networking with the people who matter at the top has assumed an ultimate significance irrespective of whether they are thieves, frauds, or pimps, because you can get plum postings through such connections too. And, very often, such scandalized cases, which unfortunately get into the police net, no longer dampen the spirits of others involved in similar transactions because "people forget these cases as soon as they perceive them".

Yes! There have been many positive strides too in the recent past to make the system of governance in India more participatory, transparent and people-friendly. We have gradually moved into a system of self-governance at national, regional and local levels, involving people and

NGOs as active participants. But, this has mainly remained in theory. Various policy documents on urban poor and their rehabilitation, empowerment of women and other marginalized sections have provided sufficient space to the NGOs and people in general. But experience has shown that a meaningful participation, both by the people as well as the NGOs, is being greatly jeopardized by the unwillingness of those already in government machinery, to share the spaces. In one of the recently conducted studies on Delhi's resettlement colonies, it was found that the NGOs working in some of these colonies have been forced to withdraw mainly due to the non-cooperative attitude of the municipal body. What we call devolution of power in theory is being interpreted by those already in power as a threat to their power and position.

We have numerous examples where people who are supposed to govern at grassroots level fail to exercise the power they are entitled to, because of the corrupt social system. For example, in a large number of cases, the dalit women, who have been elected representatives in panchayats as members or sarpanchas, have been denied their due share in power by sheer display of patriarchy and caste dominance. In a number of cases, women sarpanchas of low castes have been removed from their seats by organizing no-confidence motions against them by the male members of the panchayats. In many cases, the women representatives, who undertook the bold agenda, invited the wrath of the village men and were stripped and made to walk in the village or even murdered. Such cases occur mainly because the present wielders of power feel threatened by the new system of governance that ensures decentralization of power, democratization and transparency – in short, good governance. Merely constitutional amendments or legislative measures will not do wonders.

Is it Possible to Get Rid of Corruption?

Since the system of governance over the years has been bureaucratized to new heights, with strings of power attached all over, from top to bottom, there is little wonder that corruption stands institutionalized today, getting legitimized by not only those in power but even the public at large. To use Durkheimian terminology, it has become a social fact, both external to the individual and exercising constraint upon him. Once it has attained an independent existence, it is actually now a matter of great concern as to whether it is possible to break the nexus between governance, power and corruption. I am an optimist. Whatever the social reality may be, whatever the magnitude of corruption may be, still I have yet to come across people who would say "corruption is very good and must go on". My hope lies in this. The need is to grab this moment before it is too late and do something tangible even if it hurts some people who matter. First, the nexus between governance and power must be smashed. Power here is two-fold. One, a superior has the power over his/her subordinate since he/she can spoil the ACR and ruin his career; or he can give him a bad posting. The other is power over the general public. Both cause corruption. The subordinates are perpetually busy trying to please their bosses, spending more time on this exercise than on their jobs. The public on the other hand is forced to grease the palms of officials to get even the routine work done.

One major source of corruption in our society is the process of official appointments and postings by the politicians or the superiors, who often use this power to please their dear ones, and set the others right. One way to curb corruption would be to remove the power of appointments and postings from the hands of politicians and entrust it to an independent body of men and women. In fact, officers in all bureaucratic services spend greater money, time and energy in managing plum and glamorous postings than performing their official duties. Politicians, on the other hand, help them in this process, making the whole system highly politicized and impotent. One can get rid of this problem but only by making the whole system of transfers and appointments absolutely transparent. But, the moment this is done, politicians and senior bureaucrats shall lose their power over others. And most interestingly, they are the decision-makers, policy framers and so on. Can we expect them to act with such an altruism? The point is that it is very simple to raise the slogan of transparency in governance, but how hard it hits the existing system, must not be overlooked.

Indian bureaucracy of late has developed into a top heavy system, mainly due to successful lobbies of senior ranking officers for greater number of vacancies. This has been accompanied by an increasing magnitude of corruption among the higher ranks, eliminating all moral or legal checks on their subordinates as far as corruption is concerned. Boss' insatiable greed has to be met by his subordinates who now fearlessly indulge into money-making, because it is a joint venture. The heavy top of bureaucracy thus has a double cost – exorbitant economic burden on the state exchequer; and the complete institutionalization of corruption in official circles, where the success of an officer is measured through the postings he has enjoyed. In the present state of financial crisis, where government has been trying ruthlessly to get rid of overstaffing at lower levels, can the state afford a bureaucracy with such a heavy top? Some bold steps have to be taken in this direction.

Corruption has done the greatest harm to the common man, in that it has produced a fear psychosis among him. A common man or woman thinks hundred times before approaching a sarpanch, a municipal councillor, a police official or a Deputy Commissioner for redress of a problem. Without faith of the people, how can the system of governance be people-friendly? For this, the citizens must be encouraged to use the Right to Information Act and pursue the cases of corruption at the legal front without fear. Unless the public is sensitized against corruption and empowered to protest against it formally, the fear which has vanished among the corrupt incumbents in systems of governance cannot be restored. Finally, our children must be taught the distinction between what is corruption and what is not, with the same earnestness (or even more), as the lessons on science or mathematics. In fact, the small children receive the very first lessons on corruption in school when they get to know the networking between teachers and parents of some children, when some children are promoted at the cost of others because their parents matter for the school, and when a child is selected in the cricket team of the school because his father got the coach his job. We must stop this and punish those who indulge into such a poisoning of the next generation.

Society must acknowledge its role in having let loose the strings of corruption, by not only tolerating it, but also hailing it as the rule of the day. People have lost trust in governments and their bodies. The enthusiasm among the electorate to exercise their right to vote is fading, thanks to the electoral politics and the nuisance attached to it. Under such circumstances, how can we expect to evolve a system of governance, which is people-friendly, democratic, decentralized and transparent. We cannot just go on waiting for the state or the politicians or the elders or the younger generations to put an end to corruption. Each one of us will have to take it on to ourselves in whatever capacity we are. Let us not be opportunists in that we close our eyes to any act of corruption when it suits us while we make such a hue and cry when it suits somebody else. These are hard decisions not only for the people at the top, but equally for the common people like you and me. The functionality of corruption has started weighing heavy on our minds, taking away our earnestness to erase it from the society. Let us give up this opportunistic attitude and make our society sustainable for our next generations, so that they cannot only breathe in a clean physical environment, but a non-corrupt social environment too. Do we have the courage and will to do that?

References

Alatas, Syed Hussein. 1999. *Corruption and the Destiny of Asia,* Malasia, Simon and Schuster Asia Pvt. Ltd.

Gill, S.S. 1998. *The Pathology of Corruption.* New Delhi, Harper Collins Publication.

Noorani, A.G. 2003. 'Stop Thief'. *Hindustan Times*, November 4, p.8.

Ribeiro, Julio 2003. 'Cops and Robbers'. *The Indian Express*, November 12, p.8.

Wertheim, W.F. 1965. 'Sociological Aspects of Corruption in South-east Asia', in his *East-West Parallels*, Van Hoeve, The Hague.

17

Dwarfed State, Extended Market and Corrupt Society

RAJESH GILL

The interface between state, market and society in contemporary context can only be understood within the domain of globalization. The relationship, which was already a complex one, has gone even more intricate, with an absence of homogenization as predicted by development theorists. Instead, experiences of different societies have varied in terms of the changed interface between state and global market system; privatization, structural adjustment programmes, on the one hand; and society, especially family, gender, etc., and state and civil society, on the other. Experiences of the developed nations hardly resemble those of the less developed. The problem is primarily of theorizing and conceptualizing these processes, which though varied at micro level, of course, possess certain common thread pointing out parallels between them.

One thing is for certain; the immense worth of the powerful materialist interpretation of Marx, or functional analysis of Parsons notwithstanding, these seem to be less and less plausible today in view of the historical events that have shaped the recent history across the globe. What of course is still very relevant even today's context of market is Marx's idea of 'fetishism of commodities'. Under capitalism, Marx argued, the production of goods is determined not by their intrinsic usefulness, but by the price they can command on the market – their 'exchange value'. For Marx, the result of capitalist production is the loss by human beings of control over their own lives – must 'obey' the 'laws' of the market, which confronts them as objective, impersonal forces even though they are no more than the outcome of the activities of ordinary people. Expanding upon this idea, Lukacs uses the term 'reification' referring to the way in which imaginary entities, or abstract concepts, are treated as if they were real things. He argued, "a relation between people takes on the character of a thing and thus acquires a 'phantom-objectivity', an autonomy that seems so strictly rational and all embracing as to conceal every trace of its fundamental nature: the relation between people" (Lukacs, 1971:83). The consequence of all this is a relentless pressure towards the establishment of an all-pervading cultural system which is inauthentic in that it imposes on people ways of living which are a denial and distortion of genuine human needs. What results is the 'maimed consciousness', a by-product of mass culture produced thus in modern capitalism, according to the Frankfurt School.

This relegation of the individual got sufficient attention by Weber too, who argued that in the modern state, bureaucracy almost became a prison for the human spirit. This happened mainly due to the meaninglessness of social life driven by the forces of rationality, and the rigorous discipline and control by bureaucracy. Weber's ideas found a continuity in Frankfurt theorists who observed the ways in which the mass culture of industrialized societies, produced by the culture industry and spread by the mass media, had fundamentally ideological effects, and they created a cultural environment in which spurious needs were inculcated in people so that they would keep busy in buying commodities and fantasies, keeping them divorced from any critical thinking. The same phenomenon finds an interesting expression in Simmel's writings when he proposed the alienated character of all cultural production, culminating into an inevitable 'tragedy of culture'. All cultural objects, which were created by man for his own self, ultimately assume an independent existence, appear objective and immutable, and dominate their creators. An unprecedented array of cultural products is available in such 'rich and overburdened cultures', yet our contact with most of them is superficial.

In a very interesting observation, "there emerges the typical condition of modern humanity, the feeling of being surrounded by an immense number of cultural elements, which are not meaningless, but not profoundly meaningful to the individual either, elements which have a certain crushing quality as a mass, because an individual cannot inwardly assimilate every individual thing, but cannot simply reject it either, since it belongs potentially, as it were, to the sphere of his or her cultural development (Frisby and Featherstone, 1997:73).

There have been interesting shifts in the way social scientists have dealt with the phenomenon of globalization, particularly from the perspective of its implications on state and society. The understanding of state, market and society from the perspective of positivism was based upon the form of knowledge, which characterized capitalist culture – a form of knowledge, which not only infused the natural and the social sciences but also lay at the very root of capitalist civilization. On the contrary, later interpretations of society, market and state were based on the idea that no final, objective knowledge of society as a totality was possible. What the theorist could grasp was only a snapshot or a fleeting glimpse of some social phenomenon, which is also seen to have universal significance (Frisby, 1981). In rejecting the notion of one objective, all encompassing account of social change, the idea of historical materialism as a 'grand narrative' was also rejected by the Frankfurt School (Sharrock, Hughes and Martin, 2003). According to them, positivism and empirical science had led to the surrendering of the world to the blind force of rationalization. The aim of Critical Theory was the liberation of humanity from the condition of alienation. Proponents of this theory rejected both the disinterested pursuit of knowledge for its own sake, as well as the 'scientific' analysis of society, calling for ethical and political objectives. This was to be achieved by uncovering the alienated untruth of modern culture.

The emerging perspective on knowledge thus believed that the meaning of objects was not self-evident but has to be understood through the real-life materialistic activities of human beings. Further, the experiences of individuals as members of society are inevitably shaded by concepts and thoughts, which are given to us by the particular historical context in which we live. It follows therefore that people in different cultures, and in different historical periods, will see the world in different, rather incompatible ways and the external reality is in fact the product of human social activity. In the words of Horkheimer, there was no underlying pattern to history, and rejected the idea that the whole of human life could be explained by any one theory (Jay, 1973).

These developments in theoretical standpoints were emerging mainly because societies, states and markets had changed tremendously since Marx's times. The nature of capitalism was altogether different. 'Monopoly capitalism' had emerged in which there was an increasing concentration of capital in ever larger, but fewer, companies which had started dominating the whole society. It was certain that the age of individualistic free market capitalism, with many small firms belonging to individual capitalists and competing with each other in the market, was gone. This was also bound to make society different in that other institutional activities also became more and more specialized, less and less individualized, with an individual possessing only a fractional knowledge of the system. All this was also to be accompanied by the changed role of the state, which though looked shrunken at the national level, appeared to be enlarged in the context of globally recognized bodies, with a direct and indirect access to countries, particularly the less competent in the global power structure.

The disillusionment shown by scholars like Weber, Simmel, and particularly the Frankfurt School, with capitalist, mechanized and robotic society, where the individual had been reduced merely to a calculative being, using his instrumental rationality, pointed to the very pertinent notion of the slavery of human soul and production of a 'culture industry'. The creation of films, novels, plays etc., devoid of any sensitive creativity, as mere products, actually leads to the conception of the media as part of the 'culture industry'. Although the mass media, like positivist science, represented its portrayals of reality as neutral and objective rather than as expressions of ideology, this was precisely their power to convey ideology in the guise of freedom from ideology. The emergence of culture industry in capitalist society made it possible to understand the processes of capitalist rationalization, pseudo-individualism, standardization and commodification.

It is most interesting that while the individual in capitalist society was supposed to be an enlightened being, free as a consumer, to make his own choices economically, politically and socially, but the fact of the matter is that individual's freedom is largely illusory, a illusion projected and perpetuated through popular culture. Although making choices by the individual is treated as individualization, yet in reality, this is pseudo-individualization, where individuals are not free and autonomous but are extensively manipulated by the culture industry.

Despite the post-modernist emphasis upon the deconstructed, decentred reality, with a futility of grand narratives, objective and universal reality, divorced from the subjective mind situated at a particular space and time, the fact cannot still be denied that the individual in the modern process of getting individualized, has indeed been marginalized by the state as well as the market in a society, which is no longer to be understood within the boundaries of time and space. Globalization has no doubt blurred the boundaries between regions, languages, markets, nations and states, but this has not made the individual free. Rather, market has made its inroads not only into the state, but it has also invaded the privacy of the individual, dictating him how to fulfil which of his needs. Spaces are still ethnically defined, gendered and colonized, if not in ways these traditionally were, of course in superficial ways, with tall claims of free global economy, democratized world society, emancipated genders and securalized culture.

It has to be remembered here that while the whole world is undergoing liberalization and globalization, the experience of developing countries is substantially different in that these have not still been able to grapple with the problem of providing basic necessities to a large chunk of their populations, which continue to be reeling under an unbearable burden of poverty and deprivation. Indian society is an interesting example in this context. Despite the rigorous efforts to decentralize and democratize the state, with the help of constitutional reforms and technological know-how, India continues to confront the terrible challenges of militancy, ecological degradation, cultural invasion, unemployment, economic disparity, etc. Rather than entertaining an optimistic picture in times to come, one is forced to visualize the aggravations that are likely to happen in relation to these issues, in the light of private sector taking over the most crucial social sectors from the state.

While we boast of being one of the most liberal and secular societies on the planet, we still continue to practice patriarchy in the most barbaric form, in the garb of sophisticated technology. That is why, two of our most forward states, i.e., Punjab and Gujarat, have shown a sharp decline in the sex ratio in the census of 2001, forcing the academics, planners and women activists to sit up and introspect. It seems that the most pious efforts of our national leaders in liberating Indian women are being thwarted significantly by the damaging gender images being thrown by the western as well as our own media, commercial culture and stinkingly consumerist behaviour that has sprouted among us, irrespective of age, caste, class and gender.

We, in this age of globalized economy and culture, continue to remain highly ethnicized, almost having learnt to enjoy the persistent tussle between tradition and modernity in our everyday life. While we have landed in almost all corners of the world as successful entrepreneurs, scientists, artists, etc., we have managed to build our own ghettoized little worlds, in which we practise the same age-old patriarchal ethnic ideologies, while at the same time enjoying the Americanized way of life. In this process, however, while we have let the market invade the larger part of our life, public and private both, learning from it the way one should love and hate, compete and excel, we have grown an incapacity to understand our own surroundings. What I mean is that the individual, with a strong individual conscience, to use Durkheimian terminology, has totally lost an empathy, a sensitivity, even to throw a cursory glance at the thousands and lakhs of fellow beings who, though a part of the same society, hardly resemble him, not even in body and flesh.

The Indian society has thus moved into the global world with a heavy baggage of caste, regional and ethnic consciousness, gendered worldview, traditionalized modernity and unbridgeable human disparities – all woven together in the thread of corruption, which has gained the status of a way of life. Be it the state, market or society, we have successfully injected corruption into each of them, almost institutionalizing it into our daily life. So much so, that one wonders what would happen had there been no speed money, official perks, under-table transactions, and so on. The question is, can the sociologists, or to be more generous, social scientists, expect to understand contemporary interface between state, market and society, turning a blind eye to these realities, which are as objective as these three elements of our reality.

References

Adorno, T.W. 1973. *Negative Dialectics.* London, Routledge. Trans. E.B. Ashton.

— 1984. *Aesthetic Theory.* London, Routledge. Trans. C. Lenhardt. Ed. G. Adorno and R. Tiedemann.

— 1991. *The Culture Industry: Selected Essays on Mass Culture.* London, Routledge, Translated and edited, J.M.Bernstein.

Frisby, D. and Featherstone, M. (eds) 1997. *Simmel on Culture: Selected Writings.* London, Sage.

Frisby, D. 1981. *Sociological Impressionism: A Reassessment of Georg Simmel's Social Theory.* London, Heinemann.

Giddens, A. 1996. *In Defence of Sociology: Essays, Interpretations and Rejoinders.* Cambridge, Polity Press.

Jay, M. 1973. *The Dialectical Imagination: A History of the Frankfurt School and the Institute of Social Research, 1923-50.* London, Heinemann.

Marcuse, Herbert. 1991. *One Dimensional Man: Studies in the Ideology of Advanced Industrial Society.* London, Routledge.

Sharrock, Wes W., Hughes, John A. and Martin, Peter J. 2003. *Understanding Modern Sociology.* London, Sage.

Index